Affirmative Action

Recent Titles in
Historical Guides to Controversial Issues in America

Affirmative Action

John W. Johnson and Robert P. Green, Jr.

Historical Guides to Controversial Issues in America

GREENWOOD PRESS
AN IMPRINT OF ABC-CLIO, LLC

A B C 🗠 C L I O

Santa Barbara, California • Denver, Colorado • Oxford, England

Library of Congress Cataloging-in-Publication Data

Johnson, John W., 1946–
    Affirmative action / John W. Johnson and Robert P. Green, Jr.
        p. cm. — (Historical guides to controversial issues in America)
    Includes bibliographical references and index.
    ISBN 978–0–313–33814–4 (alk. paper) — ISBN 978–0–313–08132–3 (ebook : alk. paper)
    1. Affirmative action programs—United States—History.   2. Discrimination in employment—United States—History.   3. Discrimination in higher education—United States—History.   I. Green, Robert P.   II. Title.
    HF5549.5.A34J64   2009
    331.13'30973—dc22   2009010171

13 12 11 10 9   1 2 3 4 5

This book is also available on the World Wide Web as an eBook.
Visit www.abc-clio.com for details.

ABC-CLIO, LLC
130 Cremona Drive, P.O. Box 1911
Santa Barbara, California 93116-1911

This book is printed on acid-free paper ∞

Manufactured in the United States of America

For Maureen and Martha

Contents

Acknowledgments

Until this project materialized, I had never worked with a coauthor on any long piece of writing. But when Bob Green—a good friend and professional colleague of many years standing—asked me to join him in writing a book on affirmative action, I jumped at the chance. During our pleasant collaboration, my already high estimation of Bob's scholarly acumen, his good humor, and his basic humanity has only increased.

In the course of research and writing about race- and gender-conscious public policy, I have contracted a number of debts. First of all, I benefited from travel support furnished by the Department of History, the Graduate College, and the College of Social and Behavioral Sciences at the University of Northern Iowa. Second, I received the help of a former graduate assistant, Pavel Terpelets, in identifying and copying research materials. In addition, my colleagues in the UNI History Department once again offered sympathetic ears and constructively critical eyes for one of my scholarly projects: particularly helpful were Bob Martin, Don Shepardson, David Walker, Chuck Holcombe, Dick Broadie, and Wally Hettle. I also want to express appreciation to my bosses at UNI, Provost Jim Lubker and President Ben Allen, for looking the other way when I occasionally took some time away from "deaning" for work on this book.

My greatest debt of gratitude is to my wonderful wife, Maureen Ethel Murphy, who provides me with support and encouragement in so many ways. My portion of this book is lovingly dedicated to her.

John W. Johnson
Cedar Falls, Iowa
August 2008

John Johnson and I have been colleagues and friends for nearly 30 years and, from time to time, have contributed to each other's scholarly endeavors. As John notes, this is our first effort at coauthorship. I must say that this project has simply confirmed my belief that John is the quintessential scholar/teacher. His advice and support for my contribution are deeply appreciated.

I also thank Bill Fisk, Chair of Teacher Education, and Mike Padilla, Director of the Eugene T. Moore School of Education, here at Clemson University, for various manifestations of administrative support throughout this project. I benefited as well from the advice and moral support of a number of colleagues in the School of Education, especially Bob Horton and Suzanne Rosenblith. My colleague and former dean, Harold Cheatham, continues to be an advisor without parallel. Graduate assistant Amy Montalbano helped in a variety of ways during the final stages of the book.

My deepest gratitude, as always, goes to my most thorough critic and unselfish supporter, Martha Lancaster Green.

Robert P. Green, Jr.
Clemson, South Carolina
August 2008

In addition to our individual expressions of appreciation, both of us thank Veronica F. (Sandy) Towers, senior acquisitions editor for the Greenwood Publishing Group, for supplying appropriately timed measures of reassurance, admonition, and patience.

The individuals and organizations named above are in no way responsible for any errors, omissions, or dubious conclusions in the pages that follow. As the persons whose names appear on the title page, we must bear and accept the responsibility for this book's shortcomings.

John W. Johnson
Robert P. Green, Jr.

Introduction: The Debate over Affirmative Action

Affirmative action has been a controversial policy issue in American life for over 40 years. The notion of affording special consideration to racial minorities and/or women in employment, government contracting, and education has divided once-unified coalitions of interest groups, provoked heated discussions that have affected elections at the state and federal levels, sparked angry popular referenda, and occasioned a number of major Supreme Court decisions. The rhetoric of the Great Society and the turmoil of the mid-1960s ignited the first sparks for affirmative action; the actions of new government agencies in the late 1960s and early 1970s led to halting early steps in the policy; and a crucible of judicial decisions, legislative enactments, and political campaigns have made the subject irresistible to historians and other commentators on recent America.[1]

Affirmative action is a subject replete with irony and unintended consequences.[2] Consider, for example, the following observations, generally accepted by most who have studied the origins and unfolding nature of affirmative action: (1) Designed as a program principally to assist African Americans, affirmative action was conceived in the presidential administration of a man (Lyndon Johnson) born and raised in the segregated South; (2) The high point for affirmative action, at least in terms of jobs and government contracts for members of racial minorities, came during the administration of a president (Richard Nixon) who owed his election, in large part, to a strategy that capitalized on racial bigotry; and (3) Defended in its early days as a means of assisting people of color and women in obtaining jobs and securing admission to institutions of higher learning, affirmative action today has as its principal justification the promotion of the benefits of racial and gender diversity for all Americans in the workplace and the classroom. Such curiosities are among the topics explored in the pages that follow.

Programs providing special consideration for one group or another—for example, preferences for military veterans, employment security for workers based on seniority, jobs for children of current employees, or seats in classrooms for relatives of alumni—have long been staples in American life. Although there is some difference of opinion about when the first glimmers of *racial* or *gender* preferences became visible on the horizon, most scholars who have studied affirmative action identify the New Deal of the 1930s as witnessing the first explicit use of the term *affirmative action* in federal law. They also agree that the first deployment of the term in the context of race took place during the early days of the Kennedy Administration. The most telling political impetuses for systematic programs of affirmative action, however, arose in strident presidential oratory and the chaotic events of the Great Society era in the mid-1960s. Affirmative action then, in the late 1960s and early 1970s, moved haltingly from rhetoric to policy at the federal and state levels. From the beginning, however, critics of race- and gender-conscious policies branded them "reverse discrimination."

Although controversial from its inception, affirmative action seldom made the front pages of newspapers during the contentious years of the Vietnam War and the Watergate scandal. Essentially, it flew beneath the radar until about the mid-1970s. Thereafter, primarily as a result of Supreme Court decisions of the 1970s, 1980s, and 1990s, efforts were mounted to defeat affirmative action at the polls via public referenda. By this time, the debate over affirmative action was featured above the fold in newspapers and in lead stories on television news broadcasts. Later, in the first decade of the 21st century, another spate of court cases further inflamed public passions on affirmative action.

Today, more than 40 years after the birth of affirmative action, strident voices on all sides of the debate continue to clamor for a hearing. In the chapters that follow, we trace the genesis and development of affirmative action and the continuing controversy that constitutes the story of racial and gender preferences. We pay attention to the individuals, the events, and the ideas that spawned federal and selected state affirmative action policies—and the resistance to those policies. Perhaps most importantly, we probe the key legal challenges to affirmative action in the nation's courts. A theme of this study—sometimes explicit and almost always implicit—is that the controversy over affirmative action in America has been marked by a persistent tension between its advocates, who emphasize the necessity of overcoming historical patterns of racial and gender injustice, and its critics, who insist on the integrity of color and gender blindness.

There have been scores of good books published on race-based preferences in the last generation. Hence, it can justifiably be asked, "Is there a need at this time for yet another book on affirmative action?" We suggest three reasons why this question should be answered in the affirmative. First of all, the two of us have special knowledge of affirmative action: Johnson is a professor of history at a Midwestern state university who teaches, conducts research, and publishes on contemporary constitutional issues; and Green is a professor of education at a Southern state university who teaches, conducts research, and publishes on the history of race relations. Our knowledge of the subject matter of this study has been afforded a practical edge because each of us has served stints as academic administrators, in which capacities we have been charged with administering institutional affirmative action policies. Second, we have written extensively for popular as well as academic audiences. We have designed this book to occupy a middle ground between the once-over-lightly popular tours of the affirmative action controversy, on the one hand, and the dense law-review parsings on race and gender-based public policy on the other. And third, the timeliness of this treatment—in the wake of the U.S. Supreme Court's pupil placement/affirmative action decisions of 2007[3]—offers an occasion to bring up to date the story of one of the most embattled public policy issues of the last half century.

NOTES

1. Among the many insightful treatments of affirmative action, see especially Terry H. Anderson, *The Pursuit of Fairness: A History of Affirmative Action* (New York: Oxford University Press, 2004); William G. Bowen and Derek Bok, *The Shape of the River: Long-Term Consequences of Considering Race in College and University Admissions* (Princeton, NJ: Princeton University Press, 1998); Hugh Davis Graham, *The Civil Rights Era: Origins and Development of National Policy 1960–1972* (New York: Oxford University Press, 1990); Nancy MacLean, *Freedom Is Not Enough: The Opening of the American Workplace* (Cambridge, MA: Harvard University Press, 2006); John David Skrentny, *The Ironies of Affirmative Action: Politics, Culture, and Justice in America* (Chicago: The University Press of Chicago, 1996); Dinesh D'Souza, *Illiberal Education: The Politics of Race and Sex on Campus* (New York: The Free Press, 1991); Herman Belz, *Equality Transformed: A Quarter-Century of Affirmative Action* (New Brunswick, CT: Transaction Publishers, 1991); Howard Ball, *The Bakke Case: Race, Education & Affirmative Action* (Lawrence: University Press of Kansas, 2000); Melvin I. Urofsky, *Affirmative Action on Trial: Sex Discrimination in Johnson v. Santa Clara* (Lawrence: University Press of Kansas, 1997); Bernard Schwartz, *Behind Bakke: Affirmative Action and the Supreme Court* (New York: New York University

Press, 1988); Linda Chavez, *The Color Bind: California's Battle to End Affirmative Action* (Berkeley: University of California Press, 1998); Andrea Guerrero, *Silence at Boalt Hall: The Dismantling of Affirmative Action* (Berkeley: University of California Press, 2002); Gary Orfield, ed., *Diversity Challenged: Evidence on the Impact of Affirmative Action* (Cambridge, MA: Harvard Educational Publishing Group, 2001); Alfred W. Blumrosen, *Modern Law: The Law Transmissions System and Equal Employment Opportunity* (Madison: University of Wisconsin Press, 1993); Samuel Leiter and William M. Leiter, *Affirmative Action in Antidiscrimination Law and Policy: An Overview and Synthesis* (Albany: State University of New York Press, 2002); Terry Eastland, *Ending Affirmative Action: The Case for Colorblind Justice* (New York: Basic Books, 1996); George E. Curry, ed., *The Affirmative Action Debate* (Cambridge, MA: Perseus Publishing, 1996); Allan P. Sindler, *Bakke, DeFunis, and Minority Admissions: The Quest for Equal Opportunity* (New York: Longman, 1978); and Paul D. Moreno, *From Direct Action to Affirmative Action: Fair Employment Law and Policy in America, 1933–1972* (Baton Rouge: Louisiana State University Press, 1997).

2. John Skrentny's *The Ironies of Affirmative Action,* one of the best books on the subject, employs irony as a guiding beam for his analysis.

3. *Parents Involved in Community Schools v. Seattle School District No. 1* and *Meredith v. Jefferson County Board of Education,* 127 S.Ct. 2738 (2007).

1

Protecting White Men's Jobs

On November 2, 1920, African American orange grove owner Mose Norman, determined to vote despite threats from the Ku Klux Klan that trouble would follow any black attempts to do so, showed up at the poll in Ocoee, Florida. Expecting trouble, Norman went armed. At the poll, however, he was overpowered, disarmed, severely beaten, and ordered home. Instead he went to the house of July Perry, another well-to-do black who had also attempted to vote. Spurred by the KKK, a white mob soon formed in Ocoee, intending to teach Norman and Perry a lesson. The heavily armed mob surrounded the black settlement in town and poured kerosene on and burned some 20 houses, two churches, a school, and a lodge hall. Black residents were burned in their homes or shot down as they attempted to flee. Some fought back, among them Perry, who was wounded, captured, and taken to a jail in Orlando. (The fate of Norman remains unclear, although he was never seen again.) Later that night, a mob, given the keys to Perry's cell by the sheriff, hauled Perry out of jail and lynched him. Over 50 blacks were killed in the riot, as well as two white rioters.[1]

The incident was a thumbnail version of life for African Americans under Jim Crow, with one exception. It was easy to whip up the white mob against Norman and Perry because both were deemed "too prosperous" by whites; they held economic positions "too good for a nigger." Norman owned an orange grove that he had repeatedly refused to sell to whites. Perry was foreman of an orange grove owned by a Northerner. These were white men's jobs. The fact that they were held by blacks violated a basic understanding, imposed by whites, about race in the South.

After the Civil War, the abolition of slavery had created a vast, unemployed labor force, while former, white masters retained ownership of the land. There was no "40 acres and a mule" for every freedman. The consequent economic relationship between laborer and landowner, forged around sharecropping, tenant farming, and the crop-lien system and buttressed by cultural and racial attitudes shaped by a history of slavery, left the freedmen in yet another subservient position. By the early 20th century, the complex network of political, social, and economic features of Jim Crow served to maintain white superiority in the South.[2] Southern constitutional provisions restricted black access to the franchise, segregation laws shaped almost every aspect of social interaction between races, and economic discrimination ensured that blacks remained at the bottom of the economic ladder. When blacks stepped out of line, the gun or noose could be applied by whites with virtual impunity.

THE DEVELOPMENT OF JIM CROW

Relationships between whites and blacks in the Slave South had been defined in state laws known as slave codes. With the abolition of slavery, slave codes became defunct. Therefore, immediately after the Civil War, white leaders in the South sought to redefine white-black relations with new laws, known as black codes. While black codes recognized certain rights held by freedmen—for example, the right to hold property, to marry, to sue and be sued, to testify in court, and so on—they also imposed restrictions.[3] Black codes typically required freedmen to hold jobs (by signed contract) and provided for their return to their employer if they were to quit without good cause. They provided for the imposition of court-ordered apprenticeships for certain black minors, beefed up vagrancy laws, and targeted freedmen with an array of misdemeanors that could lead to jail sentences. Part of the Mississippi code required "That if any freedman, free negro or mulatto, convicted of any of the misdemeanors provided against in this act, shall fail or refuse, for the space of five days after conviction, to pay the fine and costs imposed, such person shall be hired out by the sheriff or other officer, at public outcry, to any white person who will pay said fine and all costs, and take such convict for the shortest time."[4] If these provisions sound a lot like the reimposition of involuntary servitude to the modern reader, so did they to many in the North after the Civil War. Reaction to laws such as these, as well as other injustices imposed on freedmen, led to the passage in the U.S. Congress of the Civil Rights Act of 1866, a law that defined citizenship to include blacks and guaranteed their legal equality.

The Civil Rights Act of 1866 immediately became embroiled in the struggle between President Andrew Johnson and Radical Republicans in Congress dissatisfied with his plan for political reconstruction of the South. Johnson vetoed the bill as a violation of states' rights and the principle of federalism. His veto was overridden, but many felt a Constitutional amendment was necessary to address his concerns. The Fourteenth Amendment was the result. Section 1 of the Fourteenth Amendment declared, "All persons born or naturalized in the United States, and subject to the jurisdiction thereof, are citizens of the United States and of the State wherein they reside. No State shall make or enforce any law which shall abridge the privileges or immunities of citizens of the United States; nor shall any state deprive any person of life, liberty, or property, without due process of law; nor deny to any person within its jurisdiction the equal protection of the laws." Another section prohibited anyone from holding public office who had taken an oath to uphold the Constitution and subsequently participated in insurrection.

While Congress debated the Fourteenth Amendment, it also provided for a more rigorous regimen for Southern states' reentry into the Union. Aspects of Congress's plan divided Southern states into military districts and required them to scrap their former state constitutions and create new ones recognizing black suffrage and to ratify the Fourteenth Amendment. The enfranchisement of adult black males at the same time that restrictions were placed on the political participation of former Confederates led to constitutions and state governments that were highly unpopular among white Southerners. Heightened taxes (caused in large measure by the need to rebuild infrastructure in the war-torn region) and corruption (a national pastime at that point) contributed to the white claim that black or black-supported government (the majority of elected officials in most states were white Republicans) was bad government. Consequently, beginning during Congressional Reconstruction and, particularly, once Southern states were readmitted to the Union and federal troops withdrawn, both extralegal and legal means were pursued by whites to dissuade black participation in government and to "redeem" government for whites.

The convergence of legal and extralegal means to regain and maintain white supremacy was reflected in a legal case that ended up before the U.S. Supreme Court, *United States v. Cruikshank*.[5] In the spring of 1873, after a disputed election between white Democrats and black Republicans, armed groups of whites rode through the countryside around Colfax, Louisiana, terrorizing blacks in the area. To protect themselves, blacks fled to the local courthouse and established defensive barricades. On Easter Sunday, a small army of whites—after allowing black women and children to flee—attacked and overran the defensive positions, forcing blacks to retreat into the courthouse. That they set on fire. From that point on, a massacre ensued. Black men were shot down as they attempted to flee the flames, and some 30 or 40 who surrendered were murdered in gruesome fashion. In all, some 100 blacks were killed.[6] While local justice could not be obtained, eventually William

Cruikshank and other whites participating in the slaughter were convicted of violating the Enforcement Act of 1870, a federal statute designed to enforce citizenship rights guaranteed by the Fourteenth Amendment.

When *United States v. Cruikshank* reached the Supreme Court on appeal, the Court reversed the convictions and severely limited the federal government's ability to protect individual rights. Expanding on their reasoning in the *Slaughter-House Cases* (1873),[7] in which a majority of justices discerned dual citizenship (state and national) in the Fourteenth Amendment and left the protection of most fundamental rights to the states, the Court found that in this case, where individual citizens had interfered with the rights of others, the Fourteenth Amendment did not apply. The Fourteenth Amendment empowered the national government to prevent states and their officers, not individual citizens, from violating equal protection and due process. Cases where individuals violated the rights of other individuals (the fundamental right to life, for example) remained to be resolved by the states.

Several years later, the reasoning in *Cruikshank* was applied again in *United States v. Harris* (1883)[8] and the *Civil Rights Cases* (1883).[9] *Harris* challenged the indictment of members of a Tennessee lynch mob under the Civil Rights Act of 1871, a federal statute designed to address the intimidating tactics of terrorist groups such as the Ku Klux Klan. The *Civil Rights Cases* challenged the constitutionality of the Civil Rights Act of 1875, a federal statute banning discrimination against blacks by inns, public conveyances, theaters, and the like. In both cases, the Court argued that the Fourteenth Amendment applied only to the states, not individual citizens; therefore, aspects of the Civil Rights Act of 1871 that punished individual actions and the Civil Rights Act of 1875 that banned discrimination by private owners were unconstitutional. The effect of this series of decisions was to leave the protection of fundamental individual rights to the states. In the redeemed South, where whites were determined to maintain white superiority, that meant no protection of the rights of blacks. Terrorist tactics pursued by private individuals and designed to keep blacks "in their place" could (and did) go unpunished by local and state authorities, and the federal government was powerless to interfere.

By the time of *Harris* and the *Civil Rights Cases,* the white power structure in the South had developed yet another legal device to maintain the subordination of blacks—segregation laws. Rationalized as the application of the police power of the state to maintain the health and safety of citizens, these laws required the separation of the races in many areas of life: for example, public accommodations, conveyances, schools, neighborhoods—even cemeteries. One such law was that of the state of Louisiana providing for "the comfort of passengers" in railroad passenger coaches. The 1890 Louisiana statute required "that all railway companies carrying passengers in their coaches in this State, shall provide equal but separate accommodations for the white, and colored races, by providing two or more passenger coaches for each passenger train, or by dividing the passenger coaches by a partition so as to secure separate accommodations."[10] Keep in mind for our later discussion that the only exception in this regulation applied "to nurses attending children of the other race."

In the early 1890s, a number of black communities in the South continued to challenge the white power structure, and one such was found in New Orleans. Blacks there sought a case testing the constitutionality of segregation laws, and when Homer Plessy, a light-skinned African American, was convicted of violating the passenger coach law, such a case presented itself. Plessy's conviction was upheld by the Louisiana Supreme Court and subsequently appealed to the Supreme Court of the United States as *Plessy v. Ferguson* (1896).[11] Before the Court, Plessy's attorney argued that the law, despite its provision for "equal but separate" accommodations, violated the equal protection clause of the Fourteenth Amendment, that its objective was simply to debase blacks and perpetuate caste distinctions derived from slavery, and that it was an expression of white superiority and white supremacy.

In its decision, however, the Court—clearly influenced by the pseudoscience of the day propounding the racial inferiority of non–Anglo-Saxons—rejected these arguments, further undermining application of the Fourteenth Amendment. "The object of the amendment was undoubtedly to enforce the absolute equality of the two races before the law, but in the nature of things it could not have been intended to abolish distinctions based upon color, or to enforce social, as distinguished from political equality, or a commingling of the two races upon terms unsatisfactory to either,"[12] wrote Justice Henry Billings Brown for the Court. Given this distinction between political and social equality, and a history of judicial support for segregation by race, the Court found that the Louisiana statute was a reasonable application of the police powers of the state. The Court rejected the claim that segregation stamped African Americans with a badge of inferiority. "If this be so," wrote Brown, "it is not by reason of anything found in the act, but solely because the colored race chooses to put that construction upon it."[13] Furthermore, legislation could not eradicate social prejudices, opined Brown. "If one race be inferior to the other socially, the Constitution of the United States cannot put them upon the same plane."

Decrying the decision of the Court in *Plessy v. Ferguson*, its lone dissenter, Justice John Marshall Harlan, foresaw the dire consequences it would have. "The present decision, it may well be apprehended, will not only stimulate aggressions, more or less brutal and irritating, upon the admitted rights of colored citizens, but will encourage the belief that it is possible, by means of state enactments, to defeat the beneficent purposes . . . of . . . the recent amendments of the Constitution."[14] That is precisely what happened as states adopted constitutions and passed laws that not only continued to isolate blacks socially (except in cases where they were employed as servants) but also restricted their political rights. Restrictions on the franchise resulting from residential requirements; convictions for a number of crimes; failure to pay taxes, including poll taxes; and literacy requirements all fell particularly heavily on blacks. That this was the intent of those who formulated these provisions was never in doubt. Senator Benjamin Tillman from South Carolina, for example, later argued before the U.S. Senate, "We did not disfranchise the negroes until 1895. Then we had a constitutional convention convened which took the matter up calmly, deliberately, and avowedly with the purpose of disfranchising as many of them as we could."[15] Later adoptions of "grandfather clauses" by Southern states—clauses that exempted those who had voted or whose fathers or grandfathers had voted before a certain date (usually prior to the beginning of military reconstruction) from these restrictions—that is, white males—provided further evidence of the targets of these provisions. By the early twentieth century, black political participation had been dramatically reduced and in some areas stamped out. Socially stigmatized and politically powerless, subject to the gun and noose, blacks were in no position to challenge the economic position imposed on them by whites.

WORKING FOR THE MAN

In 1911 *The Crisis*, the magazine of the fledgling National Association for the Advancement of Colored People (NAACP), published a letter from a black laborer in the South describing debt peonage. "If a colored man is arrested here and hasn't any money, whether he is guilty or not, he has to pay just the same. A man of color is never tried in this country. It is simply a farce. Everything is fixed before he enters the courtroom." The fix plays itself out as, after the black man is convicted, a white man appears to pay his fine, allowing the black to work off his debt on the white man's farm. However, "At the end of the month I find that I owe him more than I did when I went there. The debt is increased year in and year out. You would ask, 'How is that?' It is simply that he is charging you more for your board, lodging and washing than they allow you for your work."[16] The "convict" remains perpetually indebted to his "savior," unable to leave his employ.

Tenant farming and the crop lien system worked in much the same way, well into the 20th century. Black tenants farmed land owned by white landlords. Theoretically, after the harvest, a portion of the proceeds from the harvest went to pay off rent for the land and any credit extended for the tenant's needs. In reality, the accounting virtually always left the tenant even deeper in debt. "When word reaches us that the Lords of the Land are bent over the big books down at the plantation commissary," wrote African American author Richard Wright, "we lower our eyes, shake our heads, and mutter: A naught's a naught, / Five's a figger; / All for the white man, / None for the nigger." Wright captured the sense of repression resulting from entanglement in "this hateful web of cotton culture":

And we know that if we protest we will be called "bad niggers." The Lords of the Land will preach the doctrine of "white supremacy" to the poor whites who are eager to form mobs. In the midst of general hysteria they will seize one of us—it does not matter who, the innocent or guilty—and, as a token, a naked and bleeding body will be dragged through the dusty streets . . .

   And we cannot fight back; we have no arms; we cannot vote; and the law is white. There are no black policemen, black justices of the peace, black judges, black juries, black jailers, black mayors, or black men anywhere in the government of the South. The Ku Klux Klan attacks us in a thousand ways, driving our boys and girls off the jobs in the cities and keeping us who live on the land from protesting or asking too many questions.[17]

Blacks were expected to remain satisfied with "their place," and off the farm, as well as on, that place was at the bottom of the economic ladder.

   By the early twentieth century, economic dislocation in Southern agriculture, in large part deriving from the devastating impact of the boll weevil on cotton, forced thousands of blacks off the land. Excluded from the growing textile industry in the South, where production jobs were reserved for whites, black males were able to find some jobs in mines and factories in or near urban centers. Leon Alexander and Earl Brown, black coal miners near Birmingham, Alabama, who later became union organizers, recounted work in the mines during the 1930s. "Now, there were things back then that was called 'a white man's job,' and 'a black man's job,'" recalled Alexander. "Ninety percent of the machinery that was operated at the mine was operated by white. The cutting machines was one of the few things that the predominantly black had because that was *really* some tough work."[18] "Segregation had a great effect on the black coal miners," argued Brown, "because they didn't have the equal opportunities, the equal rights in jobs. . . . No job opportunities for advancement. You had a certain mold that you stayed in, and you couldn't get out of that mold. The best jobs went to the whites and lower jobs or the menial work went to the blacks."[19] Bathhouses, water fountains, and mine cars were all segregated, and owners manipulated race in ways that undermined the positions of both black and white miners.

   Debt peonage also played a role in the mines, as convicts were leased to the coal mining companies. Leon Alexander spoke of working in the mines for seven years with a black convict, "Hardworking man who said that he spent

17 years in prison for something he didn't do. . . . Back then, if a white man said you did it, you were guilty before you ever went to court."[20] Convict labor kept wages low and served as a weapon against union organization.

Despite some degree of union organization and sporadic successes by individuals landing skilled jobs, conditions remained much the same into the 1950s. Ralph Thompson, a military veteran and high school graduate with some business college coursework, in 1959 landed a job with International Harvester in Memphis, Tennessee. "I ended up working in the foundry for most of my time there, because it was segregated, and when you went into jobs they were basically 'white jobs' and 'black jobs.' And black jobs were basically in the foundry. . . . We couldn't drive cranes, overhead cranes . . . We couldn't run no machine. They didn't let us do that. You couldn't get no office job. All you could do was the hardest job."[21]

African American women not trapped with their husbands and families in the agricultural economy typically served as domestic workers. There, too, wages were low, and women were subject to the whims of their employers. Ann Pointer, in an interview with historians, recalled how, during the Depression, her mother "worked hard, working in people's houses. Seven days a week she had to get there and cook breakfast for them, wash all the clothes, iron all the clothes, clean up the house, and everything for four dollars a week, seven days a week."[22] The whims often went beyond the white matron's unreasonable expectations for service. Cleaster Mitchell recalled, "one of the things that they instilled in you was about being approached by the young mens. . . . A lot of people who worked and had jobs, they left on that account . . . you had no alternative. To go to the law didn't mean anything. There wasn't no law [for] you [to] go to. . . . [White men] took it for granted when they saw a black lady that they could just approach her."[23] Ann Pointer, identifying the same issue with tenancy, argued, "Everywhere the [white] man has got, maybe from eight to fifteen tenants, on his place, there is a woman there that he is messing with. Then you going to see the flowers start to blooming, the children start to popping. . . . You don't have to wonder about these flowers blooming. You can just look at the population and tell."[24]

THE GREAT MIGRATION

For hundreds of thousands of Southern blacks, oppression and economic dislocation in the South, combined with the lure of greater freedom and apparent economic opportunity in the North, contributed to a vast migration to the industrial centers of the North. The period 1916–1918 alone saw some 400,000 African Americans move to Northern cities. Between 1910 and 1920, New York's black population increased by 66 percent, Chicago's by 148 percent, Detroit's by 611 percent, and Philadelphia's by 59 percent.[25] One migrant to Philadelphia wrote the following letter to a friend in the South, revealing the attraction.

with the aid of God I am making very good I make $75 per month. . . . I don't have to work hard. dont have to mister every little white boy comes along I havent heard a white man call a colored a nigger you no now—since I been in the state of Pa. I can ride in the electric street and steam cars any where I get a seat. I dont care to mix with white what I mean I am not crazy about being with white folks, but if I have to pay the same fare I have learn to want the same acomidation. and if you are first in a place here shoping you don't have to wait until the white folks get thro tradeing.[26]

All was hardly rosy in the North, however, as blacks crowded into ghettoes and black laborers again were hired for the most menial positions—often despite skills they might have possessed. "Reality never matched the dream of the Great Migration," wrote historian Carole Marks. "Black workers were recruited for the lowest-level jobs—dirty work shunned by the native white population. They worked in vulnerable positions from which they were laid off at the first sign of economic downturn and moved into positions from which there was no upward mobility."[27] Furthermore, the presence of a low-wage black workforce was manipulated by employers to undermine the position of white workers as well. The presence of large numbers of black workers in a plant dampened overall wage levels, and blacks were sometimes employed as strikebreakers. White union workers resented these facts, and such economic realities combined with racial prejudice led many local unions either to exclude blacks altogether or to segregate them within their membership. Consequently, black unionization was low.[28] Large numbers of black women worked as well, and, as in the South, these women were employed primarily in domestic services. Their positions were insecure, low paying, and demanding. "They worked as many as fourteen hours a day, frequently on an irregular schedule, worked longer than was arranged, got less than was promised, and had to accept clothing instead of cash."[29] These jobs provided needed income for black families, but average family income remained low. "In 1900 . . . black family income was almost 57% of that of white families," summarized historian Marks. "In 1950, some thirty years after the Great Migration, ten years after the Great Depression, and a few years after the Second World War migration, it was at approximately the same level."[30]

WHEN AFFIRMATIVE ACTION WAS WHITE

The period from the early-1930s to the mid-1950s was a watershed in American economic life. Policies pursued by the federal government to counteract the impact of the Great Depression, fight World War II, and provide benefits for returning veterans created the modern welfare state and provided the basis for an amazing expansion of the American middle class. Nonetheless, the gap between black and white earning power, as the preceding quotation suggests, remained wide. Historian and political scientist Ira Katznelson, synthesizing an extensive body of research on the period, argued that the reason for this continued gap was that federal policies of the 1930s and 1940s were crafted and administered in a deeply discriminatory manner.[31] White Southern Democrats in Congress and the Senate—a key element in President Franklin Delano Roosevelt's political coalition—anxious to protect "the Southern way of life," were able to influence major pieces of legislation in ways that either excluded large numbers of African Americans from their benefits or placed the administration of beneficial programs in the hands of state or local authorities who discriminated against blacks. For example, federal relief programs such as the Federal Emergency Relief Act (FERA) were administered locally and unevenly. In the North, where blacks represented an important voting block that shifted to Roosevelt and the Democrats, African Americans, who were poorer to start with, benefited proportionately. In the South, however, white administrators, who made sure that relief did not undercut the cheap black labor market, kept relief rates for blacks disproportionately low. Important pieces of labor legislation, such as elements of the National Industrial Recovery Act (NIRA) and the National Labor Relations Act (NLRA), protecting workers' rights to organize and bargain collectively, were either interpreted or written specifically to exclude agricultural and domestic workers—some 65 percent of the black labor force nationally and 75–80 percent of that labor force in the South. Social Security, while it did benefit those blacks who qualified, excluded (until 1954) these same farm and domestic workers. Those parts of the law that provided aid to dependent children and the elderly were structured so that administration was left to state and local officials who again, in the South, applied the law in ways that discriminated against blacks. Unemployment insurance provisions also excluded farm and domestic workers. "In short," argued Katznelson, "each of the old age, social assistance, and unemployment provisions advanced by the Social Security Act was shaped to racist contours."[32]

Despite gains for some individuals, the overall impact of the racial policies of the military during World War II disadvantaged blacks. "The Second World War was the last major conflict in which the military policies of the United States accommodated undisguised racism," argued Katznelson.[33] Military units remained segregated, despite the African American community's continued effort to point out the inconsistency of that practice when fighting a war against racist, totalitarian governments. Maltreatment by Southern white officers and at Southern military bases; limited commissioning of black officers and never placing senior black officers over white officers; reservations about the effectiveness of black troops based on stereotypes rather than observation; the typical assignment of menial work to blacks; and resistance to placing blacks in key positions or training all maintained elements of Jim Crow in the military. "As with other New Deal policies," wrote Katznelson, "many blacks found and exploited openings that would not otherwise have been possible. But for most African American individuals, and certainly for the group as a whole, war service ended with a wider gap between whites and blacks, as white access to training and occupational advancement moved ahead at a much more vigorous rate."[34]

The same pattern held with the Selective Service Readjustment Act, or GI Bill of Rights. As a result of provisions that helped veterans purchase homes, farms, and businesses; provided them with grants for education and further job training; and assisted them in finding work, the GI Bill has been credited with creating postwar, middle-class America.[35] However, benefits flowed much more readily to whites than to blacks. Once again, the responsibility for implementation of the various programs under the GI Bill was left to states and localities, thus allowing local prejudices to shape that implementation. In the South, white officials discouraged blacks from participating in programs in areas such as skills training. Educational opportunities in general were restricted because black veterans weren't accepted at all-white Southern colleges and universities and historically black colleges and universities were ill-equipped to meet the demand. In both the South and North, financial institutions refused to approve loans to African Americans. Federally funded employment services channeled African Americans into black jobs. While the GI Bill did provide African Americans benefits, increasing the number of middle-class blacks, its overall performance failed to meet its promise of equitable treatment. "The differential treatment meted out to African Americans," summarized Katznelson, "sharply curtailed the statute's powerful egalitarian promise and significantly widened the country's large racial gap."[36]

MOMENTUM FOR CHANGE

As these various policies unfolded, African American reaction was divided. On the one hand, many of the New Deal policies helped blacks, whose plight had been ignored for decades, despite the fact that the policies abetted discrimination. The shift of the black electorate in the North to the Democratic Party reflected appreciation of that fact. On the other hand, many leaders in the African American community recognized the shortcomings in federal policy and worked to address them. For example, labor and civil rights leader

A. Philip Randolph, anticipating strategies that would be used in the civil rights movement of the 1950s and 1960s, in May 1941 called for mass action by African Americans in the form of a march on Washington, DC, to demand jobs in the defense industry, integration in the armed forces, and the abolition of "Jim-Crowism" in government departments.[37] Roosevelt, moving to preempt such a demonstration and not unsympathetic to black's concerns, issued Executive Order 8802, affirming nondiscrimination in defense and government employment and establishing the Fair Employment Practices Committee (FEPC) to oversee that policy.

Momentum for change accelerated as World War II drew to a close and the United States became engaged in the Cold War, yet another struggle justified in terms of freedom versus totalitarianism. As the United States and the Soviet Union competed for influence in the developing world, a world largely composed of people of color, U.S. efforts were compromised by manifestations of racism at home. Furthermore, new anthropological and sociological studies undermined traditional racial stereotypes. Anthropologists such as Ruth Benedict and Gene Weltfish, carrying on the earlier work of Franz Boas, demonstrated the importance of environment rather than race in shaping intelligence and character.[38] In his comprehensive study of African Americans in the United States published in 1944, *An American Dilemma,* Swedish economist Gunnar Myrdal claimed that a brutal cycle characterized race relations in the United States. White discrimination and injustice fostered poor health, poor education, and low standards of living among blacks, characteristics that whites then used to rationalize the actions that created these characteristics in the first place.[39]

African Americans found an ally in President Harry Truman, who proved to be a major advocate of civil rights. His Executive Order 9981 in July 1948 led to desegregation in the military by the late 1950s. Earlier, his 1946 Executive Order 9809 established the Committee on Civil Rights, and its publication, *To Secure These Rights,*[40] addressed many of the issues identified by Myrdal. Juxtaposing basic American principles in the form of four essential rights— those to safety and security of the person, citizenship and its privileges, freedom of conscience and expression, and equality of opportunity—with the record of the nation's treatment of African Americans, the report outlined a program of action that could begin to close the gap between the nation's principles and practices. The committee called for administrative changes to strengthen federal and state machinery protecting civil rights, including a permanent Commission on Civil Rights in the Office of the President; an anti-lynching act; abolition of poll taxes and enactment of laws that protected access to the franchise; and, in general, the elimination of segregation from American life, especially targeting employment, education, housing, health, and public services. Thus, the report established the legislative agenda for civil rights advocates for the next two decades. Yet another report Truman commissioned, on higher education, pointed out the barriers to equal opportunity in higher education in the United States. That report argued (with Southern whites on the commission dissenting), "The time has come to make public education at all levels equally accessible to all, without regard to race, creed, sex, or national origin . . . If education is to make the attainment of a more perfect democracy one if its major goals . . . [it] must renounce the practices of discrimination and segregation in education institutions as contrary to the spirit of democracy."[41]

THE LEGAL CHALLENGE TO JIM CROW

Soon after its founding in 1909, the NAACP began to support legal cases challenging elements of Jim Crow. These cases were based primarily on the Fourteenth Amendment's Equal Protection Clause and the Fifteenth Amendment's prohibition of disfranchisement based on race. Recall that, in *Plessy v. Ferguson,* the Supreme Court had endorsed the "separate but equal" doctrine. That is, Southern state actions that provided separate but *equal* accommodations or provisions for blacks and whites did not violate the equal protection clause of the Fourteenth Amendment. However, by the 1930s, it was clear to anyone who cared to look that separate accommodations were almost never equal. Working under the direction of Charles Hamilton Houston, NAACP attorneys attempted to craft a series of cases that would chip away at segregation laws in schooling, public accommodations, and housing. They were successful. By 1950, NAACP attorneys had convinced the Supreme Court to require Southern states to provide graduate and professional schools for blacks that were fully equivalent to those for whites—or admit blacks to the previously all-white schools. Out-of-state scholarships to avoid black admission,[42] jury-rigged professional schools,[43] and segregated accommodations within graduate schools[44] would no longer be acceptable. In 1941 the Court required the Interstate Commerce Commission to enforce its policy that interstate railroad travelers be treated equally with regard to accommodations;[45] in 1945 the Court ruled that the state-imposed, segregated, *intra*state travel of *inter*state passengers violated the interstate commerce clause of the Constitution as well as the equal protection clause of the Fourteenth Amendment;[46] and in 1950 the Court effectively invalidated carrier-imposed segregation of interstate travelers.[47] In 1944 the Court declared all-white primary elections unconstitutional under the Fifteenth Amendment[48] and, in 1948, declared state enforcement of private, restrictive covenants in housing a violation of the equal protection clause.[49]

Success in this series of cases emboldened the NAACP to challenge the doctrine of separate but equal itself. Education had always been a major concern of the African American community as blacks saw education and training as important to attaining good jobs. The focus on graduate and professional education in the series of cases from the late 1930s to 1950 was reflective of this fact, and these cases were planned as the first steps in a strategy that would eventually address inequities in the public schools of the South. Under the direction of Houston's protégé, Thurgood Marshall, NAACP attorneys crafted a set of K-12 educational test cases (from South Carolina, Virginia, Kansas, and Delaware) that, if successfully pursued, would, at the least, extend the findings of the Court to K-12 public schooling. But the real focus of the cases was the attempt to overturn *Plessy* altogether.

It was clear that separate public schools for blacks and whites were not equal. Throughout the South, school expenditures for black students were a fraction of that for whites, buildings were inferior, and teacher and principal salaries were far lower. One of the cases pursued by the NAACP, *Briggs v. Elliott,* originated in Clarendon County, South Carolina. There, during the 1949–1950 school year, per pupil expenditures averaged $179 for each white child but only $43 for each black child. Twelve "white schools," typically constructed of brick and stucco and valued at $673,850, served 2,375 students. Sixty-one "black schools," typically wooden shacks valued at $194,575, served 6,531 students.[50] Often these wooden schools were in disrepair, were heated by woodstoves, and had no running water or sewage (that is, they had outdoor toilets). Black students attended fewer days than did whites, essentially only as work schedules in the fields allowed, and they were not provided transportation by the school system. Demonstrating inequality was straightforward.

The more important effort, however, was the challenge to *Plessy.* Marshall and his colleagues sought to demonstrate that race was not, as Justice Henry Billings Brown had argued, a reasonable basis for separating students. Marshall introduced evidence drawn from contemporary social science research indicating that perceived racial differences were more likely attributable to environmental (such as inequitable schooling), rather than inherent, factors. Furthermore, research suggested that segregation produced psychological damage to black students marked as inferior by segregation. Such a system clearly violated the concept of equal protection of the law, he argued.

The Supreme Court agreed. *Briggs* and four other cases (a fifth case was not one pursued by the NAACP) were treated together under the Kansas case, *Brown v. Board of Education of Topeka.* In a unanimous decision issued on May 17, 1954, written by Chief Justice Earl Warren, the Court declared, "We conclude that in the field of public education the doctrine of 'separate but equal' has no place. Separate educational facilities are inherently un-equal." The Court delayed issuing a relief decree, however, until the next year, when it required the school systems, under the direction of the federal district courts, to pursue "all deliberate speed" in moving from dual (black and white) to unitary status.

THE CIVIL RIGHTS MOVEMENT BEGINS

Many point to the decision in *Brown* as the opening round in the modern civil rights struggle. The NAACP and allies of civil rights would continue efforts in the courts. By 1954, however, African Americans had already de-veloped other strategies to chip away at Jim Crow. Although A. Philip Ran-dolph's march on Washington never materialized (Randolph called it off when Roosevelt issued Executive Order 8802), the use of direct mass action spread. In 1953 African Americans in Baton Rouge, Louisiana, fed up with mistreat-ment on the city's segregated buses, staged a boycott. That boycott provided a model for others, most notably a bus boycott in Montgomery, Alabama. The arrest of Rosa Parks; the formation of the Montgomery Improvement Association; the leadership of Martin Luther King, Jr.; and the establishment of the Southern Christian Leadership Conference initiated the direct-action component of the movement.

A spreading movement to challenge Jim Crow had begun. One result of early efforts was broadened public support for civil rights legislation in Congress. Consequently, in 1957, the first national civil rights legislation since 1875 was signed into law. While very much a compromise—Southern senators were able to remove portions of the original bill they found too objectionable—the law created a Commission on Civil Rights, charged with investigating and reporting violations of voting rights and equal protection of the laws, provided a Civil Rights Division in the Department of Justice, and established procedures by which penalties might be imposed on those interfering with the right to vote.[51] In the view of many African Americans, however, the law had critical shortcomings. Charles H. Thompson, editor of the *Journal of Negro Education,* argued that the law's focus on voting, while welcome, left significant needs unaddressed. Those needs included the right to be free from discrimination in employment and the right to be free from economic reprisals. Pointing to the wide and growing gap in median income between black and white families in Washington, DC, Thompson wrote, "The most serious and critical disadvantage which Negroes suffer at present is economic, and much, if not most, of it is due to race."[52] The fight against discrimination in employment would remain a central element of the civil rights movement.

WOMEN AT WORK

While the focus of this chapter has been racial discrimination against African Americans, they were not the only group to suffer exclusion based on cultural perceptions of their "appropriate" place. Other racial minorities were typically treated in similar fashion.[53] The experience of women presents yet another version of cultural expectations, one with similar exclusionary results.

The experience of women in America has largely been shaped by cultural expectations associated with marriage, family, and home—the domestic sphere. From the time of the earliest colonial settlements, both religious authority and British common law made wives subject to husbands, women subject to men. "Wives, be subject to your husbands, as to the Lord," wrote Paul the Apostle.[54] The great expositor of British common law, William Blackstone, argued, "By marriage, the husband and wife are one person in law: that is, the very being or legal existence of the woman is suspended during the marriage, or at least is incorporated and consolidated into that of the husband; under whose wing, protection, and cover, she performs every thing."[55]

The history of women's rights has consisted largely of efforts to battle the constraints imposed by those traditions, and one of those constraints has been occupational role. A woman's place was in the home, involved in those pursuits suitable for women. John Winthrop, the first governor of Massachusetts Bay Colony, lamented the fate of one Mrs. Hopkins, who had "fallen into sad infirmity, the loss of her understanding and reason . . . by occasion of her giving herself wholly to reading and writing, and had written many books. . . . [If] she had attended her household affairs, and such things as belong to women, and not gone out of her way and calling to meddle in such things as are proper for men, whose minds are stronger, etc., she had kept her wits, and might have improved them usefully and honorably in the place God had set her."[56] Intellectual pursuits more suitable for men had carried Mrs. Hopkins out of her God-given, proper role, attending to household affairs, leading to her sad fate.

Such role expectations were reinforced by social and economic developments during the early national and antebellum periods. As the nation began to experience industrialization and urbanization, the nature of the family changed. In traditional, agricultural society, the family was the economic or productive unit, and, while the husband was the head, virtually every member played a role. In urban settings, the economic function of the family changed as work shifted away from the home and was perceived as the province of the husband. The home thus became the province of the wife, with concomitant cultural expectations. "It is the province of woman to make home," wrote

Presbyterian minister Jonathan Stearns in 1837, "*whatever it is*. If she makes that delightful and salutary—the abode of order and purity, though she may never herself step beyond the threshold, she may yet send forth from her humble dwelling, a power that will be felt round the globe."[57]

Women's principal role was thus confined to the home, where, as vessels of purity and virtue, they were to shape the virtuous children of the Republic. Where women did work outside the home, care was taken not to threaten their traditional roles. In the growing textile industry of New England, for example, paternalistic regulations, relatively low pay (although it often appeared attractive to farm girls), and job distribution according to sex (men were supervisors, were skilled mechanics, or did heavy work; women's options were limited), reflected an understanding that work should not inhibit future home roles.[58] But relatively few women worked for wages outside their homes—only 10 percent in 1840—and the vast majority of those were single. That year, some 70 percent of the women who worked for wages outside the home served as domestic workers; about 25 percent worked in manufacturing; and the rest held a variety of jobs such as bookbinders, typesetters, nurses, and teachers. "[B]y 1860," writes labor historian Alice Kessler-Harris, "no more than 15 per cent of all women could be found in the wage labor force at any one time."[59] Those tended to be poor women, forced to work to subsist.

Professional opportunities, as well as the more rigorous educational opportunities preparatory thereto, were limited. The sole profession to which women had access in any numbers was teaching. Catharine Beecher, forceful advocate of the training of young women for employment in that field, framed her argument in both economic and domestic terms. Women, who were more willing than men to work for the "scanty pittance that is allowed to the majority of teachers," were particularly suited "by disposition, and habits, and circumstances" to educate the children of the nation. "And, most happily," she wrote, "it is true, that the education necessary to fit a woman to be a teacher, is exactly the one that best fits her for that domestic relation she is primarily designed to fill."[60] This profession would let women step outside the home, but as an extension of their nurturing role.

With few exceptions, any formal education beyond common schooling to which a woman was exposed most typically served to deepen her understanding of her domestic role. "The female seminaries were quick to defend themselves against any suspicion of interfering with the role which nature's God had assigned to women," wrote historian Barbara Welter. "At Miss Pierce's famous school in Litchfield, the students were taught that they had 'attained the perfection of their characters when they could combine their elegant accomplishments with a turn for solid domestic virtues.'"[61] Collegiate education or professional education in medicine, law, or the ministry was simply beyond the pale. Even if women could withstand the rigors of medical training, for which their smaller brains and purer sensibilities were unsuited, general opinion held, they would have great difficulty practicing—and their practice would likely be limited to other women or children. Law was much too complicated and its practice too rough, and the Bible itself limited the ministry to men. St. Paul had declared, "Let your women keep silent in churches."[62] While a handful of women served as lonely pioneers in these fields,[63] the opening of professional schools to women on an equal basis with men was a late 19th- and early 20th-century phenomenon. Women who sought greater scope for their abilities—represented by writers such as Mary Wollstonecraft, Frances Wright, and Harriet Martineau—were perceived in the popular women's literature of the day as "only semi-women, mental hermaphrodites" who were undermining civilization.[64] While the Seneca Falls Convention of 1848 and its Declaration of Sentiments asserting women's equality with men are seen by many as the beginning of the women's rights movement in the United States, it should be no surprise that the focus of the women's movement prior to the Civil War was in securing rights with regard to married women's property, divorce, and child custody.

The idea that woman's principal job was domestic retained its preeminence, with some variation, into the mid-20th century. As industrialization and urbanization continued apace, the domestic sphere of women and the public sphere of men became even more clearly demarcated. The home was perceived as a refuge for men from the workaday world. The gentler, woman's role, beyond that of mother, was to provide comfort and solace to the man wearied from the strain of competition. If women must work, it was felt, their more fragile constitutions should be taken into consideration. The Supreme Court decision in the labor case *Muller v. Oregon* (1908) was reflective of this perspective.

In a series of cases during the late 19th and early 20th century, most famously in *Lochner v. New York* (1905),[65] the Court struck down state legislation regarding minimum wages and hours that interfered with freedom of contract. However, in *Muller v. Oregon* (1908),[66] the Court approved an Oregon law limiting to 10 the maximum number of hours a woman could work a day in any mechanical establishment, factory, or laundry. The special characteristics of women, the Court found, legitimated the state's use of its police power to protect the health, safety, and welfare of the community. "That woman's physical structure and the performance of maternal functions place her at a disadvantage in the struggle for subsistence is obvious," wrote Justice David J. Brewer for the Court. "This is especially true when the burdens of motherhood are upon her . . . and as healthy mothers are essential to vigorous offspring, the physical well-being of woman becomes an object of public interest and care in order to preserve the strength and vigor of the race." Elaborating on the differences between women and men, Brewer noted that these differences "justify legislation to protect her from the greed as well as the passion of man."[67]

Muller would prove to be problematic for women. For working women, the protections offered by statutes such as that reviewed in *Muller* were valuable. They afforded immediate benefits. Yet they were based on, and promoted, stereotypes that severely limited women's opportunities.

Nonetheless, while basic popular attitudes toward women's work changed little, opportunities for work outside the home did expand throughout the first half of the 20th century. This expansion was characterized by a number of patterns, including structural changes in the family and economy that changed home life and created new jobs, job differentiation, wage discrimination, and incremental increases—with short periods of expansion or contraction resulting from depression and war—in the number of women who worked outside the home.[68] Throughout all, the special sphere and sensibilities of women remained in mind.

Structural changes in the family and the economy played a significant role. By the end of the 19th century, women were having half as many children as they had had at the beginning of the century. Technological developments in homemaking—for example, appliances for making and washing clothes—along with smaller families, reduced the time and effort required for homemaking. Continued expansion in the textiles and foods industries made these commodities cheaper at the same time they provided opportunities for employment. Relief from demands of the home had a particular impact on middle-class women, enabling them to become active in social and community affairs—again extending their nurturing role beyond the home. During the Progressive Era, community activities led to the creation of new jobs for women, such as child labor investigators, visiting nurses, and truant officers. In a parallel development, middle-class women began to demand more education, fostering the growth of coeducation and women's colleges. These new roles for women created momentum for political change, as well; the struggle for women's suffrage culminated in the ratification of the Nineteenth Amendment in 1920. By the 1920s, technological developments as well as continued expansion in the retail, service, and distribution sectors of the economy provided new job opportunities for women as operators, clerks and bookkeepers, saleswomen, designers, and copywriters, and in human service fields such as social work, personnel work, and counseling. For a brief period during World War I, women moved into jobs vacated by men who went to war, but these jobs disappeared once men returned.

One further development resulting from women's activities during the Progressive Era was the call by some women for an Equal Rights Amendment (ERA), the goal of which was complete civic equality between women and men. The New Women's Party, a spin-off from the suffrage movement, met in Seneca Falls, New York, in July 1923 and endorsed just such an amendment. Subsequently, and unsuccessfully, the amendment was introduced in Congress every year until 1972, when new wording for an ERA was proposed.[69] This original ERA was not endorsed by all women's groups; many were concerned that the abolition of legal distinctions between men and women would prohibit protective legislation that was immediately beneficial to working women. This debate among women's activists would continue into the 1970s.

Women's proportion of the work force edged up, reaching 24.3 percent in 1930, 28.8 percent of whom were married, and 25.1 percent in 1940, 35 percent of whom were married. As job opportunities expanded, two features of those opportunities became prominent. First, women tended to be concentrated in just a few occupations. Furthermore, in many of these occupational areas, such as teaching, nursing, and social and clerical work, women were the workers and their supervisors or administrators were men. Traditionally male professions, notably medicine, law, and university teaching, remained largely closed to women. Concentration and work hierarchies fostered distinctions between "men's work" and "women's work." Second, women's wages were lower. In 1930 women's wages averaged 57 percent of men's. Historian Alice Kessler-Harris summarized these developments: "Overall, between 1910 and 1940, from 86 to 90 percent of all women worked in only ten different occupations—an occupational concentration that contributed to the ability to assign low wages and poor status to these jobs."[70]

Neither the Great Depression nor policies of the New Deal dramatically altered these developments. While economic dislocation required more women to work, efforts were pursued by government and, to some degree, industry to keep women from taking men's jobs. In fact, some defenders of tradition launched campaigns to eliminate women from the workforce altogether. Married women who worked were special targets. In 1937 a *Fortune* magazine poll asked if wives should work when their husbands had a job. Eighty-five percent of men respondents said no; 79 percent of women respondents agreed.[71] These attitudes were reflected in actions. For example, many school systems would not hire married women as teachers, and those who married in service were dismissed. While New Deal policies helped wage earners in general with reduced hours, increased wages, and support for unions, they also allowed personnel reductions targeting women and institutionalized wage differentials between men and women. Male-dominated unions tended to maintain traditional distinctions in jobs and wage levels. As noted earlier in this chapter, New Deal programs failed to help domestic workers altogether. In 1940 some 20 percent of women who earned wages worked as domestic servants. In general, however, women suffered fewer job losses than men during the Depression because jobs for women increased in gender-typed sales, service, and clerical work.

Much has been made of the role women played during World War II as a severe manpower shortage led to the recruitment of women into jobs in heavy industry previously held by men. "Rosie the Riveter" did her patriotic duty and served the nation well. However, as hostilities ended and men returned to these jobs, women were laid off at a rapid rate. The shift of women into clerical and office jobs continued, and professional women did see some gains. Where women did move into "men's jobs," government and unions made some effort to equalize pay—but mainly to prevent women from undermining men's pay levels. Job differentiation remained a key feature of the working world, and women's wages actually decreased as a percentage of men's during the war years.

Once the war was over, pressures to return to the domestic sphere renewed. A Gallup poll taken after the war indicated that 86 percent of Americans believed that married women should remain at home. A 1947 best seller by Marynia Farnham and Ferdinand Lundberg, *The Modern Woman: The Lost Sex,* accused women who sought educational or employment equality of participating in "symbolic castration" of men and claimed that an independent woman was a contradiction in terms. They argued that women "would do well to recapture those functions in which they have demonstrated superior capacity. Those are, in general, the nurturing functions around the home."[72] The 1955 White House Conference on Effective Uses of Woman-Power claimed, "The structure and the substance of the lives of most women are fundamentally determined by their functions as wives, mothers, and homemakers."[73] Along with the renewed emphasis on home life, the funneling of women who did work into stereotyped, low-wage jobs continued. For the vast majority of these women, opportunities for advancement were limited. Wrote one Michigan secretary: "We are brought up to believe in a democracy; we are told that if we have talent coupled with ambition we will go far; those of us who accept this challenge are at a definite disadvantage. We are not told that undemocratic elements are at play and that we will be hindered in our efforts simply because we are women. Someone should have told me years ago that I'd have to be content with half a loaf. . . . I wouldn't have tried so hard."[74]

NOTES

1. Walter F. White, "Election by Terror in Florida," *The New Republic,* January 12, 1921, 195–97.

2. Originally reflecting a derogatory stereotype drawn from black minstrel shows, the term "Jim Crow" came to represent the system of segregation, discrimination, and disfranchisement that maintained white supremacy in the South.

3. See, for example, *Laws of Mississippi,* 1865 (Chaps. II, IV–VI, XXIII, XLVIII), 71–194, *passim,* cited in Richard Bardolph, *The Civil Rights Record: Black Americans and the Law, 1849–1970* (New York: Thomas Y. Crowell, 1970), 37–41, *passim.*

4. Ibid., Chapter XXIII, Section 5.

5. *United States v. Cruikshank,* 92 U.S. 542 (1876).

6. Nicholas Lemann, *Redemption: The Last Battle of the Civil War* (New York: Farrar, Straus and Giroux, 2006), 15–21; Donald G. Nieman, *Promises to Keep: African Americans and the Constitutional Order, 1776 to the Present* (New York: Oxford University Press, 1991), 95.

7. *Slaughter-House Cases,* 83 U.S. 36 (1873).

8. *United States v. Harris,* 106 U.S. 629 (1883).

9. *Civil Rights Cases,* 109 U.S. 3 (1883).

10. *Acts of Louisiana,* 1890 (no. 111), 152, cited in Bardolph, 132–33.

11. *Plessy v. Ferguson,* 163 U.S. 536 (1896).

12. Ibid., 544.

13. Ibid., 551.

14. Ibid., 560.

15. *Congressional Record* (56th Congress, 1st Session), March 1900, 3223–24.

16. *The Crisis,* August 1911, 166–67. Despite the fact that the U.S. Supreme Court had struck down laws that provided the legal bases for debt peonage, see *Bailey v. Alabama,* 211 U.S. 452 (1911) and *United States v. Reynolds,* 253 U.S. 133 (1914), the practice remained common throughout the South.

17. Richard Wright, *Twelve Million Black Voices: A Folk History of the Negro in the United States* (New York: Viking Press, 1941), 41–42, 43–46.

18. Interview with Leon Alexander in William H. Chafe, Raymond Gavins, and Robert Korstad, eds., *Remembering Jim Crow: African Americans Tell about Life in the Jim Crow South* (New York: The New Press, 2001), 229.

19. Interview with Earl Brown, ibid., 237.

20. Alexander, ibid., 235.

21. Interview with Ralph Thompson, ibid., 257.

22. Interview with Ann Pointer, ibid., 47.

23. Interview with Cleaster Mitchell, ibid., 212.

24. Interview with Pointer, ibid., 52–53, passim.

25. Carole Marks, *Farewell—We're Good and Gone: The Great Black Migration* (Bloomington: Indiana University Press, 1989), 14, 121–22.

26. Emmett J. Scott, "More Letters of Negro Migrants of 1916–1918," *The Journal of Negro History,* 4, no. 4 (1919), 461.

27 Marks, 3.

28. Ibid., 111–19.

29. Ibid., 129.

30. Ibid., 135.

31. Ira Katznelson, *When Affirmative Action Was White* (New York: W. W. Norton & Company, 2005).

32. Ibid., 48.

33. Ibid., 82.

34. Ibid., 112.

35. See, for example, Michael J. Bennett, *When Dreams Came True: The GI Bill and the Making of Modern America* (McLean, VA: Brassey's Publishing, 1996).

36. Katznelson, 141.

37. A. Philip Randolph, "Call to Negro America to a March on Washington for Jobs and Equal Participation on July 1, 1941," *The Black Worker* (May 1941).

38. Ruth Benedict and Gene Weltfish, "The Races of Mankind," Public Affairs Pamphlet No. 85 (New York: Public Affairs Committee, Inc., 1943).

39. Gunnar Myrdal, *An American Dilemma: The Negro Problem and Modern Democracy* (New York: Harper & Bros., 1944).

40. *To Secure These Rights: The Report of the President's Committee on Civil Rights* (Washington, DC: Government Printing Office, 1947).

41. *Higher Education for Democracy: A Report of the President's Commission on Higher Education, Vol. 1* (New York: Harper & Brothers, 1947).

42. *Missouri ex rel. Gaines v. Canada,* 305 U.S. 337 (1938).

43. *Sweatt v. Painter,* 339 U.S. 629 (1950).

44. *McLaurin v. Oklahoma State Regents,* 339 U.S. 737 (1950).

45. *Mitchell v. United States,* 313 U.S. 80 (1941).

46. *Morgan v. Virginia,* 328 U.S. 373 (1945).

47. *Henderson v. U.S. Interstate Commerce Commission and Southern Railway,* 339 U.S. 816 (1950).

48. *Smith v. Allwright,* 321 U.S. 649 (1944).

49. *Shelley v. Kraemer,* 344 U.S. 1 (1948).

50. Richard Kluger, *Simple Justice* (New York: Alfred A. Knopf, 1976), 8.

51. Pub. L. 85-315, 71 Stat 634.

52. Editorial, *Journal of Negro Education* 26 (1957), 433.

53. A good place to start a study of the experiences of racial and ethnic minorities with patterns of discrimination and exclusion in the United States is Ronald Takaki, *A Different Mirror: A History of Multicultural America* (Boston: Little, Brown and Company, 1993).

54. Ephesians 5:22.

55. William Blackstone, *Commentaries on the Laws of England, Vol. (1765) 1:* 442, excerpted in Winston E. Langley and Vivian C. Fox, eds., *Women's Rights in the United States: A Documentary History* (Westport, CT: Greenwood Press, 1994), 7.

56. James Kendall Hosmer, ed., *Winthrop's Journal: History of New England, 1630–1649,* 2 vols. (New York: Barnes and Noble, 1908), vol. 2, 225, excerpted in Langley and Fox, 14.

57. Jonathan Stearns, *Female Influence and the True Christian Mode of Its Exercise: A Discourse Delivered in the First Presbyterian Church in Newburyport, July 30, 1837,* excerpted in Langley and Fox, 73, emphasis in original.

58. Alice Kessler-Harris, *Out To Work: A History of Wage-Earning Women in the United States* (New York: Oxford University Press, 1982), 36–37.

59. Ibid., 46–48.q

60. Catharine E. Beecher, "An Essay on the Education of Female Teachers for the United States, 1835," in *The School in the United States: A Documentary History,* ed. James W. Fraser (New York: McGraw-Hill, 2001), 63–64.

61. Barbara Welter, "The Cult of True Womanhood: 1820–1860," *American Quarterly* 18, no. 2, pt. 1 (1966), 168.

62. 1 Corinthians 14:34.

63. Elizabeth Blackwell obtained a degree in medicine in 1849, Ada Keply in law in 1870, and Antoinette Brown in theology in 1851.

64. Ibid., 172–73.

65. *Lochner v. New York,* 198 U.S. 45 (1905).

66. *Muller v. Oregon,* 208 U.S. 421 (1908).

67. Ibid., 421–22.

68. The following discussion is drawn largely from the work of Alice Kessler-Harris.

69. The original, 1923 ERA stated: "Men and Women shall have equal rights throughout the United States and every place subject to its jurisdiction." Senate Joint Resolution 21, 68th Cong., 1st Sess., 65 *Congressional Record,* 150 (1923), quoted in Langley and Cox, 236.

70. Kessler-Harris, 249.

71. Langley and Fox, 225.

72. Quoted in Stephanie Coontz, *The Way We Never Were: American Families and the Nostalgia Trap* (New York: Basic Books, 1992), 32.

73. Quoted in Kessler-Harris, 300.

74. Quoted in Kessler-Harris, 310.

2

The Great Society and the Birth of Affirmative Action

The largest racial minority in the United States, until quite recently, has been that of African Americans. As we have just seen, prior to 1960 most of the civil rights legislation and judicial activity involving race relations targeted black Americans. One of the key goals of progressive American policy from the ratification of the Fourteenth Amendment in 1868 until the end of the Eisenhower administration was to find avenues affording African Americans, in competition with white Americans, equal legal rights and equal access to education and employment. Despite some tentative steps in New Deal legislation of the 1930s, the desegregation of the military in the 1940s, and encouraging rulings by the federal courts in the 1950s, the efforts to improve the everyday lives of black Americans had not progressed very far. Something more needed to be done, it was argued, to move from equality of opportunity to equality of results.

EARLY USES OF THE PHRASE "AFFIRMATIVE ACTION"

The first explicit appearance of the words "affirmative action" in the text of a federal law was in the National Labor Relations Act (Wagner Act) of 1935. The words in that signature piece of New Deal legislation had nothing to do with special consideration for a targeted group. The Wagner Act merely empowered the newly created National Labor Relations Board to take "affirmative action" to protect workers should management in a particular industry be determined by the Board to have engaged in an unfair labor practice.[1] In this context, then, the language was more of a gentle exhortation to a regulatory agency than the promulgation of a policy mandating special employment consideration based on race. Although some Depression-era programs like the Public Works Administration (PWA) did afford a degree of special consideration for the employment of blacks,[2] the term "affirmative action" was not ascribed to those programs.

The phrase "affirmative action" was also used on at least one notable occasion by President John F. Kennedy. In Executive Order 10925, issued shortly after taking office, Kennedy decreed that federal contractors must "not discriminate against any employee or applicant for employment because of race, creed, color or national origin." Then followed the telling language: "The contractor will take *affirmative action* to ensure that applicants are employed, and that employees are treated during employment, without regard to race, creed, color, or national origin."[3] This racially neutral use of the term "affirmative action" actually runs counter to the thrust of the race-based affirmative action in late 1960s executive orders and statutes that would spring from the rhetoric and the pen of Kennedy's successor, Lyndon B. Johnson.

How did the country move from the vague, almost innocuous language of Kennedy's 1961 executive order to government programs and agencies working aggressively in support of racial preferences in the latter half of the 1960s and 1970s? This is a fascinating and complex story: it involves unexpected and traumatic national events, the surprising passion of an American president, seismic shifts in the Civil Rights Movement and the response to a confidential government report.[4]

LYNDON JOHNSON AND CIVIL RIGHTS

In the early fall of 1963, in the wake of televised racial violence in the South—especially in Birmingham, Alabama—the Kennedy administration felt compelled to offer tangible assistance to African Americans who were being brutally assaulted for engaging in peaceful acts of civil disobedience. Kennedy voiced his support for an omnibus federal civil rights bill that would, among other things, make it a violation of federal law to discriminate on the basis of race in such "public accommodations" as restaurants, hotels, and transportation. This was the most far-reaching civil rights legislation that had been proposed in Congress since the Reconstruction Era of the late nineteenth century. But the bill was going nowhere. Kennedy, a New England liberal with minimal experience in the wheeling and dealing of legislative politics, was not capable of selling his civil rights bill to enough members of Congress to achieve its passage. In particular, Kennedy had little success persuading Southern Democratic members of Congress of the value of his initiative. Then an assassin's bullet changed the course of history.

With the death of John Kennedy in November 1963, Texan Lyndon Johnson ascended to the presidency. Johnson, to those who did not know him personally, seemed an unlikely champion of civil rights. He grew up in the hill country of Texas when segregation was flourishing in the South.[5] But Johnson believed that people of color deserved more opportunity than most of his friends and neighbors were willing to extend. In the 1930s, as a young Democratic congressman, he had been an ardent proponent of New Deal liberalism. Then, as the powerful majority leader of the U.S. Senate in the 1950s, he used all of his legislative acumen and persuasive skills to achieve passage of the Civil Rights Act of 1957.[6] Now Johnson was president and wanted desperately to put his stamp on history in an even more pronounced fashion. So he once again championed civil rights legislation, stridently arguing that the Congress should pass the pending bill.

Deploying the infamous "Johnson treatment," the new president did whatever he felt necessary to achieve his objectives. He personally cajoled, praised, ridiculed, bullied, even threatened recalcitrant senators and representatives. Moreover, he was not above exploiting sad memories of the recently murdered president to secure passage of civil rights legislation. Less than a week after the assassination, with the nation still reeling from the trauma of a state funeral, Johnson went before a joint session of Congress and pleaded that "no memorial oration or eulogy could more eloquently honor President Kennedy's memory than the earliest possible passage of the civil rights bill for which he fought so long. . . . I urge you again, as I did in 1957 and again in 1960, to enact a civil rights law so that we can move forward to eliminate from this Nation every trace of discrimination and oppression that is based upon race or color."[7]

Johnson's entreaties ultimately bore fruit. Surviving tendentious opposition in the Rules Committee of the House of Representatives and a nasty Senate filibuster, the Civil Rights Act of 1964 was approved by Congress and signed into law by Johnson on July 2, 1964.[8] The introductory description of the Act aptly summarizes its purpose: "To enforce the constitutional right to vote, to confer jurisdiction upon the district courts of the United States to provide relief against discrimination in public accommodations, to authorize the Attorney General to institute suits to protect constitutional rights in public facilities and public education, to extend the Commission on Civil Rights, to prevent discrimination in federally assisted programs, to establish a Commission on Equal Employment Opportunity."[9]

Probably the two most consequential portions of the new civil rights law were Title II on public accommodations and Title VII on equal employment opportunity. In Title II, Congress stipulated: "All persons shall be entitled to the full and equal enjoyment of the goods, services, facilities and privileges, advantages, and accommodations of any place of public accommodation . . . without discrimination or segregation on the ground of race, color, religion, or national origin."[10] Included among the places of "public accommodation" specified by the law were the following: hotels and other facilities that provided lodging to overnight guests; restaurants and establishments serving food; and places of entertainment such as movie theatres and sports arenas.[11] Achievement of these simple words in federal law had come only at the expense of a decade of pain and effort through countless civil rights marches, sit-ins, and protests.

The words in Title VII were equally straightforward and gave little appearance on their face of the hardships and injustices that had occasioned them: "It shall be an unlawful employment practice for an employer . . . to fail or refuse to hire or to discharge any individual, or otherwise to discriminate against any individual with respect to his compensation, terms, conditions, or privileges of employment, because of such individual's race, color, religion, sex, or national origin."[12] Later in Title VII, Congress provided a means to enforce nondiscrimination in employment through regulations and orders promulgated by an agency named the Equal Employment Opportunity Commission, soon to be known as the EEOC.[13]

The story of how the word "sex" came to be part of the just-quoted passage in Title VII is a fascinatingly ironic vignette in legislative history. Republican Congressman Howard W. "Judge" Smith, who had long represented Virginia's northern apple orchard country, had little sympathy for the broad-based civil rights that Congress was considering in 1963 and 1964. So, in order to do what he could to defeat the bill, he rose on the House floor during the debate on Title VII and proposed an amendment to include "sex" among the protected categories of the pending legislation. He posed the rhetorical question: "This bill is so imperfect, what harm will this little amendment do?" Smith either hoped that the feminist language would bring down this entire, key section of the bill or, if passed, that no one would take sexual equality seriously. Republicans and conservative Southern Democrats joined forces, and Smith's amendment was approved by the House of Representatives by a vote of 168 to 133. However, with the entire Title before Congress, Republicans and Southern Democrats did not have the votes to defeat the "imperfect" bill. Thus, through this curious set of circumstances, protection for women was written into Title VII and, ultimately, into American history.[14]

Both Title II and Title VII were founded on the principle of colorblind treatment of persons exercising rights of public accommodations and seeking or maintaining employment. In the debate over Title VII, Congress did listen to some arguments in favor of racial quotas and racial preferences. But, when it came time to draft the specific language of the employment title, senators and representatives came down decisively on side of affording equal treatment rather than extending preferences intended to compensate for past injustices. In the words of Hugh Davis Graham, the historian who, perhaps, has studied the Civil Rights Act of 1964 most carefully, "the debate over racial quotas [in 1963–64] elicited a virtually unanimous public condemnation of the notion of racial preference, however allegedly benign."[15]

Another key section of the Civil Rights Act of 1964 was Section 601, subsumed under Title VI, "Nondiscrimination in Federally Assisted Programs." The relevant language of Section 601 decreed that "No person in the United States shall, on the ground of race, color, or national origin, be excluded from participation in, be denied the benefits of, or be subjected to discrimination under any program or activity receiving Federal financial assistance."[16] Judging from its legislative history, Section 601 was principally intended to be relied on by black or other nonwhite individuals who experienced racial discrimination in programs that received federal funds.[17] And so this section has been used on countless occasions since the passage of the Act. However, Section 601 would also become a legal hook for *white* men and women who wished to file law suits against race-based programs receiving federal funds in education or employment. As we will soon see, in challenges to affirmative action programs at public colleges and universities—all of which receive some federal as well as state-based funding—white litigants alleged that affirmative action admissions programs violated the Equal Protection Clause of the Fourteenth Amendment *and* Section 601 of the Civil Rights Act of 1964.

THE GREAT SOCIETY AND THE HOWARD UNIVERSITY ADDRESS

The Civil Rights Act of 1964 marked the high point of official expression of the principle of colorblind treatment of the races in America. But it also was the jumping off point for what President Johnson and many commentators would refer to as the "Great Society." Just a few weeks prior to the passage of the Civil Rights Act of 1964, President Johnson delivered a commencement address at the University of Michigan. In his short speech he brought together many of the hopes for economic, racial, and cultural aspiration that he had voiced up to this point in his administration. This was not the first time Johnson had used the phrase "Great Society" in a public statement, but this address offers the most concise and elegant statement of the principles that undergirded his dream for America. He put it thusly: "The Great Society rests on abundance and liberty for all. It demands an end to poverty and racial injustice. . . . It is a place where the city of man serves not only the needs of the body and the demands of commerce but the desire for beauty and the hunger for community. . . . It is a place where men are more concerned with the quality of their goals than the quantity of their goods."[18]

The American electorate, at least for a short while, was sympathetic with Johnson's vision. In November1964 Johnson was elected president in his own right. In competition with conservative Barry Goldwater, Johnson amassed 61.1 percent of the popular vote, the most decisive majority in a presidential election to that point in American history. Perhaps more importantly for the prospects of the Great Society, Johnson's coattails swept in the largest and most liberal majority of senators and representatives serving in Congress since the New Deal.

The 89th Congress that assembled in January 1965 did not disappoint the president and those who shared his vision for the country. Most of the legislation that would constitute the Great Society originated in bills drafted in the White House or the Executive Office Building. An impressive 69 percent of Johnson's proposals hammered out in 1965 found their way into law; the figure for 1966 was 56 percent. By contrast, the success rate for President Dwight Eisenhower's legislative agenda in 1957 was 37 percent, and Kennedy's in 1963 was a mere 27 percent.[19] Moreover, the laws passed in the Johnson years were hardly garden variety. Taken as a whole, the sweep and consequence of Great Society legislation was rivaled only by the laws passed in the early years of Franklin Roosevelt's New Deal, which—not so coincidentally—was the model that Johnson strove to surpass. Between January 1965 and the end of 1966, for example, Johnson and the compliant 89th Congress furnished the country with the following progressive legislation: Medicare; the first significant voting rights act since the ratification of the Fifteen Amendment in 1870; a panoply of education bills; highway beautification; funding for a "war on poverty"; endowments for the arts and humanities; new cabinet level departments for Transportation and Housing/Urban Development; and substantial increases in funding for Social Security and the minimum wage.[20]

The height of the Great Society was probably early 1965. On March 17, in the aftermath of the bloody Selma to Montgomery, Alabama march to dramatize the need for minority voting rights, Johnson sent to the Congress the most far-reaching measure to protect the franchise of African Americans since the ratification of the Fifteenth Amendment almost a century earlier. It forbade literacy tests and established procedures for the federal government to supervise voting practices in areas of the country in which blacks had historically been denied the right to vote. The measure would later be adopted by Congress and signed by Johnson.[21] As the Voting Rights Bill was working its way along the legislative gauntlet, Johnson accepted the invitation of Howard

University, the nation's most prestigious historically black institution of higher learning, to deliver its annual commencement address. Johnson could easily have used this occasion to celebrate the passage of the Civil Rights Act of 1964 and the likely passage of the pending Voting Rights Act. He could have spoken eloquently—likely to polite applause—for what his administration had done to promote colorblind racial equality. But he took a different tack.

On June 4, following his acceptance of the honorary degree of Doctor of Laws in front of the library on Howard University's main quadrangle, the president delivered his soon to be famous address. Johnson began by asking his audience to reflect on the political and social change instigated by people of color that was occurring at that very moment in Asia and Africa. He quite intentionally invoked the term "revolution" to describe what was taking place in countries that most Americans had barely read about in their newspapers. Then he segued to the domestic scene and charged that "nothing in any country touches us more profoundly, and nothing is more freighted with meaning for our own destiny than the revolution of the Negro American."[22] Thus, within less than a minute, an American president born and raised in the Jim Crow South had twice used the word "revolution" to characterize and endorse the American civil rights movement. Then this president reminded the students, their families and their friends of the Civil Rights Act of 1964 and the pending Voting Rights Bill. He submitted that an unprecedented era of freedom for people of color was dawning.

The most quoted words in Johnson's speech offered a vivid metaphor that would furnish, from that moment forward, a rhetorical rationale for policies of race-based preference: "But freedom is not enough," Johnson intoned. "You do not wipe away the scars of centuries by saying: Now you are free to go where you want, and do as you desire, and choose the leaders you please. You do not take a person who, for years, has been hobbled by chains and liberate him, bring him up to the starting line of a race and then say, 'you are free to compete with all the others,' and still justly believe that you have been completely fair."[23] For President Johnson, equality for people of color demanded "not just equality as a right and a theory but equality as a fact and equality as a result."[24]

Then Johnson's commencement address turned somber. Although the president predicted great things for graduates of Howard University, he was not as optimistic about the future prospects for most black Americans. For example, he noted that the unemployment rate among blacks was then twice as high as among whites and getting worse every year. He cited statistics to the effect that the income of blacks was declining when compared to whites. This was particularly severe among the poorest blacks, whose numbers below the poverty line continued to increase. In addition, infant mortality for blacks was climbing, a reverse of the situation among whites. Finally, he alluded to the reality of increasing residential segregation in America: blacks were clustering in greater and greater numbers in the cores of American cities, while whites were moving inexorably to the nation's suburbs. The big question, as Johnson saw it, was "Why weren't African Americans sharing in the improving quality of life enjoyed by whites?" Part of the answer he traced to lack of job training and skills among blacks, and another part of the answer he laid at the door of persistent racism. But Johnson reserved the greatest degree of blame for what he characterized as a breakdown of the black family: "Only a minority—less than half—of all Negro children," he stated, "reach the age of 18 having lived all their lives with both of their parents. . . . Probably a majority of all Negro children receive federal aided public assistance sometime during their childhood."[25]

Among the possible strategies that Johnson suggested for addressing these deeply rooted problems were: more jobs for minorities; improved housing and medical care for blacks; and the increased enrollment of persons of color in welfare and social programs. To seek more systematic, more definitive answers he called for a White House conference that fall, to be attended by black leaders and scholars/experts of all races on the theme "To Fulfill these Rights."[26]

THE MOYNIHAN REPORT

Lurking behind Johnson's Howard University address was a scholarly report on the status of the black family. That report, commissioned by the Johnson administration although not acknowledged in the president's Howard University address, provided much of the intellectual scaffolding for later policy pronouncements on affirmative action. The existence of the report was known in the summer of 1965 to a handful of scholars and political figures, but its evidence and detailed argumentation were kept under wraps. Over the next few months, slowly and awkwardly, some of the contents of the report were leaked to the media and, eventually, to the public. The story of the report and the firestorm surrounding it would figure prominently in the early debate over affirmative action.

The confidential report was drafted in late 1964 and early 1965 by Daniel Patrick Moynihan, the same man who, along with Richard N. Goodwin, would ghostwrite the president's Howard University address.[27] Moynihan had been Assistant Secretary of Labor since 1963. He was a trained social scientist and regarded as one of the deepest thinkers in the Democratic Party. His blunt diction won him some friends and more than a few critics. Following a dubious notoriety with his report on the black family, Moynihan would continue in public service as a scholar and a political figure, completing his time on the public stage as a U.S. senator from New York in 2001.[28]

In 1965 Moynihan was still a behind-the-scenes researcher and advisor in the Department of Labor. The report he drafted on the black family under the auspices of the Office of Policy Planning and Research was part social science journal article and part political position paper. He began work on the report in the fall of 1964, disturbed that some in Congress and the Johnson administration thought that the Civil Rights Act of that year had satisfactorily addressed the most glaring problems faced by blacks in the mid-1960s. Moynihan's familiarity with statistics on black poverty and employment through his position at the Department of Labor convinced him that the 1964 civil rights legislation, important as it was, would not by itself put much of a dent in the economic and cultural deficiencies from which African Americans suffered.[29]

The formal title of the Moynihan Report was "The Negro Family: The Case for National Action."[30] It was completed in March 1965 and began circulating almost immediately within the Johnson Administration. Including tables and appendices it was only 78 typed pages in length. It commenced with the assertion that "The Negro American revolution is rightly regarded as the most important domestic event of the postwar period in the United States."[31] After detailing some of the Great Society legislation and programs that had resulted from this revolution—for example, the Civil Rights Act of 1964, the Manpower Development and Training Act, and the Job Corps—the report asserted that the "revolution" was about to enter a new phase in which the principal challenge would be to make certain that "equality of results" for African Americans would be realized. If not, Moynihan predicted, "there will be no social peace in the United States for generations."[32]

The achievement of equality of results would be most difficult, Moynihan argued, because African Americans were not prepared in 1965 to take advantage of the opportunities available for advancement offered by Great Society programs. And why was this? Drawing from U.S. Census data and presenting the results in tabular form, Moynihan determined that, on average, the black family, when compared to the white family, was deficient. For example, the percentage of families with husbands absent was at least three times higher among blacks than whites; the nonwhite illegitimacy ratio was eight times the white rate; and the percentage of welfare recipients was much greater among blacks than among whites. And these percentages were becoming more divergent over time.[33] Statistics such as these led Moynihan to conclude that "the steady expansion of . . . public assistance programs in general can be taken as a measure of the steady disintegration of the Negro family structure over the past generation in the United States."[34] Moynihan traced these problems, in part, to historical factors such as the lingering consequences of slavery, the failures of Reconstruction, and the dislocations of increasing urbanization.[35] One of the saddest dimensions of the problem of the black family, as Moynihan saw it, was the inability of young black males to find jobs that could support themselves and their families. This, in turn, led to alienation, anger, and—increasingly more often—violence.[36] In the executive summary, Moynihan pointedly expressed the thrust of his argument: "The fundamental problem . . . is that of family structure. The evidence . . . is that the Negro family in the urban ghettos is crumbling. A middle-class group has managed to save itself, but for vast numbers of the unskilled, poorly educated city working class the fabric of conventional social relationships has all but disintegrated. . . . So long as this situation persists, the cycle of poverty and disadvantage will continue to repeat itself."[37]

At the end of the report, Moynihan issued a rather cryptic call to action. Referring to the problems he had identified as constituting "a tangle of pathology," he submitted that they could only be broken by heroic government efforts "to strengthen the Negro family."[38] Although Moynihan did not go into detail as to possible solutions, it is a fair assumption that he had in mind more jobs, improved housing, and high quality medical care—the very things that Johnson would mention in the Howard University address that Moynihan had helped to write.

FALLOUT FROM THE MOYNIHAN REPORT AND THE WATTS RIOTS

Few persons outside the Johnson administration had the opportunity to examine the entire Moynihan Report until the fall of 1965. Nevertheless, sections of the confidential study were leaked to the media. In a by-lined article published on July 19, for example, the *New York Times* quoted liberally from the report.[39] Many politicians, civil rights leaders, and members of the press who had learned about the existence of the report and its conclusions from the July *New York Times* article and other press accounts were critical of Moynihan for singling out the fatherless black family for the failure of African Americans to achieve good educations and good jobs. In fact, a syndicated political column, published on August 18, 1965, reported that one reason the report was kept confidential was that Moynihan's boss, Secretary of Labor Willard Wirtz, feared that the evidence presented in the report on black illegitimacy would serve as fodder for white racists' propaganda.[40]

Public comment on the report took an angry turn in early August when the heavily black community of Watts in South Central Los Angeles exploded in racial violence. With fires still smoldering after a week of turmoil, the bodies of 34 men and women were buried, and the estimated total in property damages rose to almost $50 million.[41] In terms of loss of life, the Watts riots represented the bloodiest racial strife in the United States since World War I.

National reporter John Herbers noted, for example, that "the report has come in for new attention since the Los Angeles riots, for it pinpoints the causes of discontent in the Negro ghettos and says the new crisis in race relations is much more severe than is generally believed."[42] To document this point, Herbers alluded to Moynihan's phrase "tangle of pathology" to characterize the depth and severity of racial tension in America.

The Watts riots also placed in stark relief the report's call for "preferential treatment" for African Americans. Rowland Evans and Robert Novak, in their syndicated column of August 18, 1965, focused on this controversial line of analysis: "The Moynihan Report, a much-suppressed, much-leaked Labor Department document, . . . strips away usual equivocations and exposes the ugly truth about the big-city Negro's plight. Some Administration officials view the report as a political atom bomb certain to produce unwanted fallout—mainly by bringing up the most taboo subject in civil rights, preferential treatment for Negroes."[43] Evans and Novak maintained that the country's "white majority" would never accept preferential treatment for a minority and that "Administration officials [are keeping] their fingers crossed that the forthcoming White House conference won't even mention it."[44]

Preferential treatment—it was not yet being labeled affirmative action—was, however, exactly what the Johnson administration felt compelled to propose given the depth of problems identified by the Moynihan Report and tragically underlined by the Watts riots. Johnson and his closest domestic advisors saw the constellation of policies, suggested in the most general terms by Moynihan, as a radical but justifiable approach to race relations. Johnson hoped that his much ballyhooed White House conference on civil rights would offer new ideas and policies and essentially "leapfrog" the civil rights movement.[45]

But criticism of the leaked Moynihan Report delayed the planning conference until November 1965. The full-scale White House conference, titled "To Fulfill These Rights," did not convene until mid-1966. By the time the conference finally took place it was doomed to failure, if not irrelevance. Moynihan had quit his position in the Labor Department shortly after his report was published in mid-1965. In the words of one historian, Moynihan was "hounded into resignation by . . . the liberal academic and civil rights community."[46] In fact, because of his poisonous persona, Johnson reportedly tried to keep Moynihan from attending the very conference that his ideas and rhetoric had spawned.[47] Moynihan did, ultimately, attend the conference, but hardly uttered a word. In addition, Moynihan's thesis on the deterioration of the black family was "dismissed virtually without debate," and the delegates came to no consensus as to what strategies to endorse to improve race relations.[48]

The momentous events of 1965 further undercut any effort to come to a meeting of the minds at the White House conference. The Watts riots, of course, were of seismic influence in unsettling America. But even before the riots, the civil rights consensus had begun to unravel. Martin Luther King, Jr. still commanded influence through his Southern Christian Leadership Conference (SCLC), but younger black radicals in organizations such as the Student Non-Violent Coordinating Committee (SNCC) repudiated King's leadership and began to follow a path of increasing stridency. SNCC boycotted the White House conference. In the black cores of northern cities, the Nation of Islam (NOI) preached an anti-white message and was willing, when it deemed necessary, to countenance violence. In addition, protests against America's involvement in the Vietnam War occasionally turned violent, adding further complications to the already unstable domestic scene. Finally, spending for the Vietnam War cut into the funding available for the domestic programs of the Great Society.[49] The title of one of the first published U.S. history texts on the decade of the 1960s, *Coming Apart*,[50] captures the travail and lack of cohesion in the country at the time.

Looking back on the more than 40 years that have passed since the high watermark of the Great Society, it is hard to believe that affirmative action survived its shaky first few months in the public eye. At the time the fires in southern California were being snuffed out, Americans were probably more in favor of restoring order and meting out punishments than in rewarding violent behavior with governmental assistance. In combination, the rioting in Los Angeles, the botched Moynihan Report, the failed White House conference on civil rights, the splintering of the African American civil rights movement, and the resistance to additional government spending in light of the growing unpopularity of the war in Vietnam could easily have convinced the Johnson administration to pull the plug on affirmative action. But the president and his closest domestic advisors stayed the course, forging ahead with affirmative action directives through the new Equal Employment Opportunity Commission and other federal initiatives. In addition, state agencies and institutions of higher learning began to mimic federal efforts to afford special consideration to African Americans and other minorities. The transition from the blunt rhetoric on preferential treatment in the Moynihan Report to actual affirmative action policy under Lyndon Johnson and his successor, Richard Nixon, is addressed in the following chapter.

NOTES

1. U.S. Code, 1935, vol. 29, secs. 160b, 160c. As quoted in Jo Ann Ooiman Robinson, ed., *Affirmative Action: A Documentary History* (Westport, CT: Greenwood Publishing, 2001), 32–33.

2. Terry H. Anderson, *The Pursuit of Fairness: A History of Affirmative Action* (New York: Oxford University Press, 2004), 11–24. See also our discussion in Chapter 1.

3. Executive Order 10925, *Federal Register* 26 (March 6, 1961), quoted in Robinson, ed., *Affirmative Action: A Documentary History,* 79–80.

4. On the rise of affirmative action in the Johnson administration, see especially Bruce J. Schulman, *Lyndon B. Johnson and American Liberalism: A Brief Biography with Documents,* 2nd ed. (Boston: Bedford/St. Martin's, 2007), 1–132, 181–230; and Hugh Davis Graham, *The Civil Rights Era: Origins and Development of National Policy, 1960–1972* (New York: Oxford University Press, 1990), 3–277. See also Anderson, *The Pursuit of Fairness,* 49–109.

5. Two historians, Robert Caro and Robert Dallek, have produced brilliant studies of Johnson's youth and early years in politics. See Robert Caro, *The Years of Lyndon Johnson: The Path to Power* (New York: Alfred A. Knopf, 1982); Caro, *The Years of Lyndon Johnson: Means of Ascent* (New York: Alfred A. Knopf, 1990); and Robert Dallek, *Lone Star Rising: Lyndon Johnson and His Times, 1908–1960* (New York: Oxford University Press, 1991).

6. Caro has devoted an entire volume to Johnson's legislative leadership in the passage of this law. See Robert Caro, *The Years of Lyndon Johnson: Master of the Senate* (New York: Alfred A. Knopf, 2002).

7. Lyndon B. Johnson, Address before a Joint Session of the Congress, November 27, 1963, *Public Papers of the President of the United States: Lyndon B. Johnson, 1963–64,* I (Washington, DC: Government Printing Office, 1964), 8–10.

8. Pub. L. 88–352, 78 Stat. 241, July 2,1964.

9. Ibid.

10. Ibid., Section 201 (a).

11. Ibid., Section 201 (b).

12. Ibid., Section 703 (a).

13. Ibid., Section 705.

14. Graham, *The Civil Rights Era,* 134–39; and Shulman, *Lyndon B. Johnson and American Liberalism,* 2nd ed., 77.

15. Ibid., 120.

16. Pub. L. 88–352, 78 Stat. 241, July 2, 1964, Section 601.

17. Graham, *The Civil Rights Era,* 156–61.

18. Lyndon B. Johnson, Remarks at the University of Michigan, May 22, 1964, *Public Papers of the Presidents of the United States: Lyndon B. Johnson, 1963–64,* I (Washington, DC: Government Printing Office, 1964), 704–7.

19. Schulman, *Lyndon Johnson and American Liberalism,* 2nd ed., 96.

20. Useful tables on the accomplishments of the 89th Congress can be found at ibid., 97–98.

21. Pub. L. 89–110, 79 Stat. 437, August 6, 1965.

22. Lyndon B. Johnson, Commencement Address at Howard University, June 4, 1965, *Public Papers of the President of the United States: Lyndon B. Johnson, 1963–64,* I (Washington, DC: Government Printing Office, 1964), 635–40.

23. Ibid.

24. Ibid.

25. Ibid.

26. Ibid.

27. Lee Rainwater and William L. Yancey, *The Moynihan Report and the Politics of Controversy* (Cambridge, MA: The M.I.T. Press, 1967), 4.

28. For biographical information on Moynihan, see Lee Rainwater and William L. Yancey, *The Moynihan Report and the Politics of Controversy,* 17–18; and "Daniel Patrick Moynihan, 1927–2003," *Biographical Directory of the United States Congress,* http://bioguide.congress.gov/scripts/biodisplay.pl?index=MO (accessed July 24, 2007).

29. Rainwater and Yancey, *The Moynihan Report and the Politics of Controversy,* 25.

30. "The Negro Family: The Case for National Action," Unpublished Report of the U.S. Department of Labor, March 1965, reprinted in Rainwater and Yancey, *The Moynihan Report and the Politics of Controversy,* 47–124.

31. Ibid., 47.

32. Ibid., 49.

33. Ibid., 51–60.

34. Ibid., 60.

35. Ibid., 61–65.

36. Ibid., 80–91.

37. Ibid., 43.

38. Ibid., 93.

39. John D. Pomfret, "Capital Parley Planned," *New York Times,* July 19, 1965, 1.

40. Rowland Evans and Robert Novak, "Inside Report: The Moynihan Report," quoted in Rainwater and Yancey, *The Moynihan Report and the Politics of Controversy,* 376.

41. Bruce J. Schulman, *Lyndon B. Johnson and American Liberalism,* 2nd ed., 118–21.

42. John Herbers, "Report Focuses on Negro Family," *New York Times,* August 27, 1965, 13.

43. Rowland Evans and Robert Novak, "Inside Report: The Moynihan Report," August 18, 1965, quoted in Rainwater and Yancey, *The Moynihan Report and the Politics of Controversy,* 375.

44. Ibid., 377.

45. Ibid., 274.

46. Graham, *The Civil Rights Era,* 210.

47. Nick Kotz, *Judgment Days: Lyndon Baines Johnson, Martin Luther King, Jr., and the Laws that Changed America* (Boston: Houghton Mifflin Company, 2005), 359.

48. John Herbers, "Frustration on Rights: Parley Said to Displease White House—Subject of Families Rejected or Ignored," *New York Times,* November 25, 1965, 52; Rainwater and Yancey, *The Moynihan Report and the Politics of Controversy,* 271–91.

49. See Schulman, *Lyndon B. Johnson and American Liberalism,* 2nd ed., 111–78, 230–71.

50. William L. O'Neill, *Coming Apart: An Informal History of America in the 1960s* (Chicago: Quadrangle Books, 1971).

3

Affirmative Action Takes Shape

Title VII of the Civil Rights Act of 1964 established the Equal Employment Opportunity Commission (EEOC) to investigate complaints of illegal job discrimination. Franklin D. Roosevelt Jr., the first chairman of the EEOC, argued that the commission would pursue that charge, but also that "we regard our other approach—affirmative action—as important as the . . . correction of violations." By affirmative action, Roosevelt meant to work with businesses to "go beyond the law" and foster "more aggressive leadership and participation by private business in promoting equal employment opportunity . . . more than is required by law." He emphasized the need for aggressive recruitment and special training.[1] As we shall see, "going beyond the law" was an apt phrase for the direction that affirmative action took as government agencies attempted to find practical tools to address historical discrimination, discrimination that many believed fueled the urban crisis. Before exploring the confluence of factors that shaped affirmative action during the Johnson and Nixon administrations, however, we need to take a closer look at Title VII and the broader debate over the Civil Rights Act of 1964.

AN EARLY DEBATE

While President Johnson in his Howard University address was implicitly flirting with special consideration and preferential treatment for the victims of historical discrimination, the language of the Civil Rights Act of 1964 was color-blind. Both that language and Congressional debate indicated that preferential treatment was itself discriminatory. In fact, Section 703 (j) of Title VII, crafted as a compromise to gain the support of business-oriented, Republican legislators such as Sen. Everett Dirksen of Illinois (who helped write the law), declared "Nothing contained in this title shall be interpreted to require any employer [or other entity] . . . subject to this title to grant preferential treatment to any individual or to any group . . . on account of an imbalance which may exist with respect to the total number or percentage of persons of any race, color, religion, sex or national origin employed by an employer . . . in comparison with the total number or percentage of persons of such race, color, religion, sex or national origin in any community, State, section, or other area, or in the available work force in any community, State, section, or other area."[2] Government-imposed hiring quotas, then, were specifically prohibited.

The crafting of this legislation took place against a broader background of debate in 1963 and 1964 over civil rights and preferential treatment. While some civil rights activists anticipated the thinking of President Johnson in his Howard University address, conservatives rejected many of the arguments of civil rights liberals. For example, in late 1963, the National Urban League's Whitney Young identified the potential for violent outbreaks in Northern, urban centers. "In teeming northern ghettoes, hundreds of thousands of Negro citizens—unemployed, ill-housed, disillusioned—are nearing the breaking point," he wrote. In order to prevent the eruption of violence, Young called for a domestic Marshall Plan. The Marshall Plan was the name given the expansive effort after World War II to help war-ravaged European countries. Young called for a similar, "massive program to close the intolerable economic, social, and educational gap that separates the vast majority of Negro citizens from other Americans." Without such action, "legal progress is an illusion." Young argued that such a plea was for "special effort," not "special treatment," and identified exclusion based on racial discrimination as the culprit. "Apart from historical equity," he argued, "a massive compensatory effort may well be the only means of overcoming all present results of past neglect."[3] This line of reasoning later influenced President Johnson, although his Great Society policies would be framed in the more general language of poverty rather than race.

Consider the chasm, however, between Young's thinking and that of Frank S. Meyer writing in *National Review,* the preeminent journal of conservative opinion. In an article published in June 1963, Meyer decried the nature of the civil rights movement to that point as truly revolutionary and saw as its consequence the "destruction of the constitutional order." Against the backdrop of the recent developments in Birmingham, Alabama, where footage of the brutal police reaction to black activists' mass demonstrations produced widespread sympathy for the civil rights movement and impetus for civil rights legislation (eventually the Civil Rights Act of 1964), Meyer offered a dramatically differing view, a critical assessment based on property rights, order, and federalism. "I assume the innate value of every created human being and the right of every American citizen, enshrined in the Constitution, to equal treatment before the law," he wrote. "The social, cultural and economic relations of the races, however, are another matter . . . *Laws* enforcing segregation have always been a monstrosity; and *laws* forcing private citizens to regulate their behavior in an opposite manner, that is, laws against segregation and FEPC laws [laws requiring nondiscrimination in employment], are an equal monstrosity."[4]

Soon thereafter, conservative, constitutional theorist Robert Bork took up the theme, writing in *The New Republic* and arguing, "the danger is that justifiable abhorrence of racial discrimination will result in legislation by which the morals of the majority [by which he meant those in favor of civil rights legislation] are self-righteously imposed upon a minority [segregationists]. . . . The discussion we ought to hear is of the cost in freedom that must be paid for such legislation." For Bork, the cost in terms of personal liberty was too great. With regard to elements in the bill that dealt with segregation in public accommodations and fair hiring, Bork argued, "the legislature would inform a substantial body of the citizenry that in order to continue to carry on the trades in which they are established they must deal with and serve persons with whom they do not wish to associate." Such an imposition, backed by state coercion, "is itself a principle of unsurpassed ugliness." "It is not whether racial prejudice or preference is a good thing but whether individual men ought to be free to deal and associate with whom they please for whatever reasons appeal to them," Bork argued. Principles of personal liberty trumped the moral arguments of civil rights advocates. "One may agree that it is immoral to treat a man according to his race or religion and yet question whether that moral preference deserves elevation to the level of the principle of individual freedom and self-determination."[5]

Of course, the arguments made by Meyer and Bork, despite their explicit rejection of segregation, aligned nicely with those of the defenders of segregation and the employment status quo. Segregationist James J. Kilpatrick, for example, argued that "this precious right to discriminate underlies our entire political and economic system."[6] Kilpatrick also rejected the idea of black equality, in fact arguing that blacks were innately inferior. As such, a black "has no right . . . to favored treatment in employment, promotion, or anything else."[7] Indeed, the claim of racial inferiority was frequently promoted in the conservative press. Business and industry defenders of the status quo also adopted these arguments. Materials from the National Association of

Manufacturers (NAM) labeled the civil rights bill as "perhaps the greatest encroachment ever undertaken by the Federal government into the personal and private affairs of individual citizens" and raised concern that Title VII would cause employers to "discriminate in reverse."[8] Black self-improvement and the operation of the free market, rather than government efforts, would, in time, they argued, correct employment discrimination.

Yet it was a history of choices to exclude and discriminate—either by law or practice—that created the situation in which the nation found itself in the 1960s. One might suppose that many liberals, when reading these conservative arguments against the Civil Rights Act of 1964, were reminded of Gunnar Myrdal's comment that white discrimination and injustice fostered the conditions that whites then used to rationalize the actions that created these characteristics in the first place. The editors of *The New Republic,* for example, who supported the civil rights movement and civil rights legislation, criticized, in an editorial response, Bork's abstract treatment of the principle of personal liberty as divorced from historical realities. "In discussing the law," they wrote, "we share Justice Holmes' [Oliver Wendell Holmes, Jr., a judicial pragmatist] preference for appeals to experience rather than logic." In practical terms, principles were often constrained, and the editors suggested that "to apply this principle [personal liberty] in disregard of all others" would be inappropriate.[9] As we shall see, those responsible for enforcing nondiscrimination were faced with a similar conflict: that between the color-blind principle reflected in Title VII and the perceived need to find a practical, effective way to change historical patterns of discrimination. By the mid-1960s the historical reality of discrimination was bearing ugly fruit.

THE URBAN CRISIS AND AFFIRMATIVE ACTION

With Watts, Whitney Young's predictions had come to pass.[10] Furthermore, in the summers of 1966–68, black ghettoes exploded throughout the nation, in some cases requiring military intervention. Historian Doug McAdams identified some 290 outbreaks over that period, leaving 169 individuals dead, 7,000 wounded, and 40,000 arrested.[11] But why urban violence at this point, after major civil rights legislation had been accomplished? Civil rights activists focused on employment as a key factor. At a White House civil rights conference in June 1966, NAACP Executive Director Roy Wilkins argued, "Negro unemployment is of disaster proportions. Creative and large scale action must be taken to achieve full and fair employment for the Negro working age population."[12] A year later, A. Philip Randolph pointed out, "Teenagers with jobs don't throw Molotov cocktails."[13]

One immediate response to the outbreak of urban violence was President Johnson's reaffirmation of a commitment to nondiscrimination in employment. In September, 1965, President Johnson issued Executive Order 11246, restating President Kennedy's Executive Order 10925 requiring that contractors take "affirmative action to ensure that applicants are employed, and employees are treated during employment, without regard to race, creed, color, or national origin."[14] In the new order, he divided responsibility for his assault on discrimination between the Civil Service Commission, with regard to federal employment, and the Department of Labor, with regard to federal contracts. The Department of Labor, in turn, created the Office of Federal Contract Compliance (OFCC). With the creation of the OFCC, the federal bureaucracy most responsible for ensuring equal employment opportunity was completed. With the charge of ending discrimination and, implicitly, that of improving the employment situation of the victims of historical discrimination, the OFCC and the EEOC would become the bureaucratic architects of affirmative action. Yet both bureaucracies faced significant hurdles.

The OFCC was understaffed and underbudgeted. It did, however, have considerable power to regulate, investigate, and penalize federal contractors that did not comply with Executive Order 11246. It could cancel a federal contract. Nonetheless, this power was sometimes vitiated by a lack of cooperation from the actual, federal contracting agencies, such as the Department of Defense, hesitant to disturb long-standing relationships with certain contractors.[15]

The EEOC was underfunded, understaffed, and had little authority. While it was charged with investigating and reconciling individual complaints of discrimination as well as promoting programs of voluntary compliance by employers and unions, it had no regulatory or enforcement powers. Upon receipt of a complaint from someone who believed he or she had been the victim of illegal, discriminatory actions by an employer, the EEOC's job was to investigate and attempt to settle valid complaints by conciliation and persuasion. If the EEOC were unable to resolve the issue, the individual complainant might then take his or her case to federal court. The courts had final enforcement authority, including that to "order such affirmative action as may be appropriate."[16] The EEOC could not issue regulations or cease-and-desist orders, nor could it pursue lawsuits on behalf of complainants—although the Justice Department could (as well as sue against "a pattern and practice of resistance" to employment rights). Furthermore, as soon as the office opened in 1965, it was deluged by complaints. Funded and staffed at a level anticipating 2,000 complaints in the first year, it received over 8,800.[17] Nonetheless, the agency pushed ahead, although to limited achievement.

The first successful efforts at addressing employment discrimination occurred where the EEOC and the OFCC worked in consort, focusing on companies or industries that received hefty federal contracts. For example, shortly after opening shop, the EEOC received numerous complaints against the Newport News Shipbuilding Company in Virginia, a major defense contractor. The company was still operating under Jim Crow employment policies and restrictions: blacks were not given access to apprenticeship programs, were paid less for the same work, were not assigned "white jobs," weren't promoted, and the company maintained segregated facilities. The threat of the loss of federal contracts and potential lawsuits forced the company to change policies.[18] A similar pattern occurred in the Southern textile industry, although it took several years to bring about change.

As noted in Chapter 1, jobs in Southern textile mills were generally restricted to whites, and the EEOC received hundreds of complaints to that effect. In early 1967, the EEOC held hearings in Charlotte, North Carolina, revealing the extent of discrimination, and later that year mounted a publicity campaign calling for blacks to apply for textile jobs. African American community groups and attorneys, accustomed to organizing for civil rights, joined the effort to open the mills. The OFCC targeted several large textile companies reliant on federal contracts. White workers and owners resisted, of course, sometimes violently, but the threat of the loss of federal contracts and the success in the courts of black, class-action suits (some 1,200 suits between 1965 and 1971), brought change. "By 1970," writes historian Nancy MacLean, "blacks made up approximately 15 percent of the textile labor force in the Carolinas, and almost half of those hired were women."[19] A major transformation in textile employment was taking place.

In other areas of the country, however, and other industries, successes were hard to come by. In a number of industries situated in Northern and western cities, workers belonged to unions that were highly segregated. While on the national level, unions had been part of the liberal coalition that supported civil rights, local affiliates in the skilled trades were often closed to minorities. This was particularly the case in the construction industry. For example, in the early 1960s an Oakland, California, NAACP activist pointed out that in his city, a new federal post office was "being built with federal dollars in an American Negro neighborhood without a Negro electrical worker, Negro plumber, Negro sheet metal worker, or other crafts too numerous to mention."[20] OFCC efforts often provoked resistance from the union workers, slowing down federal projects. Such was the case in St. Louis, where resistance to OFCC efforts to open the trades to blacks for work on the Gateway Arch ultimately required a lawsuit and federal court injunction to force the unions' hand.[21]

In short, the first years of effort produced limited results. Some success in the South was counterbalanced by very little change in employment patterns in Northern and western urban areas. This at the time when urban areas literally burned in the summers.

THE KERNER COMMISSION

In 1967, President Johnson created the National Advisory Commission on Civil Disorders to explore the causes of urban unrest. The Commission was chaired by Illinois Governor Otto Kerner, and its subsequent report, often referred to as the Kerner Commission Report, laid the blame for urban unrest at the feet of whites. "White racism is essentially responsible for the explosive mixture which has been accumulating in our cities since the end of World War II,"[22] wrote the Commission. While the Commission identified a number of root causes for the riots, employment issues were central to its analysis. The unemployment rate for blacks in 1967 was double that of whites and, furthermore, black underemployment was high. "Negro workers are concentrated in the lowest-skilled and lowest-paying occupations. These jobs often involve substandard wages, great instability and uncertainty of tenure, extremely low status . . . little or no chance of meaningful advancement, and unpleasant or exhausting duties."[23] Unemployment and underemployment created a culture of poverty that fed a range of social problems, those same problems identified in the Moynihan Report. The Commission recommended that the federal government "[t]ake new and vigorous action to remove artificial barriers to employment and promotion . . . including racial discrimination."[24]

Of what might this "new and vigorous action" consist? Testimony during the Commission's hearings suggested that a broader definition of discrimination might be the ticket. Obviously, if an employer refused to hire or promote someone because of that person's race or sex, then discrimination was involved. But how would one determine discriminatory intent? The vast majority of companies in the United States had no specific policies against hiring or promoting minorities, yet, as we have seen, blacks and women were not hired or, when hired, were retained in low-paying positions. In many cases, companies had policies that were not racially or sexually discriminatory in intent, such as educational requirements or seniority and testing policies for promotion, but produced an unequal—or disparate—impact on blacks or women, revealed in employment statistics. And, in 1967, employment statistics had not improved since passage of the Civil Rights Act. The aggressive recruitment and special training of minorities, identified as affirmative action by Franklin D. Roosevelt, Jr., didn't appear to be working. Thus, a number of witnesses at the Kerner Commission hearings advocated disparate impact theory; that is, identifying practices that have disparate impact as discriminatory. "Racial discrimination and unrealistic and unnecessarily high minimum qualifications for employment or promotion often have the same prejudicial effect," the Commission would report.[25] Ultimately, the Commission advocated "[u]ndertaking, through the Equal Employment Opportunity Commission, an industry and areawide enforcement effort based not only upon individual complaints but upon employer and union reports, showing broad patterns of discrimination in employment and promotion."[26]

It is important at this point to clarify the difference between a color-blind approach to discrimination and a disparate impact approach and the implication of that difference for affirmative action. Historically, blacks had been denied employment or promotion regardless of any personal merit simply because they were black. The Civil Rights Act of 1964 clearly made that discrimination illegal. In effect, the law stated that all decisions concerning training, employment, and promotion should be made in a color-blind fashion. Implicitly, this meant that only merit should be considered when making employment decisions. Affirmative action for minorities under that understanding meant, as Roosevelt had argued, aggressive recruitment and training, providing a hand up. However, the concept of disparate impact focuses on the statistical representation of minorities in the workforce rather than some identification of discriminatory intent. It focuses on the effects of employment actions. Thus, if minorities compose a very small percentage of the work force, far smaller, say, than the percentage of minorities in the population, prima facie evidence of discrimination exists. Furthermore, practices that limit the number of minorities hired or promoted, policies shaped around traditional indicators of merit—testing and seniority policies, for example—may be considered discriminatory. Affirmative action based on this concept of discrimination would focus on the numbers of minorities hired, promoted, and so on, and, in order to improve those numbers, might require the suspension of traditional practices focusing on merit.

Clearly, there are problems inherent with affirmative action policies based on disparate impact, problems related to aspects of Title VII. Race as a category becomes significant (policies are not color-blind). The focus on improving numbers of employed minorities invites the charge of reverse discrimination. This is especially the case when traditional tests of merit are suspended to achieve results. In fact, one proviso added to Title VII permitted employers to use professionally developed ability tests as long as they were not used to discriminate by race and another proviso protected "bona fide" seniority or merit systems.[27] Furthermore, when the focus is on numbers, the prohibition of preferential treatment as described in Section 703(j) of Title VII becomes an issue.

Nonetheless, disparate impact theory, with its focus on statistics, was attractive to the EEOC and OFCC and began to work its way into their enforcement toolboxes. For example, as early as 1966, the EEOC began to require employers under its purview to complete an annual survey (called EEO-1 reports) identifying their employees by job category, race, sex, and national origin. These reports would allow statistical analyses of employment patterns. Industries that showed low numbers of blacks or other discriminatory patterns were then targeted for hearings, or forums, by geographic region. The hearings were designed to draw attention to minority employment patterns, promote community action to address underrepresentation, and offer advice for voluntary action that employers might pursue. An early target of this approach was the Southern textile industry, discussed previously. Forums soon evolved into "action projects," a more focused effort to target firms identified as discriminatory through statistical analysis of the EEO-1 forms. A 1968 EEOC report clearly articulated the attractiveness of this approach: "The project is designed to obtain a maximum return for the investment of limited government effort; the return will be measured in the form of new hiring of minority employees. . . . Particularly appropriate targets would be firms located in an SMSA [standard metropolitan statistical area] having more than 10% Negro or Spanish-Surnamed population, where the establishment employs 3% or fewer Negroes or Spanish-Surnamed Americans."[28]

The OFCC was also attracted to numbers and enforcement tools that promised results. Recall that the OFCC's task was to ensure nondiscrimination in employment on projects funded by federal contracts. In traditional practice, a federal agency would call for bids on a project—like a new post office building, for example—and award the contract to the lowest bidder. Now, however, the OFCC's job was to ensure that the lowest bidder would also be nondiscriminatory and, in fact, pursue affirmative action, defined by OFCC director Edward C. Sylvester, Jr., in January 1967 as "anything that you have to do to get results."[29] That is, foster minority employment in some measurable way. We noted earlier that the OFCC ran into particular difficulty with regard to the construction industry. There, contractors had to depend on unions to supply labor, and trade unions typically had few black members. Beginning with the effort in St. Louis, noted previously, the OFCC experimented with special area plans (plans focusing on contracts in a specific geographic area) to foster compliance with EO 11246. In short order, those plans evolved into requirements that bidders provide affirmative action plans as part of the bidding process, plans that included manning tables (indicating the number of men in each trade required at each stage of the construction process) incorporating specific goals and timetables for minority hires.

Interestingly, these requirements for affirmative action plans did not impose specific numbers. Rather, it was left up to the bidder to devise a plan that might or might not be acceptable. This vagueness led the Solicitor General to declare plans for Cleveland and Philadelphia illegal. Contract law, he argued, required that expectations be clearly set forth. The plans were shelved. It would be left to the Nixon Administration to resurrect such plans, imposing specific goals and marking the high point of race-conscious affirmative action.

AFFIRMATIVE ACTION UNDER NIXON

David Skrentny argues that the greatest irony of affirmative action was that its "most advanced and explicit race-based formulation" came during the administration of Republican President Richard Nixon.[30] Nixon had won election by steering a middle ground between former Vice President Hubert Humphrey and segregationist George Wallace of Alabama. That middle ground was established by calling for "law and order" in response to urban riots and opposition to school integration through court-enforced busing—not positions endearing him to civil rights activists. He did, however, call for the development of black capitalism through technical assistance and loan guarantees to help start or expand black businesses. Once in office, his administration was marked by the pursuit of a "Southern strategy" to align the old South with the Republican Party, nominations (that ultimately failed) to the Supreme Court of federal judges with poor civil rights records, early lack of support for EEOC and OFCC efforts (for example, granting contracts to textile firms in noncompliance with OFCC equal employment opportunity standards), and, ultimately, attacks on racial quotas. However, when the opportunity arose to drive a wedge between two key elements of the liberal, Democratic coalition—civil rights activists and union members—and at the same time deflect criticism of the administration's civil rights record, Nixon moved quickly. That wedge was the revised Philadelphia Plan.

The revised Philadelphia Plan, announced by OFCC director Arthur A. Fletcher and supported by Labor Secretary George Schultz, addressed those aspects of the original plan that had led the Comptroller General to declare the plan illegal. That is, rather than allow the bidders to devise affirmative action plans that might or might not be acceptable (thus providing the vagueness that concerned the Comptroller General), the revised Philadelphia Plan required the bidders to produce plans that met standards that included specific percentage targets or ranges for minority manpower utilization. If the contractor ultimately failed to hit the target range, he would have to demonstrate that a good faith effort had been made to reach the target. In the absence of that effort, contracts could be cancelled. Fletcher argued that since these targets were ranges where good faith effort would be acceptable, they were not quotas.

The Comptroller General again disagreed, but this time he declared the revised Philadelphia Plan illegal as a violation of Titles VI and VII of the Civil Rights Act of 1964; that is, he felt that the targets were quotas. Attorney General John N. Mitchell, however, ruled that the plan was legal, arguing that it imposed goals, not quotas, so the plan was implemented. The disagreement between the legislative branch (the Comptroller General works for Congress) and the executive branch (the Attorney General) led to debate in Congress ostensibly over the issue of separation of powers, but clearly over the legality of the Philadelphia Plan. In subcommittee hearings held by Sen. Sam Ervin (R-NC), proponents and opponents of the plan debated its flaws and merits. Some proponents, such as Sen. John Pastore (D-RI), linked the plan to the need to "stabilize" the urban situation or, as Sen. Edward Brooke (R-MA) put it, effectively to address "systemic discrimination" in employment.[31] Others argued that the plan did not require proportional minority hiring, simply a good faith effort at reaching goals. Sen. Ervin, who had opposed the Civil Rights Act of 1964 and its Title VII, now playing the role of defender of color-blindness and opponent of the plan, argued in response, "I think you have made it as clear as the noonday sun in a cloudless sky that the Philadelphia Plan requires contractors actively to take the race of people into consideration when they employ them, despite the conflicting language of the Executive Order."[32] He even read definitions of "quota" from the dictionary.

The debate broadened as a rider upholding deference to the Comptroller General—and thus opposing the Philadelphia Plan—was added to a disaster-relief bill being considered in Congress. At first, the rider passed the Senate. At that point, the administration began to pressure Republican lawmakers, pointing out the dilemma the rider imposed on many Democrats. Democrats who had traditionally supported unions (which opposed the plan) *and* civil rights (equal employment opportunity in urban areas) would have to choose. In the House, the debate continued, although many Democrats raised questions concerning the administration's motives. Otherwise, the debate reflected that in the Senate. For example, Roman Pucinski of Illinois, critic of the Philadelphia Plan and its percentage targets, argued, "If these are not quotas, then the English language has lost its meaning."[33] In the final House vote, the rider lost, with Republicans supporting the Philadelphia Plan by a three to one margin and a majority of Democrats voting for the rider and against the Plan. The Senate, then, reconsidered the rider and reversed itself. Nixon had found a wedge issue. The result was tacit approval of an OFCC affirmative action plan that incorporated percentage targets.

Subsequently, in early 1970, the Labor Department published Order Number 4, the enforcement regulations of the OFCC for all contractors (not just the construction industry covered by the Philadelphia Plan). The order required each contractor or subcontractor with 50 or more employees and contracts of at least $50,000 to develop an affirmative action program. That program was defined as "a set of specific and result-oriented procedures to which a contractor commits himself" based on an analysis of minority utilization. In determining minority utilization (or underutilization), the contractor was to consider "the minority population of the labor area surrounding the facility" and "the percentage of minority work force as compared with the total work force in the immediate labor area." Identified underutilization was to be addressed by the development of "goals, timetables, and affirmative action commitments." Goals were to be "significant, measurable and attainable." Bowing to Title VII, the order clarified, "Goals are not to be rigid and inflexible quotas . . . but must be targets reasonably attainable by . . . every good faith effort."[34]

By early 1970, then, both the EEOC and OFCC were using enforcement tools that relied on elements of the concept of disparate impact: race identification, statistical analysis, and measurable results. Had they gone "beyond the law"? At least in the case of the OFCC's goals and timetables, they had received tacit endorsement from Congress. Would the courts agree?

AFFIRMATIVE ACTION AND THE COURTS: EARLY CASES

By the late 1960s, the courts began to deal with aspects of affirmative action policy in a variety of cases, some challenging the alleged discriminatory policies of employers, others challenging elements of affirmative action policy. In the final analysis, key elements or implications of the concept of disparate impact were endorsed. Here we sample precedent-setting cases dealing with seniority, goals and timetables, and educational qualifications.

In a 1968 case, *Quarles v. Philip Morris, Inc.,* black workers challenged a departmental seniority system that, on its face, did not appear to be discriminatory. Prior to 1965, blacks had been assigned to "black jobs" in departments such as the janitorial department and not placed in better-paying, "white jobs." After 1965, when Title VII went into effect, blacks were allowed to transfer to white departments, but they ended up on the bottom of seniority lists in their new departments. That is, time spent in the previous department did not carry over to the new department, thus negatively affecting blacks' potential for advancement, since seniority was one factor considered in promotion decisions. Both Phillip Morris and the union argued that

Title VII corrections did not apply as the seniority system was not intentionally discriminatory and was, in fact, a bona fide seniority system. The EEOC, in an amicus brief, argued that the system was not bona fide because it perpetuated prior discrimination. The District Court found in favor of the plaintiffs, declaring "Congress did not intend to freeze an entire generation of Negroes into discriminatory patterns that existed before the act."[35] The Court ordered modifications of the seniority system, recognizing service in previous departments. The EEOC's emphasis on the discriminatory effect of seniority systems was endorsed, at least temporarily.

When the revised Philadelphia Plan was imposed, affected contractors cooperated in a challenge to its legality. In *Contractors Association of Eastern Pennsylvania v. Secretary of Labor,* the contractors contended in part that the specific goals and timetables for minority hires would require them to classify employees by race and force them to refuse to hire whites, all in violation of Title VII. The Third Circuit Court rejected these claims and found that the Plan was "within the implied authority of the President and his designees" and that it was not a violation of Title VII.[36]

To read Section 703(a) [of Title VII] in the manner suggested by the plaintiffs we would have to attribute to Congress the intention to freeze the status quo and to foreclose remedial action under other authority designed to overcome existing evils. We discern no such intention either from the language of the statute or from its legislative history. Clearly the Philadelphia Plan is color-conscious. Indeed the only meaning which can be attributed to the "affirmative action" language which since March of 1961 has been included in successive Executive Orders is that Government contractors must be color-conscious.[37]

The OFCC's color-conscious goals and timetables were endorsed.

The most significant decision endorsing elements of disparate impact came from the Supreme Court in *Griggs, et al. v. Duke Power Co* (1971). In a situation similar to that of the aforementioned Philip Morris case, Duke Power had a history of segregating black employees in low-paying positions. After implementation of Title VII in 1965, the company allowed both black and white employees to apply for the previously "white" jobs. The company maintained a policy, however, that required either a high school diploma or an acceptable score on certain general aptitude tests to qualify for those jobs. Although this policy was color-blind, black employees argued that these requirements were discriminatory because they made it particularly difficult for blacks to qualify. The Court, recognizing the history of inferior education for blacks in segregated schools, agreed. "[P]ractices, procedures, or tests neutral on their face, and even neutral in terms of intent, cannot be maintained if they operate to 'freeze' the status quo of prior discriminatory employment practices."[38] While the law certainly did not guarantee jobs to everyone who had previously been the object of discrimination, argued the Court, it did proscribe "not only overt discrimination but also practices that are fair in form, but discriminatory in operation."[39] The Court accepted the EEOC's position that any educational requirement must be clearly related to job performance. Significantly, it accepted the idea that discrimination could be demonstrated in the absence of intent. "Congress directed the thrust of the Act to the consequences of employment practices, not simply the motivation."[40] The central element of disparate impact, the understanding of discrimination as the effect rather than intent of employment actions, was endorsed by the Supreme Court.

While disparate impact theory was gaining ground, the EEOC was not. Still understaffed and underfunded in the early 1970s, the EEOC appeared to be failing in its mission to improve equal employment opportunity. By 1972, the EEOC was nearly two years behind in processing complaints. Civil rights advocates pushed for change, and consequently, the Equal Employment Opportunity Act of 1972 was crafted to address shortcomings. The law granted the EEOC authority to bring civil suits in federal court, including pattern and practice suits; extended the coverage of Title VII to state and local governments, governmental agencies, and political subdivisions; dropped the 1964 Civil Rights Act's exclusion of educational institutions from its provisions; and expanded the EEOC's funding and staffing.

The law did not pass without resistance, however. Senator Sam Ervin proposed an amendment that would make disparate impact affirmative action illegal: "No department, agency, or officer of the United States shall require an employer to practice discrimination in reverse by employing persons of a particular race, or a particular religion, or a particular national origin, or a particular sex in either fixed or variable numbers, proportions, percentages, quotas, goals or ranges."[41] The amendment lost, 44 to 22, providing another indirect Congressional endorsement of race-conscious affirmative action. Of Ervin's effort, historian Jo Ann Ooiman Robinson writes, "Ervin set an early example of a practice later adopted by many opponents of civil rights and affirmative action: purporting to be opposed to 'discrimination' by using that term to support a status quo that has historically always discriminated against minorities."[42]

WOMEN INCLUDED

A major source of the workload of the EEOC came from an unexpected quarter. Over a third of the complaints in its first year alone were from women. Women's opportunities were constrained by cultural expectations of their roles as wives and mothers, and when they did enter the job force, they tended to be placed in low-prestige or low-wage "women's jobs." Sexual stereotyping fueled discrimination in hiring, benefits, and promotion. In 1964, most men and many women accepted these distinctions as natural. Sen. Howard Smith introduced sex as an amendment to Title VII in an effort to undermine its passage. No one, he thought, would take such a proposition seriously. Of course, his amendment was adopted, but a general lack of concern for women's issues was widespread and even found expression in the early work of the EEOC.

As the EEOC organized itself under the direction of five commissioners, only one of whom was a woman, the clear focus of effort was on race. "The message came through clearly that the Commission's priority was race discrimination, and apparently only as it related to Black *men,*" wrote Commissioner Eileen Clarke Hernandez.[43] Nonetheless, women's issues arose, but they were soft pedaled. For example, one of the most obvious manifestations of sexual discrimination in employment was separate male and female help-wanted ads. Such ads symbolized and reified distinctions between "men's jobs" and "women's jobs." Yet the commission took a very narrow view of the implications of Title VII for such practices by allowing ads for job categories "primarily of interest" to men or women in its 1965 guidelines on sex discrimination.[44] The EEOC also failed to grapple with the implications of Title VII for state legislation designed primarily to protect women workers (for example, restrictions on the amount of weight women could be allowed to lift). It allowed some applications of those laws that, in effect, served to retain women in low-paying job categories.[45]

Such foot dragging did not go unnoticed. In June, 1966, Rep. Martha Griffiths (D-MI) lambasted the commission from the floor of the House: "The whole attitude of the EEOC toward discrimination based on sex is specious, negative, and arrogant. The Commission is failing in its duty to educate the public toward compliance with the law, to inform working women of their rights under the law, and to show an affirmative and positive attitude of encouraging employers, employment agencies and unions to comply with the prohibitions against discrimination in employment based on sex."[46]

Earlier, African American attorney and women's activist Pauli Murray had argued that, if Title VII were to work for women, they needed an organization comparable to those struggling for blacks' civil rights. The idea resonated with many women, including journalist Betty Friedan, author of *The Feminine Mystique,* a 1963 critique of the limitations imposed by women's roles as wives and mothers. Soon after Griffith's address, Friedan, Murray, and others began to plan just such an organization. The result was the National Organization for Women (NOW), a "civil rights organization" for women, "the

N.A.A.C.P. of women's rights."[47] NOW quickly began to lobby and pressure the EEOC, other federal agencies, and Congress, as well as support various efforts by women and women's groups to address sexual discrimination in the workplace and equal rights in general.

NOW's work, in consort with other women's groups, paid off. In October 1967, President Johnson issued Executive Order 11375, modifying Executive Order 11246 to include the prohibition of discrimination on account of sex. In August 1968, the EEOC rescinded its earlier position on help-wanted ads, its new guidelines stating, "It is a violation of Title VII for a help-wanted advertisement to indicate a preference, limitation, specification, or discrimination based on sex unless sex is a bona fide occupational qualification for the particular job involved."[48] In June 1970, the Nixon Administration published guidelines on sex discrimination for federal contractors. NOW and other women's groups supported a new version of a proposed Equal Rights Amendment stating simply, "Equality of rights under the law shall not be denied or abridged by the United States or by any State on account of sex." The proposed amendment passed Congress and was sent to the states in March 1972. Congress also passed the Educational Amendments Act of 1972 (Title IX), prohibiting sexual discrimination in "any education program or activity receiving Federal financial assistance."[49]

At the same time, women's sexual discrimination lawsuits opened new territory. Often lawsuits were designed to reach beyond employment. In the early 1970s, the American Civil Liberties Union (ACLU) created the Women's Rights Project (WRP), codirected by Rutgers University law professor Ruth Bader Ginsburg. Under Ginsburg, the WRP pursued a series of cases, the goal of which was to have the Supreme Court overturn sexually discriminatory laws or practices under the concept of equal protection in the Fourteenth Amendment or, if a federal case, the Fifth Amendment. In general, Ginsburg and her colleagues successfully demonstrated that there was no reasonable basis for statutory distinctions between men and women, that these distinctions were often based on sexual stereotypes that should not be applied to individuals.[50] Using a similar approach, female plaintiffs successfully pursued suits under Title VII against laws and practices that limited women's opportunities in employment. For example, in 1968, a federal district court relied on Title VII to strike down a California protective labor law restricting women's overtime and proscribing their lifting weights beyond a certain limit.[51] The district court found that stereotyped characterizations of women's abilities would not suffice to establish a bona fide occupational qualification. In early 1971, the U.S. Supreme Court found a restrictive hiring policy illegal. An otherwise qualified woman was not hired because she had young children; however, men with young children were hired. The Court held in *Phillips v.*

Martin Marietta that Title VII "requires that persons of like qualifications be given employment opportunities regardless of their sex."[52]

In a number of areas, Court decisions outpaced the OFCC and EEOC. By the early 1970s, however, both were actively pursuing affirmative action with regard to sexual discrimination. In December 1971, the OFCC revised its Order Number 4 to include women as a group for which contractors must develop affirmative action programs including goals and timetables.[53] The EEOC tackled "Ma Bell," the telephone monopoly. The Bell Telephone system was the single largest employer of women in the country and the source of numerous complaints to the EEOC from women who were restricted to work as operators or secretaries. When AT&T appealed to the Federal Communications Commission for a rate increase in 1970, the EEOC argued that the increase should not be granted a company that practiced such obvious discrimination. To back up its charge, the EEOC had collected reams of evidence demonstrating systematic discrimination in all areas of employment. "The Bell monolith is, without doubt, the largest oppressor of women workers in the United States," the EEOC study claimed.[54] By 1973, AT&T and the Bell system agreed to open up "men's jobs" to women and vice versa; provide $50 million dollars in back pay, primarily to women; and establish a set of goals and timetables for the inclusion of women in "men's jobs."[55]

The successes of women's activists by the 1970s did much to reduce the long-standing split in the women's movement. The expansion of employment and promotion opportunities appeared to offset the loss of protective legislation. "Doing away with gender-based protective laws while at the same time promising working women equality with working men, [Title VII] allowed women to define themselves as full earner-citizens and to build new alliances," wrote historian Nancy MacLean. Such alliances, she argued, produced a movement that was diverse and attentive to bread-and-butter needs.[56]

The AT&T settlement, along with similar settlements in other industries, set the tone for affirmative action in employment for several years. "From the time of these agreements, forged in the light of the broad interpretation of Title VII by the EEOC and the courts," wrote Alfred Blumrosen, "industry came to accept and to internalize the 'goals and timetables' concept, and to include members of previously excluded groups in increasing numbers."[57] But the debate over affirmative action had hardly begun. Its focus would soon shift to higher education.

NOTES

1. Terry H. Anderson, *The Pursuit of Fairness: A History of Affirmative Action* (New York: Oxford University Press, 2004), 90.

2. Pub. L. 88–352, 78 Stat 241, Section 703(j), July 2, 1964.

3. Whitney M. Young, Jr., "Preferential Hiring for Negroes," *American Child,* vol. 45, 1963, 5–8.

4. Frank S. Meyer, "The Negro Revolution," *National Review,* June 18, 1963, 496; see also Nancy MacLean, *Freedom Is Not Enough: The Opening of the American Workplace* (Cambridge, MA: Harvard University Press, 2006), 61–64.

5. Robert Bork, "Civil Rights—A Challenge," *The New Republic,* August 31, 1965, 21–24.

6. Quoted in Nancy MacLean, *Freedom Is Not Enough: The Opening of the American Workplace,* 63.

7. Ibid.

8. Ibid., 67.

9. "Civil Rights—A Reply," *The New Republic,* August 31, 1963, 24.

10. In fact, urban unrest antedated the Watts riots by a year. In the summer of 1964 a series of riots broke out in Harlem, Brooklyn, and Rochester, New York, then spread to other cities in the Northeast and Midwest. See John David Skrentny, *The Ironies of Affirmative Action: Politics, Culture, and Justice in America* (Chicago: University of Chicago Press, 1996), 71.

11. Doug McAdam, *Political Process and the Development of Black Insurgency, 1930–1970* (Chicago: University of Chicago Press, 1982), quoted in Skrentny, 73.

12. Quoted in John David Skrentny, *The Ironies of Affirmative Action,* 77.

13. Ibid.

14. 30 FR 12319; September 28, 1965.

15. Ibid., 134–35.

16. Pub. L. 88–352, 78 Stat 241, Section 706(g), July 2, 1964.

17. Hugh Davis Graham, *Civil Rights and the Presidency* (New York: Oxford University Press, 1992), 103; *Facts about Title VII of the Civil Rights Act of 1964* (Washington, DC: EEOC Pamphlet, 1969), quoted in Jo Ann Ooiman Robinson, ed., *Affirmative Action: A Documentary History* (Westport, CT: Greenwood Publishing, 2001), 105–6.

18. Anderson, 97–98.

19. MacLean, 86. MacLean provides an outstanding summary of the effort against discrimination in Southern textile mills. See 78–90.

20. Quoted in Ibid., 91.

21. Ibid., 93.

22. National Advisory Commission on Civil Disorders, *Report of the National Advisory Commission on Civil Disorders* (New York: E.P. Dutton & Co., 1968), 10.

23. Ibid., 253.

24. Ibid., 24.

25. Ibid., 416.

26. Ibid., 419.

27. Alfred W. Blumrosen, *Modern Law* (Madison: University of Wisconsin Press, 1993), 49, 118.

28. "Project Outline for FY 1968, of the Office of State and Community Affairs, EEOC, 'Eliminating Discrimination by Affirmative Government Action,'" quoted in Skrentny, 133.

29. Quoted in Skrentny, 135.

30. Skrentny, 177; see also 177–221.

31. *Congressional Record* 115, Pt. 2 (December 18, 1969), 39961, 39966, quoted in Robinson, 132–33.

32. Quoted in Skrentny, 199.

33. Ibid., 206.

34. *Federal Register* 35, no. 5 (February 5, 1970), 2587, 2589, quoted in Robinson, 133–35.

35. 279 F. Supp. 505, E.D.VA (1968), 516, quoted in Blumrosen, 94.

36. *Contractors Association of Eastern Pennsylvania v. Secretary of Labor* (442 F. 2d., 3rd Circuit, 1971), 171, 174.

37. Ibid., 173. See Blumrosen, 94; Skrentny, 165.

38. *Griggs, et al. v. Duke Power Co.*, 401 U.S. 424 (1971), 430.

39. Ibid., 431.

40. Ibid., 432.

41. *Bureau of National Affairs, The Equal Employment Opportunity Act of 1972, a BNA Operations Manual* (Washington, DC: Bureau of National Affairs, 1973), quoted in Robinson, 154–56.

42. Robinson, 153.

43. Quoted in Robinson, 109, emphasis in original.

44. Quoted in Blumrosen, 135.

45. Robinson, 110–11.

46. *Congressional Record* 112, Pt. 1 (June 20, 1966), 13693, quoted in Robinson, 112.

47. MacLean, 128.

48. *Federal Register* 33 (August 14, 1968), 11539, quoted in Robinson, 116.

49. *Laws of 92nd Congress, 2nd Sess.* (June, 1972), 444, quoted in Robinson, 166.

50. See *Reed v. Reed*, 404 U.S. 71 (1971); *Frontiero v. Richardson*, 411 U.S. 677 (1973); *Craig v. Boren*, 429 U.S. 190 (1976). A useful summary of these cases and Ginsburg's strategy can be found in Mark Tushnet, *A Court Divided: The Rehnquist Court and the Future of Constitutional Law* (New York: W. W. Norton, 2005), 104–14.

51. *Rosenfeld v. Southern Pacific Co.*, 293 F.Supp. 1219 (C.D.Cal. 1968).

52. *Phillips v. Martin Marietta Corp.*, 400 U.S. 542 (1971), 544.

53. *Federal Register 36* (December 4, 1971), 17445, quoted in Robinson, 143.

54. Quoted in MacLean, 132.

55. Blumrosen, 209.

56. MacLean, 118.

57. Blumrosen, 210.

4

DeFunis and Bakke: Judicial Challenges to Affirmative Action in Higher Education in the 1970s

THE CASE OF THE ASPIRING LAWYER

Marco DeFunis wanted to become a lawyer. As many young men and women with similar ambitions, he majored in political science as an undergraduate. He completed his BA at the University of Washington in Seattle in 1970 with a grade point average of 3.6 on a scale of 4.0 (about an A-minus average). His degree was awarded magna cum laude, and he was selected as a member of Phi Beta Kappa. He took the standardized Law School Admissions Test (LSAT) three times. The mean average of his scores was 582, substantially above the average of others taking the exam in the early 1970s. DeFunis then applied to law school at an institution he already knew well, the University of Washington. Despite his relatively strong academic credentials, he soon learned that his prospect of being admitted to the principal law school in his state would be problematic. He was rejected for admission in 1970 but reapplied in 1971.[1]

In 1971 the University of Washington Law School (UWLS) received 1,601 completed applications for about 150 places in the first-year class. UWLS, like many graduate and professional schools in the country in the 1970s, possessed a complicated admissions plan. Based on estimates of the percentage of individuals who would likely attend UWLS if admitted (the so-called "yield rate"), the admissions committee decided to offer seats to about 310 applicants. Each applicant was assigned a predicted first-year average (PFYA), an index number based on a formula that mainly took into account the applicant's LSAT score and his grade point average in the junior and senior years. In 1971, the second year DeFunis applied, applicants to UWLS with a PFYA of 78 or higher were guaranteed admission and almost all of those with a PFYA of less than 74.5 were rejected. DeFunis's PFYA in 1971 was 76.23, placing him in the gray area between automatic acceptance and likely rejection.

The UWLS admissions scheme also included an affirmative action component. Applicants identifying themselves as being of one of four racial minorities—African American, Chicano, American Indian, or Filipino— were treated differently from other applicants. Those identifying themselves as black in their applications, regardless of their PFYAs, were assigned to two members of the admissions committee for review, and those identifying themselves as from one of the other minority categories were assigned to another member of the committee for screening. None of the minority applicants were reviewed in direct competition with the general applicant pool, and none of the minority applicants were summarily rejected for low PFYAs. A total of 37 minority applicants were offered seats pursuant to this procedure: all but one had PFYAs below DeFunis's 76.23, and 30 of the 37 had PFYAs below the 74.5 index that in most cases led to summary rejection.

The reasoning behind the UWLS plan and those like it at other law and professional schools was two-fold, namely (1) that racial minorities, based on their numbers in the population, were underrepresented in the legal profession, and (2) that law school admissions offices, just as in portals to private sector employment, should do their part to reverse the history of past racial discrimination.[2]

DeFunis, a Jewish male of Spanish-Portuguese descent, did not qualify as one of the preferred minorities for admission to the UWLS. He was placed on the waiting list for admission in 1971, but he learned in August that the admissions committee had not found room for him in the first-year class. DeFunis suspected that there were less qualified applicants from minority groups admitted in his stead. So he filed suit in Washington Superior Court on the grounds that he had been discriminated against because of his race—that is, white—in violation of the Equal Protection Clause of the Fourteenth Amendment to the U.S. Constitution and analogous provisions of the Washington state constitution. The court issued a temporary order, permitting DeFunis's admission to the UWLS class beginning in September 1971. Then, in a nonjury trial, the Superior Court found in favor of DeFunis on constitutional grounds.[3]

DEFUNIS IN THE COURTS

While DeFunis remained in law school, an appeal by the University of Washington worked its way through the legal process to the Washington Supreme Court. In March 1973, a majority of the judges on that court found against DeFunis and upheld the affirmative action plan of the UWLS. At the time that the state supreme court issued its ruling, DeFunis was in his second year of law school. Shortly after receiving the bad news from Seattle, DeFunis's attorneys petitioned the U.S. Supreme Court for a review of the case. Pending a hearing before the entire membership of the nation's highest Court, Justice William O. Douglas, acting in the capacity as a circuit justice, stayed the judgment of the Washington Supreme Court. This allowed DeFunis to remain in law school. The U.S. Supreme Court granted DeFunis's petition for certiorari on November 19, 1973 and held oral argument on the case on February 26, 1974.[4]

The case attracted substantial interest from institutions of higher learning and national organizations concerned about race and education. Six groups successfully petitioned the Supreme Court to file amicus curiae ("friend of the Court") briefs in support of DeFunis and against the UWLS affirmative action plan. Included among these groups were: the U.S. Chamber of Commerce, the AFL-CIO, and three Jewish organizations. On the other side of the case, urging that the Washington affirmative action plan be upheld, were fully 120 groups and individuals signing a total of 22 briefs. They included: the American Bar Association, the Association of American Law Schools, the NAACP Legal Defense and Education Fund, the Defense Fund of the National Organization for Women, the National Council of Jewish Women, and several state attorneys general.[5]

The justices met in conference on March 1, 1974 to discuss the *DeFunis* case. The major point of discussion at the conference—the point on which the case would ultimately turn—was whether the case of *DeFunis v. Odegaard* was, in legal jargon, moot. Under the U.S. Constitution, the Supreme Court is charged with deciding certain categories of cases and controversies.[6] But those disputes must involve live issues, that is, ones in which something is at stake. At the time the Supreme Court's conference on the *DeFunis* case took place, the young man in question was a student in good standing at UWLS, and law school administrators had certified that no matter how the Supreme Court ruled DeFunis would be allowed to complete his final semester of law school. Four justices—Chief Justice Warren Burger, and associate justices Harry Blackmun, William Rehnquist, and Potter Stewart—were of the opinion that there did not exist a "case" or "controversy" within the meaning of Article III. Later, Justice Powell would come down on the side of mootness, thus making the vote five to four on that crucial procedural issue.[7]

On April 23, 1974, the Supreme Court issued a per curiam ruling (a decision for the Court majority but not ascribed individually to any single justice) declaring the case to be moot. The Court's unsigned opinion acknowledged that all the principals in the case bowed to the reality that DeFunis would complete the final year of his legal program at the University of Washington no matter how the nation's highest court ruled. Also, since DeFunis had not filed a class action suit and did not make a claim for monetary damages, the injunction that he requested to keep him in law school was no longer necessary. Hence, with no legal issues outstanding, the Court declared the case moot and remanded the cause to the Supreme Court of Washington to conduct proceedings necessary to execute the decision just rendered.[8]

Two dissenting opinions were filed. The longer of the two, written by Justice William O. Douglas, hoisted the first window into what a member of the Supreme Court actually thought about the merits of affirmative action. One explanation for Douglas's long and searching dissent in *DeFunis* was simple, as he told his clerk: "I might not be around next time this issue comes up."[9] Douglas seemed especially troubled by the use of standardized examinations by educational institutions in admissions decisions. He argued that test-takers with imagination and a sense of the problems raised by certain test questions might be at a disadvantage compared to test-takers with mindsets more clearly matched to that of the test-designers. Moreover, as closely as performance on the LSAT might correlate with first-year law school grades, Douglas was not aware of any measure that the LSAT predicted a test-taker's long-term success as an attorney. The LSAT, he maintained, did not test for such intangible qualities as motivation and perseverance. He offered a hypothetical example of a black applicant from a poor background who attended a junior college before receiving his baccalaureate degree and compared him to the son of a rich white alumnus who boasted a Harvard undergraduate degree. The Harvard student had better grades and a higher LSAT. But who, Douglas queried, was more deserving of admission to law school? He then launched into an argument that overcoming disadvantages not of one's own making might be a more telling variable in the admissions mix than the race of applicants.[10]

Douglas also raised the issue of cultural bias in the LSAT. Native Americans from his own state of Washington, Douglas wrote, might have more knowledge of the philosophies of Chief Seattle and Chief Joseph than that of Adam Smith and Karl Marx. Yet it is likely that the LSAT would have more questions on European political and economic thought than on the precepts of the Muckleshoots or the Nez Perce tribes. This line of reasoning led Douglas to suggest that it might make sense to place minority groups into a separate category from mainstream applicants, perhaps even eliminating the LSAT for minorities. If it were up to him, Douglas submitted, the case should be remanded to the original trial court in the state of Washington to consider whether the LSAT should be scrapped for minorities.[11]

Another troubling issue to Douglas was the validity of the range of minorities singled out for separate attention in the UWLS affirmative action plan. Why, for example, were Filipinos applicants covered but Chinese and Japanese applicants excluded? For such a racial classification to be sustained under the Equal Protection Clause of the Fourteenth Amendment, the Supreme Court had long held there must be a "compelling" state interest. Douglas did not perceive one to exist in this case. But, as to the related question of whether Marco DeFunis individually suffered invidious discrimination under the UWLS plan, Douglas was uncertain. This was another issue that Douglas would have preferred to have seen resolved by the original trial court on remand.[12]

REACTIONS TO THE *DEFUNIS* CASE

The reactions to the Supreme Court decision in *DeFunis* were quick in coming. Several newspaper stories published on the day following the decision emphasized that the Supreme Court had temporarily avoided a tough issue but could not do so indefinitely. The lead story in the *New York Times* on April 24, for example, was headlined "High Court Avoids Ruling on Quota for Law School."[13] A *Washington Post* editorial a few days later predicted that more law suits of this type would be filed if law and other professional schools did not modify their admissions criteria.[14]

A few reporters and commentators, finding little to grapple with in the terse majority opinion, focused on Justice Douglas's dissent. Public affairs writer Nicholas von Hoffman, for example, referred to the 75-year old jurist as "the last great liberal judge" and found merit in Douglas's cryptic suggestion that there should be separate admissions standards for law school applicants from different racial groups.[15] Another theme that emerged from the press accounts was that law schools and other professional schools would be wise to heed Douglas's criticism of the heavy reliance on standardized tests in making admissions decisions. These commentators also saw in Douglas's 29-page opinion a strong admonition against the use of racial quotas in making admissions decisions.[16] Nevertheless, on April 27 the UWLS dean maintained that his institution would not change any of its admissions policies in light of the Supreme Court opinion in *DeFunis v. Odegaard.*[17]

Although there were reports that he did not appreciate being viewed by some fellow students at the UWLS as "the house bigot,"[18] DeFunis kept a low profile during his trial and the ensuing appeals. In response to reporters' request for statements in the immediate aftermath of the Supreme Court decision, he offered nothing for attribution.[19] But a few months later, at the time of his graduation (reportedly in the top 10% of his class), DeFunis stated that the U.S. Supreme Court "should have made a decision one way or the other."[20] DeFunis went on to a successful career as an attorney in his native Seattle. He died of a heart attack on January 16, 2002.[21]

At about the time the *DeFunis* case was sputtering to a halt, an intriguing dispute was emerging a few hundred miles to the south in California's Sacramento Valley. It involved the complaint of another young white man—although not quite as young as DeFunis—who felt his educational and vocational dreams were being thwarted by an affirmative action plan. The nation's highest court would not be able to duck the constitutional issue of affirmative action this time around.

THE CASE OF THE ASPIRING DOCTOR

Allan Bakke wanted to become a physician.[22] A white male, born of middle-class parents in Minnesota and raised in the Midwest and Florida, Bakke received a baccalaureate degree in mechanical engineering in 1962 from the University of Minnesota. He followed this with a tour of duty in Vietnam as a member of the U.S. Marines Corps. In the late 1960s he moved to California and accepted a position as a research engineer for the National Aeronautics and Space Administration (NASA). In 1970 he earned an MS degree in mechanical engineering from Stanford University. Bakke appeared destined for a quiet, comfortable life as an engineer, residing with his family in a sun-splashed California community. But Bakke dreamt of becoming a doctor. So he enrolled in night classes to satisfy the undergraduate science prerequisites he had not taken in his earlier college years.

In 1973 Bakke applied to 11 medical schools, including the seven-year-old University of California Davis Medical School (UCDMS). His application was rejected. He applied again in 1974. Once more he was rejected.[23] Bakke was described by Peter Storandt, a sympathetic admissions officer at UCDMS, "as a character out of . . . [an Ingmar] Bergman film—somewhat humorless, perfectly straightforward, zealous in his approach—an extremely impressive man."[24] Storandt informed Bakke that his official credentials and performance on an interview were good but not quite impressive enough among the regular pool of applicants to be offered one of the 84 places in the medical school's next first-year class. Furthermore, he indicated that there were many applicants, all racial minorities with less impressive paper credentials than Bakke, who were reviewed under a "special admissions" program designed to fill 16 additional places in the first-year medical class.[25]

Bakke felt that he was treated unfairly because, as a white, he was not given the same opportunity to compete for admission to UCDMS as the racial minorities in the special admissions pool. So he filed a complaint in Superior

Court of Yolo County, California, seeking a judicial order compelling the university to admit him to the medical school and a ruling that the special admissions program at the UCDMS had discriminated against him in violation of the Equal Protection Clause of the Fourteenth Amendment, parallel provisions of the California state constitution and Title VI of the Civil Rights Act of 1964. The university filed a cross-complaint, requesting a ruling that its special admissions program at the Davis medical school was legally and constitutionally valid.[26]

In the two years that Bakke applied to the UCDMS, the institution was highly selective, reviewing 2,644 applicants for the entering class in 1973 and 3,737 applicants for the first-year class in 1974. As Storandt told Bakke, applicants identifying themselves as one of the targeted racial minorities (297 in 1973 and 628 in 1974) were permitted to compete in the special admissions pool for 16 seats in the entering class. The thousands of nontargeted applicants, Bakke included, were only eligible to compete for the 84 seats in the regular admissions pool. All applicants submitted a dossier of materials including undergraduate transcripts and certified scores on the standardized Medical College Admissions Test (MCAT). The top applicants were invited to interviews with panels of medical school personnel and current UCDMS students. Each interviewed applicant was given a score based on a formula weighing undergraduate grades, MCAT scores, and interview performance. The highest possible score was 500 in 1973 and 600 in 1974. Bakke's undergraduate grade point average of 3.51 and MCAT scores (three of his four scores on different sections of the exam ranked him in the 94th percentile or higher of UCDMS applicants) qualified him for an interview each year. After the interviews he was assigned composite applications scores of 468 in 1973 and 549 in 1974. Bakke's application scores placed him just slightly below the group of students in the regular admissions pool offered seats in the entering classes. But close was not good enough to merit Bakke an invitation to admission in the entering class or even to obtain the toehold of a place on the waiting list. What was particularly galling to Bakke and his attorney, however, was that most of the applicants in the special pool had lower composite UCDMS application scores than Bakke. Some even had grade point averages below 2.50 and MCAT scores below the 50th percentile of test-takers.[27]

In his depositions prior to the trial, Dr. George H. Lowrey, a UCDMS administrator and head of the admissions committee, had explained that the special admissions program at his institution was designed to afford a break to applicants from "disadvantaged backgrounds," to compensate in part for generations of racial discrimination in American life, and to address the belief of UCDMS faculty and administration that the test scores and grades of minority students do not accurately reflect their capability to perform satisfactorily in medical school or function in the future as a physician. He also attested that another purpose of the special admissions program was "to promote diversity among the student body and the profession and to increase the number of doctors practicing in the minority community."[28]

BAKKE IN THE COURTS

The trial court agreed with Allan Bakke that the UCDMS special admissions program had resulted in "invidious discrimination in favor of minority races," and it ruled that the Davis affirmative action plan violated the rights of Bakke and other white applicants as protected by the Equal Protection Clause of the Fourteenth Amendment to the U.S. Constitution. However, the court denied Bakke's request for an injunction ordering his admission because it was not convinced that Bakke would have been selected for admission in the absence of the UCDMS affirmative action plan.[29] Both parties appealed, and the case was transferred to the California State Supreme court for a ruling on the important constitutional issues.

The California high court entered its ruling on September 16, 1976, splitting six to one and leaving none of the parties or their supporters entirely satisfied. The court determined that it would apply a "strict scrutiny" level of constitutional analysis to the Davis affirmative action plan. This meant that the California judges would only uphold the plan if they found that it was "narrowly tailored" to fulfill a "compelling state interest." The court did not find this to be the case: it unearthed nothing in the record to warrant the view that minority doctors would display special interest in treating the medical conditions of minority patients; in fact, it termed this assumption "parochial."[30] The court questioned whether the UCDMS had created either the least intrusive or the most effective affirmative action procedure.[31] Furthermore, the majority found that there had been no finding of racial discrimination against minorities in the short history of the UCDMS. Citing a number of employment discrimination precedents that held that preferential treatments to minorities were not justified without a judicial finding of a history of racial discrimination, the California court looked askance at the explicit reservation of 16 seats for minorities in the entering class of a medical school that had not previously practiced racial discrimination.[32]

Even supporters of affirmative action worried that the reservation of a set number of seats for selected racial minorities in each UCDMS entering class looked too much like a quota. In addition, leaders of minority groups had long felt that the University of California system, with its low percentage of racial minorities in its several student bodies relative to the state's overall non-white population, was no great friend of racial progress. They worried, too, that the California Regents' white legal team could not be counted on to represent aggressively the views of mainline civil rights organizations or, for that matter, people of color generally. Finally, the short history of the UCDMS, extending only back to the medical school's founding in 1966, did not appear to provide a solid launching pad for an argument that affirmative action was a constitutionally viable strategy to overcome a national history of racial discrimination. Better to accept the muddled result on affirmative action in the California Supreme Court, the argument went, than take the chance that the justices in Washington would use *Bakke* on appeal to void affirmative action for the entire country. If the *Bakke* decision was a loser, why not wait for a better case to come along?[33]

Despite their trepidations, the Regents of the University of California chose to appeal the *Bakke* decision to a higher authority. On February 27, 1977, the U.S. Supreme Court agreed to hear the *Bakke* case by granting, without explanation, the Regents' request for certiorari.[34] Years later, papers of Supreme Court justices deposited in the Library of Congress and other archives would reveal that the vote in favor of granting cert was five to four.[35] Interestingly, Justice Brennan, who had wanted to decide the *DeFunis* case on the merits three years earlier, was the strongest voice against accepting *Bakke* for review. Brennan was concerned that the "quotalike" feature of the UCDMS admissions policy might be so distasteful to his brethren that a majority of the Court would issue a leveling blow against all race-based affirmative action.[36]

Even more than in *DeFunis,* interested parties clamored to express their views on the case to the justices. Ultimately, 160 interest groups, academic institutions, and governmental agencies—joining together in 42 separate briefs—successfully petitioned the Court to be heard as amicus curiae. Among the groups whose views were represented in briefs urging reversal of the California Supreme Court were the American Civil Liberties Union, the American Association of University Professors, the Association of American Law Schools, the Association of American Medical Colleges, the National Association for the Advancement of Colored People, the National Association of Minority Contractors, and the Equal Employment Advisory Council. Also arguing for reversal were attorneys general from several states and some of the country's most prestigious universities. Among the 16 amici filed by groups arguing for affirmation of the California Supreme Court opinion were the American Council of Teachers, the Chamber of Commerce of the United States, the Young Americans for Freedom, and the Pacific Legal Foundation. In *Bakke,* in contrast to *DeFunis,* all the major Jewish groups were on a single side: the American Jewish Committee, the Anti-Defamation League of B'nai B'rith, and the Queens Jewish Community Council all filed amici in support of upholding the California Supreme Court decision.[37]

As notable as was the roster of interest groups participating in the review of *Bakke* on appeal, there was a virtual who's who of distinguished constitutional lawyers signing amicus briefs. For example, Ruth Bader Ginsburg, later appointed to the Supreme Court in the 1990s by President Bill Clinton, helped prepare the ACLU brief; Edgar S. Cahn, Norman Redlich, and Philip Kurland—all distinguished law professors—signed on as amici in *Bakke;* and high profile appellate attorneys like Jack Greenberg of the NAACP and Alan Dershowitz of the American Jewish Congress represented their organizations before the Supreme Court. In addition, Archibald Cox, former U.S. Solicitor General and the Special Prosecutor who was fired on the orders of President Richard Nixon in the Watergate scandal of 1972–74, wrote the brief and argued the case for the Regents of the University of California.[38] Perhaps the most interesting name affixed to one of the amici in *Bakke* was the principal author of the brief for the conservative interest group, Young Americans for Freedom. It was none other than Marco DeFunis, Jr., Esq., now a lawyer in the state of Washington.[39]

The most interesting story involving the briefs submitted to the Supreme Court in the *Bakke* case involved the travails of the office of the solicitor general within the Department of Justice. Unlike other potential amici who must earnestly beseech that the high court grant their petitions to be heard, the solicitor general has the option of submitting an amicus brief in any case before the U.S. Supreme Court. The *Bakke* case offered a difficult challenge to President Jimmy Carter's Department of Justice. Given the widely perceived flaws in the affirmative action plan of the UCDMS, would the U.S. government be prudent, perhaps, to stay on the sidelines? Or should the Department of Justice weigh in on what Attorney General Griffin Bell termed "the most significant civil rights controversy to come before the [U.S. Supreme Court] since the school segregation cases of 1954"?[40] After much behind the scenes political hand-wringing and maneuvering—some of it leaked to the press— the Department of Justice prepared and submitted a brief that straddled the fence. It endorsed the concept of affirmative action programs based on race and ethnicity. But, without much elaboration, it objected to "rigid exclusionary quotas." In addition, the solicitor general's brief acknowledged that the *Bakke* case lacked sufficient "evidentiary data" to support affirmative action; thus, it asked that the Supreme Court remand the case to the Yolo County trial court to examine some of the factual particulars of the UCDMS affirmative action plan and of race-based preferential plans in general.[41]

Most of the more than three dozen groups filing amici supporting the Regents' affirmative action plan urged the Court to decide *Bakke* on the merits and uphold the principle of race-based affirmative action. Universities and divisions of state government were, of course, protective of their own affirma-

action plans. Also weighing in on the side of affirmative action were mainline civil rights organizations, student groups, professional organizations in law and medicine, and, curiously, testing organizations. The majority of these organizations agreed with the attorneys for the California Regents, namely that the UCDMS affirmative action plan aided disadvantaged groups, satisfied a legitimate governmental purpose of diversifying the classrooms and laboratories of a state educational institution, and did not violate Title VI of the Civil Rights Act of 1964 or the Equal Protection Clause of the Fourteenth Amendment. The amici on the other side generally presented arguments that tracked the case made by Allan Bakke's lawyer. In addition to arguing that the young medical school at Davis had no history of invidious racial discrimination, they relied on what they characterized as the "plain meaning" of the relevant Act of Congress and section of the U.S. Constitution: both mandated colorblind treatment of individuals served by state institutions. The only exception to the clear constitutional and statutory language, these briefs argued, would be that, after a "strict scrutiny" of the facts in the case, it was determined that a "compelling state interest" existed to blunt the injunctions of Title VI and the Fourteenth Amendment. Neither Bakke's lawyer nor any of the amici in support of Bakke acknowledged that such a compelling state interest existed under the set of facts presented in this case.[42]

THE *BAKKE* CASE: IN CHAMBERS AND IN PUBLIC

In anticipation of the importance and complexity of the issues involved, the justices took the unusual step of preparing memoranda on the *Bakke* case in advance of the oral argument. Justice Brennan, for example, drafted a 13-page hand-written document he titled "Bench Notes—*Bakke*," in which he emphasized his belief that the use of race in the UCDMS admission program was "noninvidious" and narrowly enough tailored to meet the objective of promoting racial diversity in the medical school.[43]

The Supreme Court's elegant courtroom was packed for the oral argument in *Regents v. Bakke* on October 12, 1977. Archibald Cox presented the case for the California Regents. Cox boasted impeccable liberal credentials: he was a Harvard law professor and the solicitor general in the administration of President John F. Kennedy. Cox was also an experienced legal advocate who was personally acquainted with some of the justices. Cox maintained, in the face of persistent but not hostile questioning, that the only way to afford admission to more than a trickle of minority applicants to a professional school was to implement and practice some form of affirmative action. Furthermore, he argued that the Fourteenth Amendment does not prohibit "race conscious programs" where there is "no invidious purpose or intent." Justice John Paul

Stevens asked Cox if the Supreme Court would need to consider the relevance of Title VI of the 1964 Civil Rights Act prior to addressing any constitutional issues in the case. Cox replied in the negative, indicating that Alan Bakke's attorney did not raise this issue in the California courts.[44]

Cox was followed to the podium by Wade McCree, the Solicitor General. McCree agreed with Cox that some form of race-based affirmative action was necessary for institutions of higher learning to succeed in enrolling more than a token number of minority students. He spent some of his time defending the position presented in the government's amicus brief that the case should be remanded to the California courts because the plan failed to accommodate Asian Americans as a group deserving of preferential treatment. In response to another query from the bench, McCree agreed with Cox that the Supreme Court would not need to confront the Title VI issue in the case before reaching the constitutional questions under the Fourteenth Amendment.[45]

According to Supreme Court lore, a brilliant oral argument seldom wins a case. But, it is widely believed, a bad presentation can turn a close case into a defeat.[46] With this in mind, the choice of Reynold Colvin, Alan Bakke's lawyer in the California courts, to argue the case before the justices himself, rather than ceding the task to a more experienced appellate advocate, represented a significant risk. Colvin was, in fact, nervous and, while at the Supreme Court's lonely podium, devoted too much of his allotted time offering testimony to the glowing character and many accomplishments of Alan Bakke instead of addressing the important constitutional issues in the case. The impatience of the justices was apparent in some of their comments and their body language.[47]

Although his overall presentation before the Supreme Court might not have been compelling, Colvin may have persuaded the justices to consider one important line of reasoning. Contrary to Cox and McCree, Colvin responded in the affirmative to the justices' leading questions as to whether their review of Alan Bakke's case should concern Title VI of the 1964 Civil Rights Act as well as the Fourteenth Amendment. Five days after the oral argument, the justices met in Conference and, by a vote of five to four, issued an order instructing the solicitor general and the attorneys for UCDMS and Alan Bakke to file supplemental briefs on the statutory relevance of Title VI to the disposition of the appeal.[48] In the majority, in addition to Chief Justice Burger and Associate Justices Byron White, William Rehnquist, and John Paul Stevens, was Associate Justice Harry Blackmun. Recovering from prostate surgery back in his native Minnesota, Blackmun cast his vote in absentia. While awaiting the supplemental briefs and the return of Justice Blackmun, the Chief Justice ordered the vote on the case delayed and encouraged the brethren to share their views on the matter by "Memoranda to the Conference."[49] They did so with alacrity, dispatching a flurry of memos among their chambers throughout the fall of 1977 and continuing into 1978. Fully a dozen detailed memos were dispatched in the four months following the oral argument; every justice wrote at least one, except the convalescing Blackmun.[50]

The supplementary briefs arrived in late November 1977 and another conference was scheduled on *Bakke* for December 9, 1977. At this conference, the fault lines on the issues presented by *Bakke* began to emerge. The Chief Justice and Justices Rehnquist, Potter Stewart, and John Paul Stevens indicated that they would uphold the decision of the Supreme Court of California, but ground their position on Title VI and not reach the constitutional issue under the Fourteenth Amendment. Recall that the relevant language of Title VI states: "No person in the United States shall, on the ground of race, color, or national origin, be excluded from participation in, be denied the benefits of, or be subjected to discrimination under any program or activity receiving Federal financial assistance."[51] The belief of this "gang of four" (Brennan's description) was that the UCDMS affirmative action plan violated the statutory right of Alan Bakke not to be discriminated against on the basis of his race (white) in an application to matriculate at an institution falling under the ambit of Title VI.[52]

By contrast a group of three justices—William Brennan, Thurgood Marshall, and Byron White—argued at the conference that the decision of the California Supreme Court should be overruled on the basis of Title VI *and* the Equal Protection Clause of the Fourteenth Amendment. Their position was that the UCDMS affirmative action plan, even with its dual admission track feature, did not violate the rights of Alan Bakke. To this troika, applying a slightly lower standard of review than "strict scrutiny," the compelling state interests undergirding affirmative action warranted the noninvidious form of preferential treatment embodied in the Davis plan.[53] At the time of the second conference, Justices Lewis Powell and Harry Blackmun had not taken clear positions on *Bakke*. Chief Justice Burger elected not to assign the task of preparing the Opinion of the Court to a particular justice until all the justices had weighed in. While waiting to learn the views of Blackmun and Powell, he encouraged the members of the Court to continue to circulate memoranda to each other.[54]

Justice Lewis Powell, a jurist who was fundamentally disposed toward moderation and compromise, staked out a middle ground that would ultimately control the judgment, if not the holding, of the Court. At the December 9, 1977 conference, Powell declared that it was a "colossal blunder" for the UCDMS to pick an absolute number to be admitted under its minority admissions policy. To him, that spelled discrimination by race under the Fourteenth Amendment and turned the case in Bakke's favor. But Powell expressed hesitation about pulling the constitutional plug entirely on the principle of affirmative action. To him, the most compelling—and thus constitutional—basis for affirmative action was that important educational benefits would accrue to all Davis medical students fortunate enough to study in a racially diverse academic environment. So, at that moment, Powell indicated that he was still thinking about how to vote in the case. After Powell spoke, William Brennan made a suggestion. He encouraged Powell to vote to affirm in part and reverse in part. That is, consistent with the thinking that Powell had just outlined, Brennan said that it would be logical for him to affirm the part of the California Supreme Court opinion that struck down the Davis plan and ordered Bakke's admission to the medical school, but reverse the part of the state court's opinion that found affirmative action in principle to be unconstitutional. Powell, according to notes taken by some of the justices at the conference, saw the merit in this strategy.[55]

POWELL'S OPINION IN *BAKKE:* A PAEAN TO DIVERSITY

The resolution that William Brennan proposed to his friend and colleague William Powell would ultimately lead the Virginia lawyer and former American Bar Association president to write his soon-to-be famous brokered opinion in *Bakke*. However, before that could happen, scores of additional memoranda had to be written, circulated, and digested. In addition, there would have to more log rolling by Brennan to keep united the core of justices favoring the preservation of affirmative action while, at the same time, working to add Powell to that group. But the breakdown of the votes on *Bakke* would not be complete until the recovering Justice Blackmun made his feelings known. Blackmun returned to Court business in January 1978, but, to the consternation of some of his colleagues, he delayed announcing his position on *Bakke* until May 1, 1978. With the 1977–78 term rapidly winding down, Blackmun finally communicated his willingness to join the group of justices voting to uphold the constitutionality of affirmative action.[56] That meant that the document that Powell was crafting would become the key opinion in the case.

Although the public and the legal community did not know exactly when the *Bakke* decision would come down, the media had conducted a "*Bakke* watch" on the Court for several weeks. NBC News, for example, in anticipation of the announcement of the decision in the late spring or early summer, began stationing a camera crew at the Supreme Court Building on May 1.[57] On the morning that *Bakke* would be announced—June 28, 1978—some of the justices' wives were in attendance in the Supreme Court's public courtroom, indicating to the press and other Court watchers that this could be a historic occasion.[58] *Regents v. Bakke* turned out to be the third case on that day's Supreme Court agenda. Before an attentive but surprisingly small courtroom audience,[59] five of the six justices writing opinions in the long-awaited California affirmative action case presented summaries of their written arguments to the reporters and others in attendance; of the opinion authors, only Justice White did not offer a summary of his views.

Justice Powell expressed the judgment of the Court in a complex, multipart opinion. Each of two quartets of justices concurred in and dissented to different portions of Powell's opinion. The gang of four (Burger, Rehnquist, Stewart, and Stevens) joined Powell in affirming the California Supreme Court opinion that struck down the UCDMS affirmative action plan and ordered Bakke's admission; and the other bloc of four justices (Blackmun, Brennan, Marshall, and White) sided with him in reversing the portion of the state court opinion that had attempted to end affirmative action in the state's higher education programs. So, technically, Powell only spoke for himself. Yet his one vote controlled the nine-member Court. He saw the irony in this situation when, on the eve of the announcement of the decision, he wrote in a short memorandum to his fellow justices: "I am a 'chief' with no 'indians.' "[60]

After a recitation of the facts and the procedural twists in the lower courts, Powell held that Bakke had legal standing to argue his complaint and then addressed the Title VI issue. Citing a number of recent precedents, he declared for the five-justice bloc that it was not incumbent upon the Supreme Court to rule on matters not decided by the courts below or argued by the lawyers presenting the case on appeal.[61] If this was not sufficient to dispatch the Title VI question, Powell concluded that the racial classifications forbidden by the statute were the same racial groupings that would fall under the sweep of the Equal Protection Clause of the Fourteenth Amendment.[62] Thus, Powell was able to avoid the statutory annoyance that troubled several of the other justices and move smartly to the constitutional issue.

Determining the appropriate standard of review under the Equal Protection Clause took up a large portion of the opinion. After reviewing the history of cases decided under this clause, Powell concluded that any state action establishing a racial classification—such as a special admissions program for racial minorities at a tax-supported medical school—was inherently suspect and would demand the highest level of constitutional scrutiny in order to pass muster.[63] Were any of the published purposes of the Davis special admissions program, Powell queried, compelling enough to survive this most searching level of constitutional review? The first three purposes articulated by the UCDMS were the following: (1) to mitigate the historic discrimination against racial minorities by American medical schools; (2) to counter the general societal discrimination against racial minorities; and (3) to augment the number of doctors willing to open practices in communities underserved by minority physicians. UCDMS was a relatively new medical school with no historic pattern of racial discrimination. So Powell found the first purpose unsupported. He deemed the second purpose to be too general and, thus, not offering a sufficient justification for the rather specific numbers in the Davis affirmative action plan. And the third purpose did not appear to Powell to be based on any solid evidence about where doctors locate their practices.[64]

Only the fourth purpose undergirding the UCDMS special affirmative action program—the attainment of a racially diverse student body—held weight for Powell and his slender majority. In support of the constitutional virtue of diversity, Powell waxed almost rhapsodic: "Physicians serve a heterogeneous population. An otherwise qualified medical student with a particular background—whether it be ethnic, geographic, culturally advantaged or disadvantaged—may bring to a professional school of medicine experiences, outlooks and ideas that enrich the training of its student body and better equip its graduates to render with understanding their vital service to humanity."[65] He then sung the praises of Harvard College's affirmative action plan, where an applicant's race was seen as a "plus factor" but not, by itself, deemed a magic bullet to automatic admission.[66]

The UC Davis plan, by contrast, was deficient. In the second confidential conference on the case back in December 1977, Powell had termed the rigid reservation of 16 seats for racial minorities in each Davis medical school class a "colossal blunder." In his written opinion he termed it a "fatal flaw."[67] Although it may have advanced the opportunities for African Americans and other minorities, it impaired the individual rights of Alan Bakke as guaranteed by the Equal Protection Clause of the Fourteenth Amendment. Thus Powell's opinion attempted to cut the Gordian knot: it affirmed the portion of the California Supreme Court opinion that had held the UCDMS special admissions program unconstitutional, and it upheld the injunction that had ordered Bakke admitted to medical school. However, perhaps most importantly, it reversed the anti-affirmative action portion of the California court opinion and preserved the principle of race-based admissions to an institution of higher learning if predicated on the use of racial diversity as a plus factor rather than a quota.[68]

THE OTHER OPINIONS IN *BAKKE*

Justice Brennan issued the main opinion of the four-justice bloc—Harry Blackmun, Thurgood Marshall, Byron White, and himself—supporting Powell in voting to preserve affirmative action. He commenced by acknowledging the complexity of the case and how it had splintered the Court. Then he directed attention to what he saw as the "central meaning" of the several opinions: "Government may take race into account when it acts not to demean or insult any racial group, but to remedy disadvantages cast on minorities by past racial prejudice at least when appropriate findings have been made by judicial, legislative, or administrative bodies with competence to act in this area."[69] He and his cohort went beyond Powell, however, in arguing that the California Supreme Court opinion should be reversed in all respects.[70]

Brennan saw Title VI of the Civil Rights Act of 1964 and the Equal Protection Clause of the Fourteenth Amendment as operating in tandem in terms of the restraints and opportunities for race-conscious affirmative action programs. One of the strengths of Brennan's opinion was that he summarized much of the legislative history of Title VI and identified race-conscious programs that had sprung from Title VI that, nevertheless, operated without legal question. Among such programs were the federal grants to segregated hospitals, vocational training courses in historically black schools, and agricultural extension services to groups of black citizens. When challenged in the courts, Brennan emphasized, such programs had been consistently ruled constitutional.[71] He wrote: "[W]here there is a need to overcome the effects of past racially discriminatory or exclusionary practices engaged in by a federally funded institution, race-conscious action is not only permitted but required to accomplish the remedial objectives of Title VI."[72] He made a similar point in a discussion of remedial racial preferences in the areas of employment and the selection of contracts for public works projects.[73]

The standard of review under the Fourteenth Amendment that Brennan and his group of four supported was one that permitted a race-conscious program that was benign rather than stigmatizing. It should be strict and searching, but not "strict in theory and fatal in fact."[74] Brennan saw the UCDMS affirmative action plan as offering a constitutionally realistic way of admitting members of racial minority groups into competitive institutions of higher learning. In the years that the UC Davis medical school operated without affirmative action—1968 and 1969—only one Chicano and two African Americans had been admitted. Brennan, accordingly, accepted the argument of the Regents of the University of California that the goal of diversifying the medical school at Davis could only be practically achieved by a program of race-conscious admission.[75]

Justices Marshall, Blackmun, and White expressed idiosyncratic views in favor of affirmative action in solitary opinions. Marshall, the Court's lone minority justice, began his concurrence with a powerful statement: "[D]uring most of the past 200 years, the Constitution, as interpreted by this Court, did not prohibit the most ingenious and pervasive forms of discrimination against the Negro. Now, when a State acts to remedy the effects of that legacy of discrimination, I cannot believe that this same Constitution stands as a barrier."[76] He then proffered a short history of legally enforced racial discrimination and its consequences.[77] Finally, drawing from the briefs of the solicitor general and some of the amici, he noted what would be the disrupting consequences of a decision voiding affirmative action generally: at least 27 federal agencies would have to scrap race-conscious programs, and hundreds of state and local affirmative action programs would similarly have to be terminated.[78]

Blackmun's principal contribution to the Court's national seminar on affirmative action was to note in his concurrence that colleges and universities had long practiced "non-racial" affirmative action by affording admissions preferences to applicants possessing athletic skill and to the sons and daughters of alumni, the affluent, and celebrities.[79] He concluded his short opinion thusly: "In order to get beyond racism, we must first take account of race. There is no other way. And in order to treat some persons equally, we must treat them differently. We cannot—we dare not—let the Equal Protection Clause perpetuate racial supremacy. So the ultimate question . . . is: Among the qualified, how does one choose?"[80] Justice White argued in a short concurrence that Title VI did not hold out a private right cause of action for an aggrieved party.[81]

Justice Stevens, representing the bloc that included Burger, Rehnquist, Stewart, and himself, began by challenging Brennan's assertion that he had captured the "central meaning" of the Court's *Bakke* decision in his opinion. In a short but blunt footnote, Stevens admonished Brennan that "only a majority can speak for the Court or determine what is the 'central meaning' of any judgment of the Court."[82] The Stevens bloc agreed with Powell's ruling that the UCDMS affirmative action plan was flawed. But these four justices arrived at this position via their analysis of the statute in question, Title VI of the Civil Rights Act of 1964; they did not reach the constitutional question presented by the Equal Protection Clause of the Fourteenth Amendment. Enunciating the classic tenet of judicial self-restraint that constitutional rulings should only be issued as a last resort, the group of justices that Brennan called the gang of four maintained that it was possible to dispose of the *Bakke* case by means of statutory construction and, thus, never need to address the question of whether affirmative action was constitutional under the Fourteenth Amendment.[83] In their view, the gravamen of the dispute came down to the plain meaning of the words in Section 601 of the Civil Rights Act of 1964: the law proscribed discrimination on the basis of race in any program receiving funds from the federal government. The medical school of UC Davis received federal funds; Bakke was denied admission to the UCDMS even though his credentials were stronger than some racial minorities who had applied; therefore the program that snubbed him violated federal law. The syllogism seemed obvious to this cohort of justices.[84] The remedy would be to void the UCDMS affirmative action program and admit Bakke to medical school.

Stevens and the justices who concurred with his opinion found nothing in the legislative history of Title VI that ran counter to the plain meaning of its statutory language. In the debate over the relevant section of the Civil Rights Act of 1964, they emphasized that the bill's sponsors—noted liberals like Hubert Humphrey (D–MN) and William Proxmire (D–WI)—assured opponents that, should the bill be enacted into law, it would be "colorblind" in his application.[85] For Stevens, a statement by Senator John Pastore (D–RI) stood out. During the Senate debate, Pastore promised that the soon-to-be historic bill would make it illegal "to say 'yes' to one person but 'no' to another person, only because of the color of his skin."[86]

POSTMORTEMS ON *BAKKE*

Postdecision commentary on the *Bakke* decision was intense and immense. On the day following the decision, the television networks and all the major newspapers in the country made the Supreme Court's affirmative action ruling their top headline. A front page *New York Times* story, for example, described the *Bakke* decision as "the most significant civil rights pronouncement the high court has made since it outlawed public school segregation in 1954."[87] As further testimony to the significance of the case, the *Los Angeles Times* alone carried 13 articles on *Bakke* in its June 29 issue.[88] As the U.S. Supreme Court's first full-dress decision on affirmative action, *Bakke* elicited extensive media analyses, with many newspapers reprinting long excerpts of the six opinions in the 154-page decision. A common theme in the media analysis was that the *Bakke* decision provided solace for all sides in the controversy. The lead editorial in the *Washington Post* put it succinctly: "Everybody won." It then went on to point out that the decision ordered Bakke's admission to medical school, struck down admissions quotas based solely on race, but sanctioned the right of universities to institute plans to increase the number of racial minorities in their student bodies, provided that those plans take various factors—in addition to race—into account.[89]

Numerous experts in constitutional law, who had been eagerly awaiting the decision, were called on for their instant analyses. Many saw the decision as a wise compromise resolution of an explosive issue. For example, Harvard Law School's Alan Dershowitz characterized it as "an act of judicial statesmanship,"[90] and A. E. (Dick) Howard, a constitutional law professor at the University of Virginia Law School, termed the decision "Solomonic."[91] Philip Kurland, a University of Chicago law professor, sounded a more tentative note: "This is a landmark case, but we don't know what it marks."[92] The confusing nature of the *Bakke* decision was also captured brilliantly in a syndicated Herblock editorial cartoon showing a football official declaring a penalty while a frantic announcer exclaims in the caption: "He's signaling 'illegal procedure'—the affirmatives still have the ball."[93]

Views expressed in the wake of the decision by those with intimate knowledge of the case and representatives of various interest groups underline how easy it was to read the *Bakke* decision in decidedly different ways. Attorney General Griffin Bell, for example, declared that the decision marked a "great gain for affirmative action" because the Court supported race-conscious admissions in "as strong a way as possible."[94] Bell added that President Jimmy Carter was also "pleased" by the ruling.[95] Similarly, Benjamin L. Hooks, executive director of the NAACP, termed the decision "a clear-cut victory for voluntary affirmative action."[96] Daniel Patrick Moynihan, U.S. Senator from New York, and previously the executive department official responsible for the Moynihan Report that in 1965 had attempted to lay the historical and social groundwork for affirmative action, maintained that the *Bakke* decision "gets us back into a good, sensible, mainstream idea of what affirmative action should be."[97]

By contrast, James Prestige, academic affairs vice president at Southern University (a historically black institution), expressed disappointment that the Supreme Court had voided the set-aside plan for admitting racial minorities at UCDMS and submitted "This is a sad day for minorities."[98] Jesse Jackson, director of Operation PUSH, was even more emphatic in his criticism of the Supreme Court ruling in *Bakke*. Jackson compared the decision to the withdrawal of federal troops from the South at the end of Reconstruction in 1876. "Black people," he stated, "will again be unprotected. We must not greet this decision with a conspiracy of silence. . . . We must rebel."[99]

A few interest groups emphasized the significance of Bakke's personal victory and the fact that the Supreme Court had struck down what they saw as an offensive set-aside program. For instance, Ron Robinson, executive director of the Young Americans for Freedom, saw the decision as "an important step in eliminating the practices of reverse discrimination and quotas."[100] In a similar fashion, Howard M. Squadron, president of the American Jewish Congress, expressed satisfaction that the high court had ruled in favor of the "elimination of quota systems and the use of race as the sole criterion for university admission."[101]

Representatives of higher education contacted for comment expressed general satisfaction with the resolution of the case. Jack Peltason, president of the American Council of Education, a body representing hundreds of institutions of higher learning, maintained that the *Bakke* decision should not threaten voluntary affirmative action plans at American colleges and universities because "we have more [affirmative action] programs like Harvard than like Davis."[102] Even the president of the University of California system, David Saxon, although now compelled to admit Allan Bakke and oversee the retooling of the set-aside program at Davis, put a positive spin on the Supreme Court decision, calling it "a great victory for the university."[103] Within a few weeks of the announcement of the *Bakke* decision, colleges and universities set in motion plans to assess the impact of the Supreme Court's ruling. The College Entrance Examination Board, with financial support from the Ford Foundation, scheduled a series of conferences around the country, seeking to "illuminate the meaning of the decision for undergraduate admission." Notably, the Universities of California and Washington—institutions directly party to the Supreme Court's 1974 and 1978 affirmative action decisions— announced their own post-*Bakke* conferences.[104] The general feeling in higher education appeared to be that affirmative action admissions plans with race-based admissions set-asides, like the Davis plan, would need to be scrapped, but that programs that employed race as one nonarbitrary factor in admission decisions would not need to be revamped.

The *Bakke* decision, not surprisingly, led to speculation about how the Supreme Court might handle pending affirmative action litigation in the federal courts involving employment and government contracting. Eleanor Holmes Norton, director of the Equal Employment Opportunity Commission, asserted that the *Bakke* decision would not derail efforts in private industry to pursue hiring and promotion goals or achieve greater minority success in the receipt of government contracts. She declared: "My reading of the decision is that we are not compelled to do anything differently from the way we've done things in the past, and we are not going to."[105] Whether Norton's confidence would be borne out regarding affirmative action's persistence in employment and contracting arenas is the subject of our next chapter.

Years after the opinions in *Bakke* were issued, private papers of several of the justices on the Court in 1978 were made available to scholars and others interested in the Supreme Court. Among the hundreds of archived internal memoranda and notes of the justices were scores of fascinating letters, written by members of the public who felt moved to communicate with the justices. The collection of letters that Justice Blackmun saved for posterity was the most interesting. Blackmun's endorsement of affirmative action drew praise from several scholars and friends. For example, Blackmun's Methodist minister, Bill Holmes, wrote glowingly: "[T]he opinions rendered by you and your three colleagues [Brennan, Marshall, and White] clearly represented the most profound awareness of our nation's history in regard to race, as well as the most morally incisive interpretation of the Constitution as it pertains to the redress of that history. . . . I confess to be deeply proud and grateful that you came out where you did."[106]

The majority of the letters in the Blackmun file, however, were critical of the position the justice ultimately took in *Bakke.* For instance, a writer from New Hampshire, typing his remarks shortly after the oral argument in the case, posed this rhetorical question of Blackmun and his brethren: "Did Jackie Robinson ask for 4 strikes? And would you approve that the rules for baseball or tennis be made elastic?"[107] A few of Blackmun's correspondents even strayed into ad hominem attacks, such as a writer from Reno, Nevada, who vented: "You Sir, are a lousy Supreme Court Justice. YOUR MIND IS CLUTTERED WITH CLAPTRAP. The *Bakke* case didn't call for a decision as to whether 'affirmative action' be good or bad, desirable of not—it was simply whether using RACE as a criteria [sic] for anything be CONSTITUTIONAL."[108]

Finally, what about the man who occasioned all the attention and the Supreme Court decision that will forever bear his name? Allan Bakke went to work, as usual, at NASA's Ames Research Center in Palo Alto, California on June 28, 1978. At about 10 A.M. PDT he was asked by his secretary if he had heard the news. He just smiled and ducked into his office.[109] In a statement released later that day through his attorney, Bakke said: "I am pleased with the decision and that's all I have to say. I'd like to keep my private life private."[110]

As a legal denouement to the landmark case of *Regents v. Bakke,* the Supreme Court on July 3, 1978 vacated the stay in the California judgment that had been issued back in 1976, pending a definitive ruling by the nation's highest court.[111] Thus Bakke was officially cleared to enter UCDMS. So he did, beginning his medical studies in September 1978 and receiving his MD in June 1982. Bakke practiced as an anesthesiologist in the Mayo Clinic in Rochester, Minnesota for most of his medical career. In addition to administering anesthetics, Bakke invented a device that warms refrigerated blood prior to transfusions. He is now retired.[112]

In the early 1990s, a young man from Iowa drove to the Mayo Clinic to undergo an outpatient medical procedure. While navigating the twisting halls of the hospital complex, he encountered a middle-aged, balding man in a white coat with a name plate that said "Dr. Allan Bakke." The Iowan asked if the physician was indeed *the* Dr. Allan Bakke. The doctor reluctantly acknowledged that he was, but he promptly added a dismissive comment: "I do not talk about my case."[113]

NOTES

1. Personal information on Marco DeFunis is drawn from the Supreme Court opinion in *DeFunis v. Odegaard,* 416 U.S. 312 (1974); Allan P. Sindler, *Bakke, DeFunis, and Minority Admissions: The Quest for Equal Opportunity* (New York: Longman, 1978), 38–40; Howard Ball, *The Bakke Case: Race, Education, and Affirmative Action* (Lawrence: University Press of Kansas, 2000), 22–25; and Bernard Schwartz, *Behind Bakke: Affirmative Action and the Supreme Court* (New York: New York University Press, 1988), 32–33.

2. Sindler, 32.

3. Procedural information on the case in the state superior court is found in *DeFunis v. Odegaard,* 82 Wn. 2d 11, 13–14 (1973).

4. On the procedural history of the case in the U.S. Supreme Court, see *DeFunis v. Odegaard,* 416 U.S. 312, 315 (1974).

5. For a complete listing of the participating amici in *DeFunis,* see Ibid., 313–14. See also Ball, 33–36.

6. United States Constitution, Article III, Section 2.

7. Del Dickson, ed., *The Supreme Court in Conference (1940–1985): The Private Discussions behind Nearly 300 Supreme Court Decisions* (Oxford: Oxford University Press, 2001), 737–38; and Lewis Powell to Warren Burger, March 11, 1974, in Papers of Harry Blackmun, Folder 186, Library of Congress, Washington, DC.

8. *DeFunis v. Odegaard,* 416 U.S. 312, 314–20 (1974).

9. Quoted in Bruce Allen Murphy, *Wild Bill: The Legend and Life of William O. Douglas* (New York: Random House, 2003), 467.

10. Ibid., 227–332.

11. Ibid., 333–36.

12. Ibid., 338–44.

13. Warren Weaver, Jr., "High Court Avoids Ruling on Quota for Law School," *New York Times,* April 24, 1974, 1. See also John Field, "Justices Sidestep Bias Case," *Washington Post,* April 24, 1974, A10.

14. "The *DeFunis* Ruling" [editorial], *Washington Post,* April 26, 1974, A30.

15. Nicholas von Hoffman, "Justice, Injustice," *Washington Post,* May 3, 1974, C1.

16. Donald Johnston and Caroline Rand Herron, "Court Permits Schools to Keep Their Quotas," *New York Times,* April 28, 1974, E11; Cheryl M. Fields, "High Court Avoids Ruling on Preference to Minorities in Law-School Admissions," *Chronicle of Higher Education,* April 29, 1974, 1; and Cheryl M. Fields, "Court's Ducking of Admissions Issue Weighed," *Chronicle of Higher Education,* May 6, 1974, 3.

17. "Law School to Continue Minority Admissions," *Washington Post,* April 28, 1974, A13.

18. Nine Totenberg, "Discrimination to End Discrimination," *New York Times Magazine,* April 14, 1974, 9.

19. Warren Weaver, Jr., "High Court Avoids Ruling on Quota for Law School," 21.

20. "Follow-Up on the News: Marco DeFunis," *New York Times,* June 30, 1974, 23.

21. David J. Garrow, "Lessons from Affirmative Action's Past," *AAD Project,* March 31, 2003, http://aad.english.ucsb.edu/docs/op61.html (accessed December 6, 2006).

22. On Bakke's background, see *Allan Bakke v. Regents of the University of California,* 18 Cal. 3d 34 (1976); *Regents of the University of California v. Allan Bakke,* 438 U.S. 265 (1978); Sindler, 63–64; Ball, 46–61; and Schwartz, 1–10.

23. Bakke actually initiated his first application to the UCDMS in late 1972. Records at UC Davis indicate that Bakke might very well have been admitted to the class beginning the following fall if he had completed the application before the end of 1972. However, due to his family's decision to spend time in Iowa with his seriously ill mother-in-law, Bakke did not submit his application until January 9, 1973. By then most of the "regular" seats in the class had been filled. So, were it not for the sad turn of events delaying his application, there might never have been a Bakke case. See Robert Lindsey, "Focus of Historic Battle in Civil Rights Law: Allan Paul Bakke," *New York Times,* June 29, 1978, A22.

24. Ibid., A22.

25. Storandt would later be fired from UCDMS for disclosing to Bakke confidential information on other candidates for admission to the medical school. See Schwartz, 6–7; and Ball, 55.

26. *Bakke v. Regents,* 18 Cal.3d 34, 38–39 (1976).

27. Ibid., 39–44.

28. Ibid., 43–44.

29. Ibid., 44.

30. *Bakke v. Regents,* 18 Cal. 3d 34, 49–53 (1976).

31. Ibid., 56–57.

32. Ibid., 56–61.

33. Skepticism by friends of affirmative action regarding the appeal of California Supreme Court decision in Bakke is discussed in Sindler, 236–41; and Ball, 62–67.

34. *Regents of the University of California v. Bakke,* 429 U.S. 1090 (1977).

35. Ball, 67.

36. Schwartz, 41–42.

37. A roster of the amici in *Bakke* can be found as *Regents of the University of California v. Bakke,* 438 U.S. 265, 266–68 (1978). See also Ball, 70–85.

38. *Regents of the University of California v. Bakke,* at 267–68.

39. Ball, 77. Although DeFunis was the principal author of the YAF brief, he was not afforded formal billing in the roster of authors included in the introductory material to the Supreme Court opinion in *Bakke.*

40. Quoted in Ball, 74. See also Schwartz, 45–47.

41. Ball, 72–77.

42. Ibid., 80–85.

43. Schwartz, 43.

44. Ball, 91–94; Schwartz, 48–52.

45. Ball, 94–96; Schwartz, 52–53.

46. Kermit L. Hall, ed., *The Oxford Companion to the Supreme Court of the United States,* 2nd ed. (Oxford: Oxford University Press, 2005), 710–11.

47. Schwartz, 53–54; Ball, 96–98.

48. Schwartz, 63.

49. Ibid., 62.

50. Ball, 113–14.

51. Civil Rights Act, 78 Stat. 252, Title VI, Section 601 (1964).

52. Dickson, 738–41; and Justices' Conference Notes and Tally Sheet on *Regents v. Bakke,* October 14, 1977, in Papers of Harry A. Blackmun, Folder 261, Library of Congress, Washington, DC.

53. Dickson, 738–41; and Justices' Conference Notes and Tally Sheet on *Regents v. Bakke*, October 14, 1977, in Papers of Harry A. Blackmun, Folder 261.

54. Ball, 113.

55. Dickson, 738–41; and Justices' Conference Notes and Tally Sheet on *Regents v. Bakke,* October 14, 1977, in Papers of Harry Blackmun, Folder 261. See also Schwartz, 96–97.

56. Schwartz, 99–136; Ball, 107–35.

57. Jerrold K. Footlick, "The Landmark *Bakke* Ruling," *Newsweek,* July 10, 1978, 31.

58. "Bakke Wins, Quotas Lose," *Time,* July 10, 1978, 9; Schwartz, 142.

59. Warren Weaver, Jr., "Guidance Is Provided: Medical School Racial Quota Voided, but Advantage for Minorities Is Allowed," *New York Times,* June 29, 1978, A22.

60. Lewis F. Powell, "Memorandum to the Conference," June 27, 1978, Papers of Harry Blackmun, Folder 260, Library of Congress, Washington, DC.

61. *Regents of the University of California v. Allan Bakke,* 438 U.S. 265, 283–84 (1978).

62. Ibid., 287.

63. Ibid., 287–305.

64. Ibid., 305–11.

65. Ibid., 314.

66. Ibid., 311–19. Powell even added an appendix to his opinion laying out the terms of the Harvard College Admissions Program. See Ibid., 321–24.

67. Ibid., 320.

68. Ibid., 319–20.

69. Ibid., 324–25.

70. Ibid., 325–26.

71. Ibid., 328–40.

72. Ibid., 344.

73. Ibid., 341–55.

74. Ibid., 361.

75. Ibid., 370–79.

76. Ibid., 387.

77. Ibid., 387–400.

78. Ibid., 402.

79. Ibid., 404.

80. Ibid., 407.

81. Ibid., 379–87. White was the only member of the Supreme Court who appeared to care much about this arcane issue. The bloc of Stevens, Burger, Rehnquist, and Stewart did suggest, although not belabor, that White's view was incorrect. See Ibid., 418–21.

82. Ibid., 408.

83. Ibid., 411–12.

84. Ibid., 412–13.

85. Ibid., 415–16.

86. Quoted at ibid., 418.

87. Warren Weaver, Jr., "Guidance Is Provided: Medical School Racial Quota Voided, but Advantage for Minorities Is Allowed," *New York Times,* June 29, 1978, A22.

88. Jerrold K. Footlick, "The Landmark *Bakke* Ruling," *Newsweek,* July 10, 1978, 31.

89. "The *Bakke* Decision" [editorial], *Washington Post,* June 29, 1978, A26.

90. Quoted in Linda Greenhouse, "Bell Hails Decision, *New York Times,* June 29, 1978, A1.

91. Quoted in Jerrold K. Footlick, "The Landmark *Bakke* Ruling," *Newsweek,* July 10, 1978, 20. Anthony Lewis, perhaps the most respected legal commentator among journalists at that time, also used this phrase to describe Powell's opinion. See Anthony Lewis, "A Solomonic Decision," *New York Times,* June 29, 1978, A25.

92. Quoted in Footlick, 31.

93. In *Washington Post,* June 29, 1978, A26.

94. Greenhouse, "Bell Hails Decision," A1.

95. Cheryl M. Fields, "In Bakke's Victory, No Death Knell for Affirmative Action," *Chronicle of Higher Education,* July 3, 1978, 12.

96. Greenhouse, "Bell Hails Decision," A1.

97. Greenhouse, "Bell Hails Decision," A23.

98. Quoted in Fields, "In Bakke's Victory, No Death Knell for Affirmative Action," 12.

99. Quoted in ibid., 12.

100. Quoted in Charles R. Babcock and Loretta Tofani, "The Reaction: A Ruling with Something for Every Group," *Washington Post,* June 29, 1978, A23.

101. Quoted in ibid., A23.

102. Ibid., A23.

103. "Bakke Wins, Quotas Lose," *Time,* July 10, 1978, 15.

104. Cheryl Fields, "Officials Ponder Impact of *Bakke* Decision," *Chronicle of Higher Education,* July 10, 1978, 1.

105. Quoted in "Bakke Wins, Quotas Lose," *Time,* July 10, 1978, 16. See also, "Impact of *Bakke* Decision," *U.S. News and World Report,* July 10, 1978, 17.

106. Bill Holmes to Harry Blackmun, June 30, 1978, Papers of Harry Blackmun, Folder 262, Library of Congress, Washington, DC.

107. N. Landy to Harry Blackmun, October 17, 1977, ibid.

108. John M. Sperry to Harry Blackmun, July 3, 1978, ibid.

109. Dennis A. Williams, "Dr. Bakke?" *Newsweek,* July 10, 1978, 24.

110. Ibid., 12.

111. *Regents v. Bakke,* 438 U.S. 912 (1978).

112. Peter Schmidt, "'*Bakke*' Set a New Path to Diversity for Colleges," *Chronicle of Higher Education,* June 20, 2008, A18.

113.   Anecdote related by William O'Dell to John W. Johnson, n.d.

5

The Limits of Employment Affirmative Action, 1970s–1990s

Accepting the Republican Party's nomination to run for a second term in 1972, Richard Nixon had argued, "Let us commit ourselves to rule out every vestige of discrimination in this country of ours. But . . . the way to end discrimination against some is not to begin discrimination against others."[1] With this statement, Nixon tapped into a growing disaffection with affirmative action among many Americans. Nixon's comments were part of a broader effort to appeal to middle-American voters who were becoming more conservative, as political analyst A. James Reichley claimed, "in the sense that they [were] more likely to lose than to gain from social change."[2] Many middle-Americans were white ethnics who had relatively high-paying, unionized, blue-collar jobs or good white-collar jobs and had recently achieved middle-class status. They were less concerned with social justice than they were with issues such as urban violence, high taxes, inflation, and protecting their jobs and homes. Republican guru Kevin Phillips argued that, at a time when the Democratic Party had become closely associated with "the Negro socioeconomic revolution," the Republican Party could create a new popular majority based on these white voters.[3]

Historian Nancy MacLean describes how conservatives in the Republican Party did just that, exploiting fear and resentment over affirmative action in the 1970s to build an electoral base for the policies of Ronald Reagan in the 1980s.[4] Aided by economic restructuring and dislocation that lost or threatened jobs, conservatives were successful in convincing many whites that affirmative action was a zero-sum game. Affirmative action, they argued, took

third party, why should he "be made to pay for . . . what someone did 150 years ago?"[13] He filed a class-action suit under Title VII of the Civil Rights Act of 1964 on behalf of himself and other white employees. The district court upheld Weber's claim that the affirmative action plan violated Title VII and granted an injunction prohibiting Kaiser and USWA from discriminating against Weber and other whites on the basis of race. The Fifth Circuit Court of Appeals affirmed that decision, "holding that all employment preferences based upon race, including those preferences incidental to bona fide affirmative action plans, violated Title VII's prohibition against racial discrimination in employment."[14] The case was appealed to the U.S. Supreme Court.

Weber dealt squarely with the issues of reverse discrimination and quotas at the heart of the controversies surrounding efforts to dismantle historic job discrimination. It followed by only a year the decision in *Bakke* striking down the affirmative action policy of the University of California-Davis Medical School. For that reason, it was dubbed the "blue-collar *Bakke*" case. Much was at stake. Employers covered by Title VII were particularly in a bind. Already threatened by antidiscrimination lawsuits from individuals and the EEOC if they maintained a racially imbalanced workforce, would they now face reverse-discrimination lawsuits if they pursued affirmative action? By the time the case reached the Supreme Court, some 325,000 employers with 30 million workers had some form of affirmative action program based on goals and timetables.[15] The majority decision in the case and the key dissent marked out basic positions in the debate over affirmative action in employment.

The Supreme Court, voting five to two (two justices did not take part), reversed the Fifth Circuit Court and found that the voluntary affirmative action plan adopted by Kaiser and the USWA did not violate Title VII. Justice William Brennan, writing for the majority, noted that the lower courts had relied on a literal construction of the wording of Title VII and failed to understand its spirit. Rather, the legislative history and historical context of the act revealed "Congress' primary concern in enacting the prohibition against racial discrimination in Title VII . . . was with 'the plight of the Negro in our economy.'" "It would be ironic indeed if a law triggered by a Nation's concern over centuries of racial injustice and intended to improve the lot of those who had 'been excluded from the American dream for so long' constituted the first legislative prohibition of all voluntary, private, race-conscious efforts to abolish traditional patterns of racial segregation and hierarchy."[16] Nor did Section 703 (j) and its prohibition of quotas apply here. If Congress had wanted to prohibit all race-conscious affirmative action, 703 (j) would have read, "that Title VII would not require or *permit* racially preferential integration efforts."[17] Voluntary affirmative action plans such as the one under review, then, were permissible. "The purposes of the [Kaiser-USWA] plan mirror those of the statute," wrote Brennan. "Both were structured to 'open employment opportunities for Negroes in occupations which have been traditionally closed to them.'"[18] Furthermore, the plan did not unnecessarily trammel the interests of white employees; it neither discharged white employees nor created an absolute ban to their advancement. Finally, the plan was temporary, designed to reach a specific goal and then be abandoned.

Justice Rehnquist offered a vehement dissent. Rejecting the majority's interpretation of the spirit of the law in contrast to its literal reading, Rehnquist argued, "Were Congress to act today specifically to prohibit the type of racial discrimination suffered by Weber, it would be hard pressed to draft language better tailored to the task than that found in . . . Title VII. . . . Quite simply, Kaiser's racially discriminatory admission quota is flatly prohibited by the plain language of Title VII."[19] Furthermore, "the legislative history of Title VII is as clear as the language . . . and it irrefutably demonstrates that Congress meant precisely what it said . . . that no racial discrimination in employment is permissible under Title VII, not even preferential treatment of minorities to correct racial imbalance."[20] Rehnquist then provided a long analysis, replete with quotations, of the debate over Title VII in both the House and Senate, focusing on proponents' responses to concern that the law would spark the very situation that kept Weber from admission to the Kaiser training program. Clearly, argued Rehnquist, the bill prohibited discrimination against *anyone* on account of race. That meant no racial balancing, no preferential treatment, no quotas.

There is perhaps no device more destructive to the notion of equality than the *numerus clausus*—the quota. Whether described as "benign discrimination" or "affirmative action," the racial quota is nonetheless a creator of castes, a two-edged sword that must demean one in order to prefer another. In passing Title VII, Congress outlawed all racial discrimination, recognizing that no discrimination based on race is benign, that no action disadvantaging a person because of his color is affirmative. With today's holding, the Court introduces into Title VII a tolerance for the very evil that the law was intended to eradicate, without offering even a clue as to what the limits on that tolerance may be.[21]

But the majority had spoken, and at least some kinds of affirmative action fell, in the words of Justice Brennan, "on the permissible side of the line."[22] The history of affirmative action litigation over the next two decades would determine "what the limits on that tolerance" were.

LIBERAL LIMITS

Throughout the 1980s, a liberal construction of affirmative action generally held sway, although the majority of justices reflected a concern for fairness (that the interests of whites not be unnecessarily trammeled) that in some cases identified restrictions on remedial measures. In those cases, the more conservative justices helped form the majority. In general, the justices grappled with the distinction between a permissible remedial action and an impermissible racial preference.

In the late 1970s, associations of contractors and subcontractors challenged a provision of the federal Public Works Employment Act of 1977 that required at least 10 percent of federal funds granted for public works projects be used to obtain services or materials from businesses owned by minorities (defined as Negroes, Spanish-speaking, Orientals, Indians, Eskimos, and Aleuts). The contractors argued that the requirement violated the concept of equal protection under the law embedded in the Fifth Amendment's Due Process Clause as well as statutes such as Title VI of the 1964 Civil Rights Act. In *Fullilove v. Klutznick* (1980), the Court found six to three that there was no constitutional or statutory violation. Chief Justice Burger, writing for the Court, noted that Congress had evidence of a long history of marked disparity in the percentage of public contracts awarded to minority business enterprises. This disparity resulted "not from any lack of capable and qualified minority businesses, but from the existence and maintenance of barriers to competitive access which had their roots in racial and ethnic discrimination, and which continue today, even absent any intentional discrimination or other unlawful conduct. . . . [W]e are satisfied that Congress had abundant historical basis from which it could conclude that traditional procurement practices, when applied to minority businesses, could perpetuate the effects of prior discrimination."[23] Thus, Congress adopted a plan that was narrowly tailored to remedy the present effects of past discrimination. With regard to the question of the burden placed on innocent third parties, the Court argued, "When effectuating a limited and properly tailored remedy to cure the effects of prior discrimination, such 'a sharing of the burden' by innocent parties is not impermissible."[24] In a separate, concurring opinion, Justice Powell noted that "the set-aside would reserve about 0.25% of all the funds expended yearly on construction work in the United States for approximately 4% of the Nation's contractors who are members of a minority group." That would allow the remaining 96 percent of the contractors to compete for 99.75 percent of the funds—not a significant burden. "In my view," he wrote, "the effect of the set-aside is limited and so widely dispersed that its use is consistent with fundamental fairness."[25]

Here, the majority crafted an opinion that allowed Congress to address historic discrimination yet not unnecessarily trammel the rights of whites. This was nonetheless objectionable, argued Justice Stewart, joined in dissent by Justice Rehnquist. "The equal protection standard of the Constitution has one clear and central meaning—it absolutely prohibits invidious discrimination by government. . . . Under our Constitution, the government may never act to the detriment of a person solely because of that person's race. . . . The rule cannot be any different when the persons injured by a racially biased law are not members of a racial minority."[26] The fault line on the right, at least, was clear. Interestingly, however, the majority decision expressly avoided taking a stand on the test required in equal protection cases. Recall that in *Bakke,* Justice Powell examined the UC Davis Medical School affirmative action program under strict scrutiny, while those in dissent argued that, when racial classifications were used for remedial purposes, a less rigorous standard should be used (see Chap. 4). "This opinion does not adopt, either expressly or implicitly," wrote Chief Justice Burger, "the formulas of analysis articulated in . . . *Bakke.*"[27]

Boundaries on the extent to which innocent third parties might be burdened by remedial actions were established in cases that came before the Court in the mid-1980s. *Firefighters v. Stotts* (1984)[28] and *Wygant v. Jackson Board of Education* (1986),[29] both five to four decisions, protected seniority, building on an earlier case, *Teamsters v. United States* (1977).[30] These two cases also marked the limited influence that the arguments of the Reagan administration had on the Court at this time. *Teamsters* had reversed district-level decisions like that in *Quarles* (see Chap. 3), decisions finding that seniority systems that perpetuated prior discrimination were not protected. In *Stotts,* a district judge had allowed white firefighters with seniority to be laid off to protect the jobs of junior, black firefighters hired under an affirmative action plan. The Court ruled that under Title VII, in order to disregard seniority, evidence had to be provided that the seniority system was intentionally discriminatory or that the black firefighters who were retained had themselves been victims of illegal discrimination. No such evidence was provided, so the judge had violated Title VII's protection of bona fide seniority systems.

In *Wygant,* a similar situation arose when a collective-bargaining agreement provided that white teachers with seniority might be laid off to protect the jobs of minority teachers recently hired by a school system. White teachers laid off under the policy sued, arguing that the policy was a violation of the Equal Protection Clause of the Fourteenth Amendment. A plurality of the justices applied Justice Powell's test and found that the policy was a violation of the Equal Protection Clause because it failed to pass the strict scrutiny required whenever racial classifications were used by the state. In order to pass such an examination, the policy must reflect a compelling state interest and be narrowly tailored to achieve that interest. In this case, the Jackson policy of retaining less-senior minority teachers was adopted to address "societal discrimination" (as reflected in the much lower percentage of minority teachers than minority students in the system) rather than past discriminatory practices of the school system. In the absence of "a strong basis in evidence" of prior discrimination, compelling interest was not demonstrated. Furthermore, the remedy, laying off nonminority teachers, was not sufficiently narrow. Here the burden on innocent third parties, teachers who lost their jobs, was too heavy. Where the Court in the past had endorsed *hiring* goals, layoffs were a different matter. "While hiring goals impose a diffuse burden, often foreclosing only one of several opportunities, layoffs impose the entire burden of achieving racial equality on particular individuals, often resulting in serious disruption of their lives. That burden is too intrusive."[31]

Two major cases in the mid- to late 1980s found the Court endorsing key elements of affirmative action revolving around the use of quotalike formulations. Recall that in *Weber,* the Court endorsed *voluntary* affirmative action programs incorporating percentage formulas. In the following cases, however, formulas were *required* by court order.

Sheet Metal Workers v. EEOC arose out of the long-term refusal of New York City Local #28 to end discriminatory practices.[32] In fact, it had been held in contempt of court on two occasions. Finally, the district court imposed both a fine (the proceeds from which went to a fund to help increase nonwhite membership) and an affirmative action goal (29.23% minority membership) and timetable for desegregating the local. Local #28 challenged the district court's actions on a number of grounds, but principally contended that the membership goal and fund exceeded the scope of remedies available to the court under Title VII because they extended race-conscious preferences to individuals who were not the identified victims of unlawful discrimination. The Supreme Court, however, upheld the district court's order.

Among the variety of opinions offered by the justices, two are of particular interest. A plurality opinion penned by Justice Brennan argued that both the fund and the membership goal were appropriate applications of Title VII in the face of the local's "long and egregious racial discrimination" and resistance to court orders. The goal was perceived not as an attempt to achieve and maintain racial balance (illegal under Title VII), but rather as a "benchmark" against which the court might gauge the local's efforts to remedy past discrimination. It was not "a strict racial quota."[33] Furthermore, it was a temporary measure and did not needlessly trammel the interests of white employees. Nor did the membership goal violate the Constitutional right to equal protection. While still failing to adopt Justice Powell's strict scrutiny, Justice Brennan argued that "the relief ordered in this case passes even the most rigorous test—it is narrowly tailored to further the Government's compelling interest in remedying past discrimination."[34] Newly appointed Justice Sandra Day O'Connor (replacing Potter Stewart) issued an opinion that concurred in part and dissented in part with the majority. Justice O'Connor disagreed with the Brennan plurality over the nature of the membership goal. While accepting a distinction between a "quota" and a "benchmark" or "goal" requiring "good faith effort," Justice O'Connor found that, upon close examination, the district court's order in this case imposed a quota, thus it violated Section 703(j) of Title VII.[35] She did not address the constitutional issue. Justice O'Connor's much more cautious approach in accepting goals and timetables, in tailoring a remedy to the violation, would loom large in future cases.

Alabama's resistance to desegregating its state patrol presented another opportunity to review percentage targets on equal protection grounds. In *United States v. Paradise*,[36] the Supreme Court reviewed a district court order requiring the Alabama Department of Public Safety to promote one black state trooper for every white state trooper, as long as qualified black candidates were available, until the state trooper force was 25 percent black and the department implemented an acceptable (without disparate impact) promotion procedure. In a five to four decision, the Court upheld the district court order. Again side-stepping a commitment to strict scrutiny, Justice Brennan, writing for a four-justice plurality, nonetheless claimed that the relief ordered survived that high level of review. Pointing out that in 1972, the district court had found that the Department had failed to hire a single black trooper for 37 years and again, in 1979, that of 232 state troopers at the rank of corporal or above, there was still not one black, Justice Brennan argued, "[T]he pervasive, systematic, and obstinate discriminatory conduct of the Department created a profound need and a firm justification for the race-conscious relief ordered by the District Court."[37] The plurality argued that the hiring ratio was narrowly tailored to address the government's compelling interest in eradicating illegal discrimination. The requirement was temporary and did not impose an unacceptable burden on innocent third parties.

Justice O'Connor, joined by Justice Rehnquist and the newly appointed, conservative Justice Antonin Scalia, dissented. Specifically applying the strict scrutiny standard, O'Connor recognized the Department's egregious history of discrimination and the establishment of a compelling interest to remedy such. However, the remedy failed the second prong of the analysis. Justice Brennan's "standardless view of 'narrowly tailored'" was "far less stringent than that required by strict scrutiny." "In my view, whether characterized as a goal or a quota, the District Court's order was not 'manifestly necessary' to achieve compliance."[38] There were other alternatives, not relying on quotas or goals, that might have been used by the district court. Justice O'Connor's uneasiness with reverse discrimination was clear: "There is simply no justification for the use of racial preferences if the purpose of the order could be achieved without their use because '[racial] classifications are simply too pernicious to permit any but the most exact connection between justification and classification.'"[39]

The Brennan-led effort to craft a balance between the need to address historical discrimination and sensitivity to the rights of nonminorities was extended to sex discrimination in *Johnson v. Transportation Agency of Santa Clara County* (1987).[40] Before treating that case, however, it is important to review developments with regard to sexual discrimination in employment from the early 1970s to the late 1980s. During that period, women's rights in employment expanded.

WOMEN AND EMPLOYMENT OPPORTUNITY, 1970–1990

There had been considerable dissatisfaction among women's rights activists with the treatment of sexual discrimination by the EEOC in its early years. This dissatisfaction was reflected when Congress, in 1972, considered amendments to Title VII. "Discrimination against women," the House report stated, "is no less serious than other forms of prohibited employment practices and is to be accorded the same degree of social concern given to any type of unlawful discrimination."[41] Of course a major manifestation of sexual discrimination in employment was the segregation of women into low-paying, "women's jobs." This was not the only issue, however. Women employees also faced discrimination in terms of standard benefits such as disability insurance and pensions. And there was the issue of sexual harassment. In its 1972 guidelines, the EEOC stated that denial of disability insurance benefits to women who missed work while pregnant, when men were covered for all disabilities, was illegal under Title VII. The Supreme Court in *General Electric Co. v. Gilbert* (1976)[42] rejected this interpretation, but Congress clarified Title VII with the Pregnancy Disability Act (PDA) of 1978. The PDA asserted that discrimination on the basis of sex in Title VII included discrimination on the basis of pregnancy, childbirth, or related medical conditions, thus overturning *Gilbert.* In a series of cases following passage of the PDA, the Court held that the act applied to pregnant spouses of male employees,[43] rejected an argument that a state law requiring employers to give pregnancy leave without pay violated the equal treatment language of Title VII,[44] and found an employer's policy excluding women of childbearing age from a job with a potential health hazard to their unborn children a violation of Title VII.[45] Legal scholar Alfred Blumrosen argues that the latter case "constitute[d] the ultimate rejection of the paternalism which had permeated the case of *Muller v. Oregon.*"[46] With regard to pensions, employers had frequently increased the cost to female employees or reduced the benefits because women tended to live longer than men. The Court rejected this reasoning on the basis of stereotyping.[47] That is, just because women as a group live longer, that doesn't mean that an individual woman will. Such policies discriminated on the basis of sex and were illegal.

Sexual harassment was addressed by the EEOC under the leadership of African American attorney and activist Eleanor Holmes Norton, appointed chair of the commission by Jimmy Carter in 1977. In 1980, the EEOC adopted guidelines that declared sexual harassment a form of sexual discrimination under Title VII. In 1986, the Supreme Court, in *Meritor Savings Bank, FSB v. Vinson,*[48] adopted the EEOC's position and ruled that sexual discrimination in Title VII was not limited to economic or tangible discrimination (as in loss of employment status) but also included the creation of a hostile or abusive work environment.

But the key issue remained dead-end jobs; that is, the segregation of women into low-paying women's jobs. There were a number of dimensions to this issue. One was access to "male" jobs. In *Dothard v. Rawlinson* (1977),[49] the Supreme Court extended the disparate impact principle in *Griggs* to women by finding that a height and weight requirement for employment as an Alabama prison guard, while neutral on its face, arbitrarily discriminated against women. While some employment requirements might be exempt from Title VII prohibitions as "bona fide occupational qualifications," such qualifications had to be closely related to the job. The case was followed by a number of decisions in the 1980s serving to open positions for women previously considered men's jobs.[50]

A second dimension was low pay resulting from the fact that women's jobs were paid at lower rates because, well, they were women's jobs and were, historically, simply valued less. While the Equal Pay Act (EPA) of 1963 prohibited unequal pay for equal jobs "the performance of which requires equal skill, effort and responsibility and which are performed under similar working conditions,"[51] the law was applied narrowly to apply to male and female job situations that were virtually identical. It also authorized exceptions in certain situations. When Congress passed Title VII prohibiting discrimination in compensation because of sex, one provision incorporated the standards and exceptions of the EPA. Some employers used these standards and exceptions to justify sex wage differentials. Sex discrimination in wages, they argued, could only be established in cases of equal jobs. If the jobs were not equal, women did not have the right to sue. In *County of Washington v. Gunther,*[52] the Supreme Court rejected this reasoning, five to four, and found that women could sue over sex-based wage discrimination even if the jobs were not equal. The decision in *Gunther* opened up a wide range of actions in support of pay equity including lawsuits, state studies and legislation, union activity, and efforts to pass a federal pay equity statute.

A third dimension related to women's jobs was the potential role that affirmative action under Title VII might play in opening positions for women. The issue was considered by the Supreme Court in *Johnson v. Transportation*

Agency of Santa Clara County (1987).[53] The Transportation Agency of Santa Clara County adopted a voluntary affirmative action plan to address the historical underrepresentation of women in various, skilled, craft-worker positions. In 1979, there were 238 skilled positions at the agency, and none were filled by women. The plan attempted to achieve statistically measurable improvements in the hiring and promotion of women and minorities, with the long-term goal that the composition of the agency's workforce reflect the proportion of women and minorities in the area labor force. It also established adjustable, short-term goals to serve as annual guides for hiring and promotion decisions. In promoting individuals into skilled positions, the agency was authorized by the plan to consider sex as one factor. When a road dispatcher position (a skilled position) became vacant, a qualified woman was selected over a number of qualified men, one of whom scored slightly higher than she did in the interview process. The latter sued, arguing that the affirmative action plan violated Title VII's prohibition of sex discrimination.

In a six to three decision written by Justice Brennan, the Court extended the principles enunciated in *Weber* to this case, endorsing the affirmative action plan. The plan was voluntary, it addressed manifest imbalances in traditionally segregated job categories, sex was only one factor among many considered in promotion (paralleling Justice Powell's argument in *Bakke*), it didn't unnecessarily trammel the rights of male employees (no one was fired or lost standing), and the agency had "no intention of establishing a work force whose permanent composition is dictated by rigid numerical standards."[54] In a separate, concurring opinion, again reflecting her caution with affirmative action, Justice O'Connor argued that voluntary affirmative action plans of public agencies, subject to the Equal Protection Clause as well as Title VII, are appropriate only in cases where that agency itself has a history of discrimination. A statistical imbalance such as that presented here (no women in the skilled positions) sufficed to establish that basis. Justice Scalia, joined by Justices Rehnquist and White, disagreed. This was a case, plain and simple, of reverse discrimination. "The Court today completes the process of converting [Title VII] from a guarantee that race or sex will not be the basis for employment determinations, to a guarantee that it often *will*."[55]

Justice Scalia argued that, contrary to the positions of the majority, "the plan's purpose was assuredly not to remedy prior sex discrimination by the Agency. It could not have been, because there was no prior sex discrimination to remedy."[56] While the majority here accepted the statistical absence of women in skilled positions as indicative of prior discrimination, Scalia rejected that claim. "The most significant proposition of law established by today's decision is that racial or sexual discrimination is permitted under Title VII when it is intended to overcome the effect, not of the employer's own discrimination, but of societal attitudes that have limited the entry of certain races, or of a particular sex, into certain jobs."[57] That, to Scalia, was a travesty. "Today's decision does more . . . than merely reaffirm *Weber,* and more than merely extend it to public actors. It is impossible not to be aware that the practical effect of our holding is to accomplish . . . what the law—in language even plainer than that ignored in *Weber*—forbids . . . in many contexts it effectively requires employers, public as well as private, to engage in intentional discrimination on the basis of race or sex."[58]

Johnson would be the high point of William Brennan's effort to craft a position that he saw as balancing the spirit of Title VII—that is, the reduction of racial and sexual discrimination in employment—with the rights of non-minorities. Changes in the Court's composition would, over the next several years, shift its position further toward that of Scalia.

CONSERVATIVE LIMITS

While the Reagan administration's efforts to change the course of affirmative action had met limited success with the Court, personnel changes had begun to shift the Court's position in an anti–affirmative action direction. Conservative Presidents such as Richard Nixon, Ronald Reagan, and George H. W. Bush, elected in 1988, tended to appoint conservative justices. President Reagan's first appointment (some claimed an ironic, affirmative action appointment) was Justice O'Connor.[59] We have already noted the caution with which she approached affirmative action. Chief Justice Warren Burger's retirement in 1986 gave President Reagan a particularly good opportunity to strengthen conservative elements of the Court. He appointed Justice William Rehnquist as Chief Justice and, in Rehnquist's seat, Antonin Scalia. As we have seen, both were staunchly anti–affirmative action. One more opportunity was provided President Reagan when Lewis Powell retired in 1987. After a bruising political battle in which one conservative appointee, Robert Bork, was rejected and another, Douglas Ginsburg, withdrew, Reagan appointed conservative Anthony Kennedy in 1988. President Bush appointed David Souter in 1990 upon William Brennan's retirement (although Souter turned out to be much more liberal than anticipated) and Clarence Thomas, arguably the most conservative justice in recent years, in 1991 upon the retirement of Thurgood Marshall, arguably one of the most liberal—certainly with regard to civil rights and affirmative action. Thus, by the early 1990s, the Court had a definitely conservative cast, with three staunch conservatives, Chief Justice Rehnquist, Justices Scalia and Thomas, and two moderate conservatives, Justices O'Connor and Kennedy. Furthermore, the 12 years of Presidents Reagan and Bush provided many opportunities for the appointment of conservatives throughout the federal judicial system. Personnel changes portended a reexamination of affirmative action in the years ahead.

The first reexamination occurred in cases reviewed in the 1988–1989 term. In a series of decisions, the Court tightened aspects of discrimination law. Two of the cases are particularly instructive, one that saw the adoption of strict scrutiny for the first time by a *majority* of the Court and one that, at least temporarily, redefined the concept of disparate impact under Title VII. These two cases provide a sense of the Court's more skeptical treatment of affirmative action.

In 1983, the City of Richmond, Virginia, adopted an ordinance requiring that nonminority prime contractors awarded city contracts had to subcontract at least 30 percent of the award to minority business enterprises (defined as businesses at least 51% owned by U.S. citizens who were blacks, Spanish-speaking persons, Orientals, Indians, Eskimos or Aleuts). A nonminority business that failed to receive a contract because of its inability to meet the 30 percent set-aside sued the city, arguing that the ordinance violated the Equal Protection Clause of the Fourteenth Amendment. Upon reaching the high court on appeal, the claim was endorsed. Writing for the majority in *City of Richmond v. J. A. Croson Company*,[60] Justice O'Connor asserted, "Absent searching judicial inquiry into the justification for such race-based measures, there is simply no way of determining what classifications are 'benign' or 'remedial' and what classifications are in fact motivated by illegitimate notions of racial inferiority or simple racial politics."[61] Strict scrutiny was required in all such cases, and in this case, the ordinance failed both prongs of the test.

While recognizing "that any public entity, state or federal, has a compelling interest in assuring that public dollars, drawn from the tax contributions of all citizens, do not serve to finance the evil of private prejudice,"[62] Justice O'Connor argued that the city would need to show that it was at least a "passive participant" in a system of racial exclusion that injured individuals in Richmond. The city failed to do this. The city claimed that the measure was designed to remedy past discrimination, evidenced, for example, by the fact that contractors' associations in the area had virtually no minority membership. Historically, blacks had been excluded from skilled trades, access to which might have led to entrepreneurship. Such "an amorphous claim that there has been past discrimination in a particular industry cannot justify the use of an unyielding racial quota," argued O'Connor. "The 30% quota cannot in any realistic sense be tied to any injury suffered by anyone."[63] The city also pointed out that 50 percent of the city's population was black, but only 0.67 percent of the city's prime construction contracts between 1978 and 1983 had gone to minority businesses. Gross statistical disparities can provide prima facie evidence of discrimination, agreed Justice O'Connor, "But where special qualifications are necessary, the relevant statistical pool for purposes of demonstrating discriminatory exclusion must be the number of minorities qualified to undertake the particular task,"[64] not the number in the general population. "In sum, none of the evidence presented by the city points to any identified discrimination in the Richmond construction industry. . . . [T]he city has failed to demonstrate a compelling interest in apportioning public contracting opportunities on the basis of race."[65]

The city also failed to narrowly tailor its remedy. It was grossly overly inclusive, there being no evidence whatsoever of discrimination against the other, named minorities. There had been no consideration on the part of the city of race-neutral remedies it might have adopted. "[T]he 30% quota cannot be said to be narrowly tailored to any goal, except perhaps outright racial balancing."[66]

In *Croson,* the Court majority's application of strict scrutiny, independent of the race of those benefited or burdened and regardless of whether or not the classification was meant to be remedial (or benign), marked a clear shift away from Justice Brennan's reasoning in *Johnson.* In the future, references to general, societal discrimination—at least by the states and their subdivisions—would be inadequate to provide the strong basis in evidence necessary to demonstrate a compelling interest for the use of racial classifications. Remediation would have to be closely tailored to address the effects of the evidenced discrimination.

Later in the same term, the Court handed down a number of decisions that modified earlier affirmative action jurisprudence.[67] For our purposes, one of those cases, *Wards Cove,* is instructive. The case originated with the claim by minority, low-skilled workers in Alaskan canneries that, under the concept of disparate impact articulated in *Griggs,* their employers practiced discrimination. While there were many minorities hired in unskilled positions, skilled positions went to whites. Thus, from the disparate numbers, they inferred discrimination. The Supreme Court, in a five to four decision, rejected the claim. Justice White, writing for the majority, argued that the proper measure in such a case would be "a . . . comparison between the racial composition of the *qualified* persons in the labor market and the persons holding at-issue [skilled] jobs."[68] The original inference was nonsensical. "If the absence of minorities holding such skilled positions is due to a dearth of qualified nonwhite applicants (for reasons that are not [the employers'] fault), selection methods or employment practices cannot be said to have had a 'disparate impact' on nonwhites." If it were, then any employer with a racial imbalance might be "haled into court" to defend the business necessity of his actions. And here was the real rub: "The only practicable option for many employers would be to adopt racial quotas, insuring that no portion of their work forces deviated in racial composition from the other portions thereof . . . a result that Congress expressly rejected in drafting Title VII."[69] In order to ease the plight of employers facing disparate impact suits and reduce the likelihood of the adoption of quotas, the majority modified elements of the *Griggs,* disparate impact precedent. First, the plaintiff had to show how a specific employment practice created disparate impact; second, the standard of exemption from disparate impact was modified from "business necessity" to the lower standard of "legitimate employment goals" (that is, the employer needn't demonstrate that the practice was "essential" or "indispensable" to the business); and third, the burden of proof was placed on the plaintiff.[70] In short, the decision made it much more difficult to prove disparate impact.

The decision in *Wards Cove* was perceived as so damaging to disparate impact that civil rights and affirmative action advocates launched a major effort in Congress to overturn the decision, as well as a number of the other controversial decisions of the term. Eventually, Congress passed and President Bush signed into law the Civil Rights Act of 1991, repudiating the new standards in *Wards Cove* and endorsing the case law prior to it. Thus, disparate impact was specifically recognized as part of Title VII. Among other provisions addressing the Court's 1989 decisions, the law also provided for compensatory and punitive damages in cases of intentional discrimination, including sexual harassment. Sexual harassment had been a hot, national topic as a result of the nomination of Clarence Thomas to fill the seat of Thurgood Marshall in 1991. During the Senate's hearings on the nomination, a former employee of Thomas's, Anita Hill, had accused the nominee of sexual harassment while he was head of the EEOC. Thomas survived the charge, however, and his nomination was confirmed, creating the conservative block described earlier. Finally, the act noted that "despite a growing presence in the workplace, women and minorities remained underrepresented in management and decision-making positions" and established the Glass Ceiling Commission to study impediments in the private sector to the their advancement.[71]

ADARAND: STRICT IN THEORY, FATAL IN FACT?

In *Croson,* the Court had applied strict scrutiny under the Equal Protection Clause of the Fourteenth Amendment, a clause restricting the actions of states and their subdivisions (such as the City of Richmond). It had left open to question the appropriate test for federal actions. In fact, during the next term, Justice Brennan was able to craft yet one more majority in support of affirmative action, upholding a Federal Communications Commission policy promoting minority ownership of broadcasting stations. The policy derived from a Congressional mandate to foster diversity in broadcast programming. In the case, *Metro Broadcasting, Inc. v. Federal Communications Commission* (1990),[72] the majority applied an intermediate, rather than strict, standard of review. That is, the Court examined whether or not a benign policy served "important governmental objectives" and was "substantially related to those objectives." "We hold," wrote Brennan, "that the FCC minority ownership policies pass muster under the test we announce today . . . [T]hey serve the important governmental objective of broadcast diversity . . . [and] they are substantially related to the achievement of that objective."[73] In dissent, Justice O'Connor argued that federal actions should also be submitted to strict scrutiny.

In 1995, with a solid conservative block behind her, O'Connor's view would become the law of the land. By that time, Justice Brennan had retired (replaced by David Souter), as had Justices White and Blackmun. President Bill Clinton appointed Ruth Bader Ginsburg, of ACLU women's rights fame, to White's seat in 1993 and Stephen G. Breyer, a judicial pragmatist, to Blackmun's seat in 1994. Both Ginsburg and Breyer were academics, although Ginsburg had held a seat on the U.S. Court of Appeals in the Washington, DC Circuit since 1981, and both were liberal in their judicial philosophies. These appointments established the Rehnquist Court for the next 11 years. A number of cases would pit the conservative block, Rehnquist, Scalia, Thomas, Kennedy, and O'Connor (although the latter two were often swing votes) against the more liberal Stevens, Souter, Ginsburg, and Breyer. *Adarand* was just such a case.

In *Adarand Constructors, Inc. v. Pena*,[74] a case arising from a federal set-aside program, the Court adopted strict scrutiny as the standard of review for federal affirmative action policies. "Our action today," wrote Justice O'Connor for the five to four majority, "makes explicit what Justice Powell thought implicit in the *Fullilove* lead opinion: federal racial classifications, like those of a State, must serve a compelling governmental interest, and must be narrowly tailored to further that interest."[75] Especially critical of the majority opinion in *Metro,* she argued that it deviated from three fundamental principles enunciated in earlier decisions: "congruence between the standards applicable to federal and state racial classifications," "skepticism of all racial classifications," and "consistency of treatment irrespective of the race of the burdened or benefited group."[76] All of these derive from a basic principle.

[T]he Fifth and Fourteenth Amendments to the Constitution protect *persons,* not *groups.* It follows from that principle that all governmental action based on race—a *group* classification long recognized as "in most circumstances irrelevant and therefore prohibited"—should be subjected to detailed judicial inquiry to ensure that the *personal* right to equal protection of the laws has not been infringed. These ideas have long been central to this Court's understanding of equal protection, and holding "benign" state and federal racial classifications to different standards does not square with them. "[A] free people whose institutions are founded upon the doctrine of equality" should tolerate no retreat from the principle that government may treat people differently because of their race only for the most compelling reasons. Accordingly, we hold today that all racial classifications, imposed by whatever federal, state, or local governmental actor, must be analyzed by a reviewing court under strict scrutiny. In other words, such classifications are constitutional only if they are narrowly tailored measures that further compelling governmental interests. To the extent that *Metro Broadcasting* is inconsistent with that holding, it is overruled.[77]

In dissent, Justice Stevens, joined by Justice Ginsburg, reflected the thinking of advocates of affirmative action and offered an impassioned critique of the reasoning of the Court's majority. He was particularly concerned with the failure of the Court to discriminate "between a decision by the majority to impose a special burden on the members of a minority race and a decision by the majority to provide a benefit to certain members of that minority notwithstanding its incidental burden on some members of the majority." He wrote, "There is no moral or constitutional equivalence between a policy that is designed to perpetuate a caste system and one that seeks to eradicate racial subordination."[78] In effect, such reasoning would equate a "no trespassing" sign with a "welcome mat."[79]

As a matter of constitutional and democratic principle, a decision by representatives of the majority to discriminate against the members of a minority race is fundamentally different from those same representatives' decision to impose incidental costs on the majority of their constituents in order to provide a benefit to a disadvantaged minority. Indeed, as I have previously argued, the former is virtually always repugnant to the principles of a free and democratic society, whereas the latter is, in some circumstances, entirely consistent with the ideal of equality.[80]

Justice Souter, joined by Ginsburg and Breyer, and Justice Ginsburg, also joined by Breyer, wrote dissenting opinions as well.

Justice O'Connor recognized that the decision "alters the playing field in some important respects," but argued that in doing so, she wished to "dispel the notion that strict scrutiny is 'strict in theory, but fatal in fact.'" "The unhappy persistence of both the practice and the lingering effects of racial discrimination against minority groups in this country is an unfortunate reality, and government is not disqualified from acting in response to it."[81] At a minimum, however, it appeared that compelling interest required the government to provide "a strong basis in evidence" of prior discrimination, and narrow tailoring required the consideration of race-neutral and limited-term remedies. Even then, it was not clear that a race-based policy would survive the Court's review. In separate, concurring opinions, Justices Scalia and Thomas were unambiguous. "In my view, government can never have a 'compelling interest' in discriminating on the basis of race in order to 'make up' for past racial discrimination in the opposite direction,"[82] wrote Justice Scalia. "I believe," wrote Justice Thomas, "that there is a 'moral [and] constitutional equivalence' between laws designed to subjugate a race and those that distribute benefits on the basis of race in order to foster some current notion of equality. Government cannot make us equal; it can only recognize, respect, and protect us as equal before the law."[83]

Adarand "altered the playing field" for remedial affirmative action. But what were its implications for nonremedial affirmative action, policies supporting diversity? The following chapters will pursue the history of that debate.

NOTES

1. Quoted in Jo Ann O. Robinson, *Affirmative Action* (Westport, CT: Greenwood Press, 2001), 157.

2. Quoted in Godfrey Hodgson, *America in Our Time* (New York: Random House, 1976), 422.

3. Kevin Phillips, *The Emerging Republican Majority* (New Rochelle, NY: Arlington House, 1969).

4. Nancy MacLean, *Freedom Is Not Enough* (Cambridge, MA: Harvard University Press, 2006), 225–49; 300–314.

5. Allan Ornstein quoted in ibid., 233

6. Quoted in ibid., 236.

7. Quoted in ibid., 245.

8. Quoted in ibid., 247, 246.

9. See, for example, Donald T. Critchlow, *Phyllis Schlafly and Grassroots Conservatism: A Woman's Crusade* (Princeton, NJ: Princeton University Press, 2005).

10. Alfred W. Blumrosen, *Modern Law* (Madison: University of Wisconsin Press, 1993), 268–70; MacLean, 302–5.

11. Quoted in MacLean, 250.

12. Blumrosen, 221.

13. Quoted in MacLean, 250.

14. *United Steelworkers of America v. Weber,* 443 U.S. 193, 200 (1979).

15. "What the Weber Ruling Does," *Time,* July 9, 1979.

16. *Steelworkers v. Weber,* 202, 204.

17. Ibid., 205, emphasis in original.

18. Ibid., 208.

19. Ibid., 226, 228.

20. Ibid., 230.

21. Ibid., 255–56.
22. Ibid., 208.
23. *Fullilove v. Klutznick,* 448 U.S. 448, 478 (1980).
24. Ibid., 484.
25. Ibid., 514, 515.
26. Ibid., 525–26.
27. Ibid., 492.
28. *Firefighters Local Union #1784 v. Stotts,* 467 U.S. 561 (1984).
29. *Wygant v. Jackson Board of Education,* 476 U.S. 267 (1986).
30. *Teamsters v. United States,* 431 U.S. 324 (1977).
31. Ibid., 277, 283.
32. *Sheet Metal Workers v. EEOC,* 478 U.S. 421 (1986).
33. Ibid., 478.
34. Ibid., 480.
35. Ibid., 499.
36. *United States v. Paradise,* 480 U.S. 149 (1987).
37. Ibid., 167.
38. Ibid., 197.
39. Ibid., 199.
40. *Johnson v. Transportation Agency of Santa Clara County,* 480 U.S. 616 (1987).
41. House Report 238, 92d Congress, 1st Session, 1971, 5, quoted in Blumrosen, *Modern Law,* 149.
42. *General Electric Co. v. Gilbert,* 429 U.S. 125 (1976).
43. *Newport News Shipbuilding and Drydock Co. v. EEOC,* 462 U.S. 669 (1983).
44. *California Federal Savings and Loan Assn. v. Guerra,* 479 U.S. 272 (1987).
45. *UAW v. Johnson Controls, Inc.,* 499 U.S. 189 (1991).
46. Blumrosen, 187.
47. See *City of Los Angeles v. Manhart,* 435 U.S. 702 (1978).
48. *Meritor Savings Bank, FSB v. Vinson,* 477 U.S. 47 (1986).
49. *Dothard v. Rawlinson* 433 U.S. 321 (1977).
50. See, for example, *Hishon v. King and Spaulding,* 467 U.S. 69 (1984); and *Price Waterhouse v. Hopkins,* 490 U.S. 228 (1989).
51. *U.S. Code* 29, sec. 206-d (1963), quoted in Robinson, *Affirmative Action,* 87.
52. *County of Washington v. Gunther,* 452 U.S. 161 (1981).
53. An excellent treatment of this case can be found in Melvin I. Urofsky, *Affirmative Action on Trial: Sex Discrimination in Johnson v. Santa Clara* (Lawrence: University Press of Kansas, 1997).
54. *Johnson v. Transportation Agency,* 641.
55. Ibid., 658, emphasis in original.
56. Ibid., 659.
57. Ibid., 664.
58. Ibid., 675–76.
59. Reagan had made a campaign pledge to nominate a woman to the court. Responding to one of Scalia's rants against affirmative action during a court conference,

O'Connor remarked, "Well, Nino [Scalia's nickname], how do you think I got my job?" Quoted in Barbara A. Perry, *The Michigan Affirmative Action Cases* (Lawrence: University Press of Kansas, 2007), 30.

60. *City of Richmond v. J. A. Croson Company*, 488 U.S. 469 (1989).

61. Ibid., 493.

62. Ibid., 492.

63. Ibid., 499.

64. Ibid., 501–2.

65. Ibid., 505.

66. Ibid., 507.

67. See *Wards Cove v. Atonio*, 490 U.S. 642 (1989); *Martin v. Wilks,* 490 U.S. 755 (1989); *Patterson v. McLean Credit Union,* 491 U.S. 164 (1989); *Price Waterhouse v. Hopkins,* 490 U.S. 228 (1989); *Lorance v. AT&T Technologies,* 490 U.S. 900 (1989).

68. *Wards Cove,* 650, emphasis added.

69. Ibid., 651–52.

70. Ibid., 657–61.

71. *Congressional Quarterly Almanac* 47 (1991), 259, quoted in Robinson, 312.

72. *Metro Broadcasting, Inc. v. Federal Communications Commission,* 497 U.S. 547 (1990).

73. Ibid., 556.

74. *Adarand Constructors, Inc. v. Pena*, 515 U.S. 200 (1995).

75. Ibid., 235.

76. Ibid., 226–27.

77. Ibid., 227.

78. Ibid., 243.

79. Ibid., 245.

80. Ibid., 247–48.

81. Ibid., 237.

82. Ibid., 239.

83. Ibid., 240.

6

Affirmative Action Defended and Attacked: The 1970s, 1980s, and 1990s

Near the beginning of his dissenting opinion in *Regents v. Bakke,* Justice Harry Blackmun proclaimed: "I yield to no one in my earnest hope that the time will come when an 'affirmative action' program is unnecessary and is, in truth, only a relic of the past. I would hope that we could reach this stage within a decade at the most. But . . . that hope . . . [may be] a slim one. At some time, however, beyond any period of what some would claim is only transitional inequality, the United States must and will reach a stage of maturity where action along this line is no longer necessary."[1] Blackmun's "slim hope" would not be realized.

After the *Bakke* decision, affirmative education in higher education did not wither away. In fact it would soon become a fixture in the admissions policy of virtually every institution of higher learning in the country. Its actual impact would be felt primarily in the nation's most elite educational institutions. In symbolic terms, however, affirmative action would persist, even advance, its hold on higher education throughout the remainder of the 20th century and into the first decade of the 21st century. Not surprisingly, intense criticism of affirmative action—both inside and outside the academy—accompanied the growth of the policy.

A generation following *Regents v. Bakke*—fully 25 years after Justice Lewis Powell tendered his compromise opinion—the Supreme Court would decide another pair of higher education affirmative action cases, commonly referred to as "the Michigan affirmative action cases."[2] Before focusing on these and other cases in the current century, the complex debate over affirmative action in education that took shape between the mid-1970s and the turn of the century requires our attention.

The putative rationale for affirmative action in Justice Powell's opinion in *Bakke* serves as a good point of departure for understanding what transpired in the history of affirmative action in these years. Recall that Powell cited four possible justifications for affirmative action in higher education: (1) to mitigate the historic discrimination against racial minorities by American graduate and professional schools; (2) to counter the general societal discrimination against racial minorities; (3) to augment the number of professionals willing to provide services in communities underserved by racial minorities; and, most importantly, (4) to attain a racially diverse student body in order to afford minorities and white students alike with the socially beneficial experience of functioning in a real-world environment of different racial and ethnic populations.[3]

Powell not only found that the provision of a racially diverse student body was the most compelling justification for affirmative action; it was the only one of the four pretexts he proposed that was agreed on by the five-justice bloc on the Court—that is, Powell, William Brennan, Harry Blackmun, Thurgood Marshall, and Byron White—that accepted the principle of affirmative action as passing constitutional muster under the Equal Protection Clause of the Fourteenth Amendment. Taking their lead from Powell, defenders of affirmative action for the remainder of the 20th century took great stock in the diverse student body rationale. However, all four of Powell's plausible justifications were trotted out on countless occasions, and in varying combinations and permutations, between 1978 and the end of the century, to provide grist for defenders of affirmative action.

To survey even a small fraction of the defenses mounted in favor of race-based affirmative action in education in the 1980s and 1990s would take a very long book. Perusing it would try the patience of even the most patient reader. Therefore, for purposes of illustration, we will focus on two such sources. One is an influential article published in November 1977, shortly after the Supreme Court agreed to hear the *Bakke* case. The other is a heavily statistical book published in 1998. Both have the virtue of marrying social justice concerns with empirically based findings.

WHO GETS AHEAD IN AMERICA?

The 1977 article appeared in *The Atlantic,* one of the country's most respected opinion journals. It was written by McGeorge Bundy, President of the Ford Foundation, former dean at Harvard University, and former national security advisor under presidents John F. Kennedy and Lyndon B. Johnson. It is titled "The Issue before the Court: Who Gets Ahead in America?"[4] According to an unnamed source for *Newsweek* in 1978, it was Bundy's powerful defense of affirmative action in this article that persuaded Justice Harry Blackmun to join the "Brennan bloc" in *Bakke,* which supported affirmative action, rather than the "Stevens bloc," which favored dismissing the appeal of the Board of Regents of the University of California and thus striking down affirmative action on statutory grounds.[5] The folder on the *Bakke* case in Justice Blackmun's Supreme Court papers in the Library of Congress does in fact contain a copy of Bundy's *Atlantic* article.[6]

Even if Justice Blackmun had not relied on this article in his opinion, Bundy's *Atlantic* piece can still be regarded as an important apologia for affirmative action on the eve of the *Bakke* decision. Bundy commanded great respect as an intellectual and as a former advisor to two Democratic presidents in the 1960s. Moreover, the Ford Foundation, which Bundy then headed, had invested about $150 million in research on affirmative action in the 1960s and 1970s. Fragments of that research were presented in the *Atlantic* article.[7] So Bundy's comments resounded with clout as well as conviction.

Bundy focused principally on the advancement of African Americans, as opposed to other racial minorities. Near the beginning of the article he presented statistics, attesting to the success of race-conscious admissions policies in placing more blacks in professional schools and selective undergraduate colleges. To wit: in 1967–68, before most institutions of higher learning installed affirmative action policies, Bundy noted that there were 735 blacks studying medicine at American universities. Fully 71 percent of these were enrolled at Howard University and Meharry Medical College, the nation's two historically black medical schools. The slightly more than 200 black students studying medicine at that time in all other U.S. medical schools constituted only 0.6 percent of their student bodies. African Americans then numbered about 12 percent of the country's general population. By 1977, the number of blacks at American medical schools (not counting those at Howard and Meharry) had grown to about 3,000, fully 5 percent of the total number of medical students. The numbers of blacks in law schools and selective undergraduate colleges, in the same 10-year period, had shown similar patterns of growth.[8]

Could such an explosion in minority enrollment have been accomplished by means other than race-based admissions policies? Bundy said no. He advanced the argument frequently presented by advocates of affirmative action that the quantifiable social, economic, educational, and cultural deficits of racial minorities have resulted in substantially lower undergraduate grades and scores on standardized tests than that of white students and, thus, that "*there is no racially neutral process of choice that will produce more than a handful of minority students in our competitive colleges and professional schools.*"[9] Bundy granted that the 16-seat quota for racial minorities in the University of California-Davis Medical School (UCDMS) plan might have been arbitrary and politically unwise, but that the practical effect of using a more benign alternative, such as racial "targets" or "goals," is the same—provided that the goals or targets are met.[10] By contrast, if professional schools and selective undergraduate colleges were to cease practicing affirmative action, the consequences would be "catastrophic." Medical schools would return to the lily-white student bodies that were the norm in the early 1960s, as would law schools and selective undergraduate colleges.[11]

The argument over affirmative action, however, is generally not predicated on whether the policies succeed in bringing more people of color into heretofore preponderantly white environs. It is almost a given that they do. A more relevant question is: What are the consequences of bringing more blacks into selective institutions in the academy? Another is: Are unqualified racial minorities being admitted in lieu of whites? And, concomitantly: Are a significant number of qualified whites being denied the opportunity for higher learning in the most competitive colleges and universities?

What are the appropriate "qualifications" for attending a highly competitive institution? Is it possible, with a reasonable degree of probability, to determine one's future by performance on a single standardized examination? Bundy argued the position that colleges and universities should be permitted to adopt admissions policies that offer flexibility of choosing entering classes rather than being bound to lock-step formulae.[12] In fact, these institutions have for decades deviated from numerical criteria to give breaks in admissions to applicants who had nonquantifiable talents or attributes—for example, special skills or family members of previous graduates. Why should not membership in a racial minority be considered a form of "qualification"?[13] This point would be echoed by Justice Powell in his plurality opinion in *Bakke:* the achievement of racial diversity is a compelling state interest that serves as a constitutional justification to permit treating the races differently in medical school admissions.

The best test of whether one is qualified for admission may be his or her performance in the admitted class and, ultimately, his or her graduation. Bundy alluded to, but did not cite specifically, evidence that the rate of attrition of minorities in professional schools was comparable to the rate of attrition of white males.[14] So, in his view, the issue of qualifications was settled. It was not a matter of some unqualified racial minorities being accepted. Many qualified individuals were competing for a limited number of seats. It was a reality in 1977 when Bundy wrote just as it is today: there is a greater demand for physicians in America than there is a supply. The real question then becomes: How shall we choose among the qualified?

Yet what about the "damage" to disappointed white applicants to medical school in the face of affirmative action plans at UCDMS and other American medical schools? To answer this not-too-rhetorical question, Bundy presented an interesting statistical argument. In 1975–76 there were about 35,000 white applicants for medical school; only about 13,000 were accepted. By comparison, about 1,400 members of racial minorities were ultimately accepted and enrolled. Assume that all of the 1,400 members of minority groups had been denied admission, and that the number of available seats in medical schools had not changed; then the entering classes in all American medical schools could have found places for fewer than 7 percent of the disappointed whites. Thus, as Bundy read these figures, 93 percent of the "majority's problem" lay in an "excess of demand over supply"; only 7 percent lay in affirmative action.[15] Pushing this point further, he observed that the greatest competition for whites in being admitted to medical school came from other whites. Among the white applicants, the percentage of female medical students increased from 8 percent of the total in 1968 to fully 25 percent in 1976.[16] Women, according to most anecdotal evidence, achieved their increasing number of places in medical school largely without the aid of affirmative action. They clearly took the places of more white men than did blacks via affirmative action plans. Thus, wouldn't it be more logical for white men to assign greater blame to white women than to racial minorities for limiting their opportunities to attend medical school?

Bundy concluded his essay by noting that racial disparities in American life are not only substantial but have existed for hundreds of years. Affirmative action, however, at the time he wrote his article had only been in operation for a decade. How much longer would it have to be practiced to achieve substantial equality? He did not know and would not predict. But he did think it worth the cost even if it kindled anger among some whites: "it seems clear that to take race into account today is better than to let the doors swing shut because of the head start of others. We must hope and believe that in the long run our effort for equal opportunity will put the need for special programs behind us. . . . But what special admissions, and only special admissions, can do today is to make access to the learned professions a reality for non-whites."[17]

Then Bundy supplied the crucial words that Justice Blackmun adapted (or appropriated) for his own use in his *Bakke* opinion: "To get past racism, we must here take account of race. There is no other present way."[18] Blackmun's opinion in *Bakke* contains the following two sentences: "In order to get beyond racism, we must first take account of race. There is no other way."[19] Did Blackmun fail to credit Bundy with this felicitous phrasing? Or did a clerk forget to add a footnote?[20] In either case, Bundy's article should be understood as an unseen source of reinforcement for the Supreme Court's shaky but still enduring affirmative action edifice.

THE RIVER

McGeorge Bundy's 1977 article provided an eloquent defense of affirmative action on the eve of the *Bakke* decision. Two decades later, when cases involving affirmative action plans for admission to the University of Michigan were starting their slow journey to the Supreme Court for decisions that some predicted would reverse *Bakke,* another intriguing justification for affirmative action appeared in the form of a statistically laden book. Titled *The Shape of the River: Long-Term Consequences of Considering Race in College and University Admissions,* this volume presented the findings of a team of researchers assembled by two distinguished university administrators, William G. Bowen, former president of Princeton University, and Derek Bok, former president of Harvard University.[21] Published in 1998, two decades after the *Bakke* decision, Bowen and Bok's *The Shape of the River* serves as a convenient bookend to pair with McGeorge Bundy's "Who Gets Ahead in America?"

The Shape of the River focused on a sample of 28 of the nation's most distinguished and competitive institutions of higher learning. The sample included prestigious liberal arts colleges like Oberlin, Swarthmore, and Williams and well-funded research universities such as Duke, Princeton, Michigan, and Yale.[22] Most of the narrative in the book was wrapped around 76 figures and 71 tables attesting to the status and consequences of affirmative action at the elite colleges and universities in the United States.[23] The authors were quick to point out that the practical case for affirmative action, at least at the undergraduate level, rises or falls at the elite institutions. It is only at those institutions that the pressure for entrance is competitive enough to compel any appreciable choice along racial lines by admissions offices. At the vast majority of colleges and universities in the country, the issue of affirmative action is more symbolic than real. The authors state: "[O]nly about 20 to 30 percent of four-year colleges and universities (approximately 300 institutions) are sufficiently selective at the undergraduate level that the issue of whether or not to consider race in making admissions decisions comes into play."[24] The focus of *The Shape of the River* is further narrowed because it stresses comparisons mainly between African American and white students. Other racial minorities, the authors maintain, were not of sufficient critical mass in the years surveyed—the mid-1970s through the mid-1990s—to warrant meaningful comparisons.[25] Were this book ever to be issued in a second edition, the increasing numbers of Asian and Hispanic students would have to be taken into account.

The title of Bowen and Bok's book is a metaphor appropriated from the quintessential American writer, Mark Twain. The Mississippi River, to Twain, was "physically central to the United States and symbolically central to the progress of the country." Bowen and Bok see the river as a figure of speech that aptly describes "the flow of talent—particularly talented black men and women—through the country's system of higher education and on into the marketplace and the larger society." A river is a naturalistic motif that suggest twists and turns, clear passage at times but muddied and delayed progress at others. It better reflects the reality of the movement of talent by students of color through higher education and into the job market than does the more mechanistic term "pipeline."[26]

As we have seen, the river of talented black students in elite institutions constituted barely a trickle prior to the 1970s. The statistics reported in *The Shape of the River* bear this out. For example, in 1951, black students accounted for only 0.8 percent of the entering classes in 19 institutions in the Bowen/Bok data set; the other 9 institutions in the sample did not even see the need to keep adequate records of the race of enrollees. At the graduate school level, in 1965 only about 1 percent of law students in America were African Americans, with about one-third of this number attending historically black law schools. In the same year, about 2 percent of American medical school students were black, with about 75 percent enrolled at the two historically black schools, Howard and Meharry.[27]

The federal government's affirmative action initiatives beginning in the 1960s, together with similar state-supported, race-based admissions policies that soon followed, contributed to the increasing flow of talented students of color into elite colleges and universities. On the eve of the *Bakke* decision, Bowen and Bok reported that blacks made up 6.3 percent of the undergraduate student bodies at Ivy League colleges, 6.3 percent of the enrollment in medical schools, and 4.5 percent of the student bodies in the nation's law schools.[28] Capitalizing on the qualified blessing that the Supreme Court issued for race-based admissions in *Bakke*, admissions offices at the nation's premier colleges and universities were successful in slightly increasing black student enrollment in the 1980s and 1990s. In 1995, for example, blacks accounted for 7.5 percent of the enrollees in law schools and 8.1 percent of those matriculating at American medical schools.[29] Thus, by the mid-1990s the river was not at flood tide, but the current was visible and growing in intensity.

Absent affirmative action measures, would the increases in minority student enrollment at the nation's top postsecondary institutions have taken place? Bowen and Bok answer a resounding "No." In one revealing figure, bearing the convoluted legend "Black Matriculants as a Percentage of All Matriculants at Five Selective Institutions, Actual and Hypothetical Percentages, 1989," the authors compare the actual undergraduate enrollment of African Americans in selected institutions in a given year (7.1%) to what would have been the case had the black applicants' probability of admission, based on admissions formulae, been the same as the probability of admission of white students. In other words, if blacks applying had had their credentials assessed strictly by the numbers without any accommodation for race, what would have been their numerical presence in the student bodies? Using one set of assumptions, Bowen and Bok found that blacks would have constituted 2.1 percent of the selected student bodies; using another set of assumptions, their finding was that the black presence among matriculants would have been 3.6 percent. Both hypothetical "yields" were significantly less than the 7.1 percent of the student bodies actually constituted by black students at these schools in 1989.[30] Affirmative action made a difference in minority enrollment—not a surprising conclusion.

Although it is fairly easy to document that affirmative action brought more students of color into elite institutions than would have been the case absent the policy, it is more of a challenge to provide evidence that the beneficiaries of race-based admissions policies performed well in the schools that admitted them. Much of *The Shape of the River* is dedicated to providing evidence to support this proposition. Although black graduation rates in baccalaureate programs in the institutions surveyed by Bowen and Bok were slightly below those of white and Asian students, one interesting statistical finding was that black students graduated at higher rates the more selective schools they attended.[31] When adjusted for socioeconomic status, the difference between graduation rates of white and black students virtually disappeared.[32] The authors found similar graduation patterns for black and white students pursuing advanced degrees such as the JD, the MD, and the PhD.[33]

Bowen and Bok looked beyond graduation rates, and even beyond the time of graduation itself, to assess the relative success of affirmative action. They found, for example, that black students who had attended elite institutions had lower divorce rates than blacks who had attended all colleges and universities.[34] They also offered evidence that income for minority graduates of elite colleges was higher than income for all minority college graduates.[35] They even concluded from their surveys that the rate of "satisfaction with one's life" expressed by blacks was correlated positively with the competitiveness of the institution attended.[36] The authors of *The Shape of the River* sought to reinforce their statistical comparisons by enlisting anecdotal accounts attesting to the benefits of affirmative action for people of color. One such comment was offered by the well-known black intellectual and scholar Henry Louis Gates, Jr.: "By 1990, the black middle-class, perilous though it might feel itself to be, had never been larger, more prosperous, nor more relatively secure."[37]

To Bowen and Bok, just as to Justices Powell and Blackmun, the principal contribution of affirmative action to higher education was the positive contribution of racial diversity to the nation's campuses. Although recognizing that affirmative action had led to racial tensions at some colleges, including minorities segregating themselves in certain sections of student unions or cafeterias and the stigmatization that some attached to "affirmative action enrollees," Bowen and Bok were enthusiastic about the overall benefits of racial diversity on campus. In fact, they found that the support for institutional commitments to diversity among whites as well as minorities was greater for students enrolled in the 1990s than for alumni going back to the 1950s.[38] They concluded their chapter on the perceptions and realities of diversity thusly: "Of the many thousands of former matriculants who responded to our survey, the vast majority believes that going to college with a diverse body of fellow students made a valuable contribution to their education and personal development. There is overwhelming support for the proposition that the progress made over the last thirty years in achieving greater diversity is to be prized, not devalued."[39]

Yes, affirmative action has redressed some societal wrongs. And, yes, a racially diverse campus may be a healthier place to educate the leaders of the future who will need to navigate a racially more complex world than did their parents. Those are clear benefits of race-based admissions policies in higher education. But what are the costs? In particular, what about the white students who were thwarted by affirmative action in their quest for admission to elite colleges and universities? The authors of *The Shape of the River* emphasize that affirmative action has not been responsible for *any* white rejections at the approximately 80 percent of American institutions of higher learning that do not practice competitive admissions.[40] Even at the top-tier schools, Bowen and Bok maintain that the toll of affirmative action on whites has not been heavy. Had policies of affirmative action not been in place, the probability of acceptance to the institutions in *The Shape of the River*'s data set of white applicants would have increased from about 25 percent to 27 percent. It is a fair assumption that the 2 percent of white applicants falling just on the wrong side of the cusp at Williams and Harvard would have likely found college homes at other very good institutions. By contrast, the authors conclude that, without affirmative action, about half of the black students who had actually been admitted to the top schools would not have been found acceptable for enrollment at *any* American colleges. The authors pose the not so rhetorical question: If this counterfactual scenario (no affirmative action) had been the reality over the last generation, would we as a society be better off? Their answer: "Considering both the educational benefits of diversity and the need to include far larger numbers of black graduates in the top ranks of the business, professional, governmental, and not-for-profit institutions that shape our society, we do not think so."[41]

WHAT'S WRONG WITH DIVERSITY?

The case for affirmative action as set forth in *The Shape of the River* is a compelling one. But there is another side to the story. The argument against affirmative action, as we have seen, at first rested on the plain meaning of the U.S. Constitution and Title VI of the Civil Rights Act of 1964. Early critics of affirmative action asked, "What is it about the clear legal injunctions against discrimination on the basis of race—even for avowedly benign social purposes—that the supporters of race-based admissions policies don't understand?" Following the *Bakke* decision, the case against affirmative action shifted from stressing the plain meaning of legal words to a presentation of specific examples of where race-based admissions policies at elite colleges and universities had led to unsatisfactory results for whites or Asian applicants. In addition, the post-1978 argument against affirmative action also questioned whether diversity based on racial differences was as important in a student body as diversity predicated on intellectual tenets.

Both these strains of post-*Bakke* criticism of affirmative action are forcefully represented in a book titled *Illiberal Education: The Politics of Race and Sex on Campus.*[42] Its author, Dinesh D'Souza, is a social commentator and native of India who emigrated to American in 1978—the same year as the announcement of the *Bakke* decision. D'Souza's own story gives a special edge to his analysis of affirmative action. He grew up in a multiracial, multicultural, yet democratic society. His country of birth was struggling (and still struggles) to balance an ancient caste system, pervasive religious differences, and extreme poverty with the inevitable but often dangerous lure of modernization. Then D'Souza came to the United States—a country with many of these same characteristics and challenges. He attended Dartmouth College, where he would edit a contentious student publication that frequently criticized affirmative action. After graduation from Dartmouth, he undertook graduate study at Princeton University and served as a policy advisor for President Ronald Reagan. D'Souza became an American citizen in 1991, the year that *Illiberal Education,* his first book, was published. Over the last two decades he has been affiliated with conservative think tanks and has appeared regularly on the lecture circuit, principally before university and corporate audiences. Including *Illiberal Education,* he has written eight books.[43]

D'Souza's thesis in *Illiberal Education* is that a variety of political and cultural forces coalesced in the last third of the 20th century to make American colleges and universities inhospitable to free inquiry. His analysis derives from a decade of personal study and visits to some of the country's most renowned educational institutions. Interestingly, most of the institutions highlighted by D'Souza are part of the data set in *The Shape of the River.* In the course of his academic sojourns, D'Souza interviewed scores of students, professors, and academic administrators. The intolerance that he found on American campuses—what one of his interviewees termed a "McCarthyism of the left"—D'Souza attributed first and foremost to affirmative action.[44]

D'Souza's chapter on affirmative action highlights the University of California, Berkeley.[45] Prior to the mid-1990s, Berkeley was the poster child for affirmative action. According to statistics provided to D'Souza by Berkeley's Office of Student Research, only about 40 percent of UC Berkeley's first-year classes in the 1980s were composed of students accepted on the basis of academic merit; the other 60 percent were selected to meet various diversity rubrics.[46] D'Souza offers the extended example of two applicants to UC Berkeley to illustrate what he saw as the injustice of affirmative action. Yat-pang Au, an Asian American, applied for admission to Berkeley in 1987. Au was the valedictorian of his San Jose high school class, earning a straight-A average (4.0 on a 4.0 scale). He received a combined score of 1340 on the verbal and mathematical sections of the SAT, placing him in the 98th percentile of those taking that standardized test at that time, even above the high average of Berkeley students. He also boasted an impressive array of extracurricular activities.[47] Au was initially denied admission to Berkeley. After threatening to sue for racial discrimination, however, Au was finally admitted in 1989 as a junior.[48]

Contrast Au's situation to that of Melanie Lewis, a young black woman who also applied to UC Berkeley in 1987. Lewis's high school GPA was 3.6 (on a scale of 4.0), and she received a combined score of 1000 on the verbal and mathematics sections of the SAT. Lewis's parents were middle-class professionals. During her interview with D'Souza, she acknowledged that she could not recall even a single time that she had been a victim of racial prejudice. Lewis was admitted to Berkeley. She confessed to D'Souza that she felt she was not given sufficient credit for her accomplishments, constantly having to face the spoken and unspoken charges that she was only at Berkeley because of her race.[49]

The cases of Au and Lewis are just two of many D'Souza cites in an endeavor to put faces on what he sees as the unequal playing field constructed by affirmative action. But D'Souza also proffers statistics to display the bigger picture. He notes, for example, that Berkeley compiled an academic index in the late 1980s that took account of high school grades, SAT scores, and honors achievement. Out of a possible 8,000 points, blacks were routinely admitted with scores of 4,800. But white students needed at least 7,000 for admission, and students of Asian background had only a 50 percent chance of admission with a score of 7,000.[50]

Inequities in admission are only part of the problem that D'Souza attributes to affirmative action. He maintains that, once admitted to elite colleges,

underqualified race-based admittees (mostly African Americans) have diffi-
cultly keeping up in their studies, despite being eligible for an array of special
tutoring. In addition, blacks often feel uncomfortable in the face of hostility
(usually unspoken but nevertheless real) expressed by their white and Asian
classmates. So, not surprisingly, D'Souza points out that most blacks do not
persist until graduation. According to statistics quoted in *Illiberal Education,*
only about 18 percent of blacks admitted to Berkeley's undergraduate programs via affirmative action in 1982 persisted to graduation five years later.
Five-year graduation rates in the same years for white and Asian students at
Berkeley were in the 65–75 percent range.[51]

As an immigrant from a poor country, D'Souza claims that he is sympathetic with applicants to elite American universities such as UC Berkeley
who are trying to overcome disadvantages not of their own making. But he is
against race-based admissions programs because, in his view, such enterprises
result in a small number of elite institutions of higher learning competing
for a relatively small pool of generally black applicants. As a result, too many
members of this limited cohort of black applicants end up being admitted to
institutions for which, at least by traditional admissions formulae, they are
not qualified. Most of them struggle to keep up with their better-prepared
classmates, and many end up leaving without degrees. Along the way, the
beneficiaries of affirmative action often segregate themselves in corners of the
campus library or student union; they demand special curricula and remedial
assistance; and they are often disruptive of campus life. In other words, affirmative action does not promote a good "fit" between the minority applicant
and an elite college. A Melanie Lewis, for example, would perform better, be
happier, and be more accepted by her classmates at a less selective institution,
such as UC Irvine or UC Davis, as opposed to the highly selective UC Berkeley. Most importantly, she would have a better chance of staying in school
until graduation.[52]

D'Souza traces much of the racial hostility that has recently flared on
America's most elite campuses to affirmative action. "Ordinarily," he argues,
"white students may be expected to show some sympathy and understanding for the difficulties endured by black and Hispanic students, but since
they consider that affirmative action benefits are awarded at their expense,
many respond with callousness and derision to struggling minority peers. . . .
[W]hite hostility to preferential treatment and minority separatism is a major
force behind many of the ugly racial incidents that have scarred the American
campus."[53]

Notwithstanding all these problems with affirmative action, D'Souza suggests that it still might be worth all the trouble and expense if it could be
deemed successful in promoting the positive consequences that its proponents

claim stem from racial diversity. D'Souza paraphrases the case for racial diversity thusly: "This logic resides in the conviction that a more diverse student body with a broad variety of backgrounds and viewpoints is likely to produce a more dynamic intellectual environment and a richer undergraduate experience."[54] Justices Powell and Brennan cited the benefit of diversity as the linchpin of their opinions in *Bakke*. And McGeorge Bundy, in his 1977 *Atlantic Monthly* article, and Bowen and Bok, in their lengthy tome, celebrate racial diversity as the key contribution of affirmative action that will ultimately lead to widespread social benefits.

To those arguments, D'Souza says, essentially: "It hasn't worked out that way." Based on his interviews at Berkeley and other elite campuses, D'Souza concludes that racial diversity in a student body does not lead to a rich academic experience. Most often, he insists, it leads to a balkanization within the student body, a sense of victimization expressed by racial minorities, confusion or resentment on the part of white and Asian students, and, most regrettably, a constriction of intellectual discourse. D'Souza argues that challenging the view that racial diversity is worth pursuing through affirmative action is a risky position for a person of any racial background to advocate on a college campus. It is simply deemed "not politically correct." As a result, much of the white or Asian disagreement with affirmative action on campus descends underground and emerges in anonymous hostility toward blacks and, occasionally, overt acts of bigotry or racism.[55] D'Souza is not against diversity per se. But, rather than racial diversity, he endorses a "diversity of mind." "Such diversity," he argues, "would enrich academic discourse, widen its parameters, multiply its objects of inquiry, and increase the probability of obscure and unlikely terrain being investigated."[56]

D'Souza does not blame affirmative action for all the forms of intolerance in American higher education. But he sees race-based admissions as running parallel to or being linked to some of the other manifestations of intellectual dishonesty pervading America's most prestigious campuses. At Stanford, for example, he sees the dalliance with multiculturalism as leading to the championing of mediocre third-world texts;[57] at Howard University he flays the historically unsound search for an Afro-centric curriculum;[58] at Michigan he dissects episodes of racial hostility that occasioned censorship in public discourse;[59] at Duke he skewers the hiring of fashionable professors—for example, deconstructionists, postmodernists, reader-response theorists—who appear bent on discrediting neutral and/or objective standards of scholarship;[60] and at Harvard he attacks what he sees as unsupportable accusations of racism against some of the institution's best known scholar/teachers.[61] In his final chapter, D'Souza advances several "modest proposals" to reverse the momentum of illiberal education, the first and most important of which is to dispense with race-based affirmative action and, in its place, institute plans that offer preference for students of low socioeconomic status.[62]

THE RESISTANCE TO AFFIRMATIVE ACTION GATHERS MOMENTUM

In 1992, William Jefferson Clinton, former governor of Arkansas, was elected the nation's 42nd president. Clinton owed much of his electoral success to black voters. But he also styled himself as a "new Democrat." Attempting to appeal to middle-of-the-road white voters as well as African Americans and other traditional Democratic constituencies, Clinton was adroit at straddling the political fence. Nowhere is this more apparent than in an address that he delivered on affirmative action at the National Archives in Washington, DC, on July 19, 1995. Often termed the "Mend It, Don't End It" speech,[63] Clinton began by testifying eloquently to his lifelong support of civil rights. But near the end of the speech he addressed some of the problems and complexities that he saw in affirmative action. He referred to the 1995 decision, *Adarand Constructors, Inc. v. Pena,* in which the Court ruled by a bare five to four majority that race-based classifications in selecting contractors can only be constitutionally permissible if they survive the high threshold of strict scrutiny.[64] With the message sent by the Court in *Adarand* in mind, the president offered this statement: "My fellow Americans, affirmative action has to be made consistent with our highest ideals of personal responsibility and merit, and our urgent need to find common ground. . . . Today I am directing all federal agencies to . . . apply . . . four standards of fairness . . . to all our affirmative action programs: no quotas, in theory or in practice; no illegal discrimination of any kind, including reverse discrimination; no preference for people who are not qualified for jobs or other opportunities; and as soon as a program has succeeded, it must be retired. Any program that doesn't meet these four principles must be eliminated or reformed to meet them. But let me be clear: affirmative action has been good for America. Affirmative action has not always been perfect, and affirmative action should not go on forever. . . . So here is what I think we should do. We should reaffirm the principle of affirmative action and fix the practices. We should have a simple slogan: Mend it, but don't end it."[65]

This less than ringing endorsement of affirmative action spoke volumes about the shaky stature of race-conscious programs at the national level. This is evidenced by the ambiguous employment decisions of the Supreme Court, particularly *Adarand,* discussed in the previous chapter. At the state level, especially in the context of higher education, affirmative action was even more on the defensive. California proved to be the bellwether state.

In 1994, the University of California, Berkeley—the institution high-lighted by D'Souza's impressionistic analysis—received in excess of 22,000 applications for 3,500 seats in its first-year class. An astounding 9,000 of the 22,000 applications were submitted by students who had earned 4.0 aver-ages (straight A grades) in their high schools.[66] Notwithstanding the likely reality of grade inflation, how could a conscientious admissions committee distinguish among such high-achieving students? The answer arrived at by Berkeley and other elite institutions placed in similar situations was the use of a formula that weighted most heavily standardized test scores and nonmerit considerations such as affirmative action.

It was the vexing admissions dilemma at Berkeley and other campuses in the University of California (the "UC system") that brought an African American businessman, Ward Connerly, to state and national prominence. In the late 1960s Connerly, a land-use planning consultant, made the acquain-tance of a California legislator named Pete Wilson. In 1993, Wilson was elected governor of the Golden State; shortly thereafter Wilson appointed Connerly to the Board of Regents of the UC system. Although Connerly had occasionally taken advantage of his status as a minority contractor in promot-ing his consulting company,[67] he had for years been a harsh critic of affirma-tive action. Ascending quickly to the chairmanship of the Board of Regents, Connerly pushed strenuously for the termination of race-based admissions at UC institutions.

Besides crusading against affirmative action in the UC system, Connerly became the most visible spokesperson for the California Civil Rights Initia-tive (CCRI), also known as Proposition 209. This initiative sought to end all preferences by race and gender in California public life. The language of Proposition 209 reads simply: "The state shall not discriminate against, or grant preferential treatment to, any individual or group on the basis of race, sex, color, ethnicity, or national origin in the operation of public employ-ment, public education or public contracting."[68] In November 1996, the voters of California approved Proposition 209 by a vote of 54 percent to 46 percent.[69]

Capitalizing on the passage of Proposition 209, Connerly and the Board of Regents made the final push to terminate affirmative action in the UC sys-tem. At a stormy public meeting in early 1997, the Board of Regents acceded to Connerly's campaign and voted to dismantle affirmative action in the UC system.[70] This is exactly what Dinesh D'Souza had so passionately advocated in *Illiberal Education*. The adverse impact on minority enrollment in the UC schools was quick in coming. For example, freshman admissions of African Americans at UC Berkeley stood at 562 in 1997; the number plummeted to 191 in 1998, an astounding 66 percent decline. In the same year, sizeable declines also took place in Latino and Native American admissions. By contrast, admissions of white and Asian American students to UC campuses increased.[71]

The retreat from affirmative action in California was reinforced by a 1996 decision of a circuit court of appeals in another part of the country. The case arose as a challenge to the affirmative action plan at the law school of the University of Texas. In the early 1990s, the law school had in place an affirmative action admission plan designed to give special consideration to African Americans and Mexican Americans, two groups that had endured lengthy patterns of discrimination in the state's history. Each applicant's file generated a Texas Index ("TI") number, essentially an algorithm based on the student's undergraduate grade point average and her score on the Law School Aptitude Test (LSAT). Applicants were grouped by racial category—white, black, or Mexican American. In each category, cut points were determined to place candidates for admission in one of three subcategories—"presumptive admit," "presumptive deny," or a "discretionary zone." The cut points were several points higher for white applicants than black or Mexican applicants. Most of the discussion among admissions officials focused on candidates in the discretionary zone.[72]

Cheryl Hopwood was a married white woman with a disabled child. At the time of her application to the law school she was 29 years of age. Her LSAT score placed her at about the 83rd percentile of national takers of the exam; her undergraduate grade point average was 3.8. Her initial TI number was 199, exactly at the lower limit of the presumptive admit zone. However, the admissions committee reduced her TI number by one point because of what it saw as the relative weakness of her undergraduate institutions. She was ultimately rejected for admission. Along with a handful of other white applicants, she sought an injunction in federal court to be admitted to the law school as well as monetary damages. She made the same claim that Allan Bakke had raised almost 20 years earlier, that is, that the denial of her admission to this professional school violated her right to equal protection under the Fourteenth Amendment to the U.S. Constitution and Title VI of the Civil Rights Act of 1964 on account of her race.[73]

After a bench trial, a federal district court in Texas found in favor of Hopwood. But that ruling was a hollow victory, at best. The district court judge found that Hopwood's equal protection rights had been violated by the law school's affirmative action policy, but granted her only one dollar in nominal damages and ordered that she be allowed to apply a second time without paying an application fee. Most tellingly, the district court refused to prohibit the law school from continuing to use race as a factor in admissions decisions.[74]

Hopwood wanted more, specifically outright admission to the law school and a declaration that the plan that thwarted her career aspirations violated the U.S. Constitution. So she appealed the lower court ruling to the Fifth Circuit Court of Appeals.

In a decision issued in March 1996, a majority of a Fifth Circuit panel acceded to Hopwood's entreaties. In a long and surprisingly activist opinion, written by Circuit Judge Jerry E. Smith, the Fifth Circuit reversed the Texas district court. Judge Smith ruled that the affirmative action plan of the law school of the University of Texas violated the Equal Protection Clause of the Fourteenth Amendment. He further held that Cheryl Hopwood was entitled to reapply to the law school under an admissions plan that was not constitutionally flawed, and he ordered that the matter of damages should be revisited by the district court.[75]

The law school at the University of Texas identified the achievement of racial diversity as the principal justification for its affirmative action plan. Judge Smith acknowledged that the leading precedent for sustaining race-based admission as flowing from the goal of racial diversity was the opinion of Justice Powell in *Regents v. Bakke*. Smith focused on what he saw as the tenuousness of this precedent. Although Powell controlled the opinion of the Court in *Bakke*, Smith read the opinion as being shaky because no other justice agreed with all the points made by Powell's lonely opinion. Further, he maintained that Powell's opinion on diversity as a compelling justification for affirmative action had been undercut by more recent Supreme Court decisions, particularly *Adarand*.[76] Smith observed that diversity can assume many forms and noted that Cheryl Hopwood, now a 32-year-old woman married to a member of the Armed Forces with a severely handicapped child, presented a type of diversity that might bring a different perspective to the law school that could be as compelling as another candidate's racial minority status.[77]

Although Judge Smith did not explicitly say that he was overruling the *Bakke* decision, his brethren on the Fifth Circuit—one concurring and one in dissent—believed that that was just what he had done. The dissenting opinion, in particular, took Judge Smith to task for "going out of his way to break ground that the Supreme Court itself has been careful to avoid."[78] Then it chided him for "the radical implications of . . . [his] opinion, with its sweeping dicta . . . [that] will literally change the face of public educational institutions throughout Texas, the other states of this circuit, and this nation."[79]

The media reaction to Judge Smith's decision was quick and generally critical. For example, Jeffrey Rosen, George Washington University Law Professor and legal affairs editor of *The New Republic*, termed Smith's opinion "freewheeling," "cynical," and "clumsy." Rosen also accused Smith of misreading and misapplying Powell's opinion in *Bakke* and posing as an "inept" predictor of what the Supreme Court might do about affirmative action when it next confronts the issue.[80]

After the circuit court opinion in *Hopwood,* speculation ensued as to what the nation's highest court would do about Cheryl Hopwood and the issues she raised in her challenge to affirmative action. That question was answered quickly but not definitively. On July 1, 1996, the Supreme Court issued an order refusing to grant certiorari in the case, thus leaving intact the ruling that affirmative action in the Fifth Circuit was no longer prevailing law. The explanation offered by Justices Ruth Ginsburg and David Souter, who con-curred in the order, was that the law school at the University of Texas had scrapped its affirmative action plan and disposed of its TI numbers sometime after the commencement of Hopwood's legal action. Hence, there remained no case or controversy for the Court to decide.[81]

This unsatisfactory resolution left affirmative action in American higher education in a state of limbo. Shortly after the Supreme Court refused to hear the *Hopwood* case, Martin Michaelson, a Washington attorney specializing in higher education law, cautioned that "educators must make the case for affirmative action themselves; the courts are unlikely to do it for them." He also predicted—correctly it would turn out—that there would be no oppor-tunity for the Supreme Court to furnish clear guidance on affirmative action for many years because there were no cases comparable to *Bakke* or *Hopwood* currently in the pipeline.[82]

As the 20th century, thus, stumbled to an end, affirmative action in educa-tion was in an anomalous position. President Clinton was on record in favor of race-based admissions in higher education—but only in a tepid way. *Regents v. Bakke* was still the affirmative action decision with the most precedential value, although experts disagreed as to how substantially it had been qualified or undercut by *Adarand.* In California, moreover, affirmative action had been essentially buried by Ward Connerly and Proposition 209. Similarly, Judge Jerry Smith's opinion in *Hopwood v. Texas* had brought an end to race-based admissions in the Fifth Judicial Circuit—Texas, Louisiana, and Mississippi.

A set of affirmative action cases involving admissions to two divisions of the University of Michigan—cases that would offer a bit more clarity for those interested in the curious status of race-based admissions in American higher education—would finally wend their way to the U.S. Supreme Court in 2003. We turn to those cases now.

NOTES

1. *Regents v. Bakke,* 438 U.S. 265, 403 (1978).
2. *Jennifer Gratz and Patrick Hamacher v. Lee Bollinger, et al.,* 539 U.S. 244 (2003) and *Barbara Grutter v. Lee Bollinger, et al.,* 539 U.S. 306 (2003). These two cases are

commonly referred to as the Michigan affirmative action cases. See, especially, Barbara A. Perry, *The Michigan Affirmative Action Cases* (Lawrence: University Press of Kansas, 2007).

3. *Regents v. Bakke,* 438 U.S. 265, 305–20 (1978).

4. McGeorge Bundy, "The Issue before the Court: Who Gets Ahead in America?" *The Atlantic,* November 1977, 41–54.

5. Jerrold K. Footlick, "The Landmark *Bakke* Ruling," *Newsweek,* July 10, 1978, 25.

6. See Papers of Harry A. Blackmun, Folder 261, Library of Congress, Washington, DC.

7. Robert Manning, "The Editor's Page," *The Atlantic,* November 1977, 4. On Bundy and affirmative action, see Tamar Jacoby, "McGeorge Bundy: How the Establishment's Man Tackled America's Problem with Race," *Alicia Patterson Foundation Reporter* 13 (1990), http://www.aliciapatterson.org/APF1303/Jacoby (accessed January 6, 2008).

8. Bundy, "Who Gets Ahead in America?" 43–44.

9. Ibid., 44, emphasis in original.

10. Ibid., 45.

11. Ibid., 44.

12. Ibid., 46–47.

13. Ibid., 48.

14. Ibid., 47.

15. Ibid., 49.

16. Ibid., 49–50.

17. Ibid., 54.

18. Ibid., 54.

19. *Regents v. Bakke,* 438 U.S. 265, 407 (1978).

20. Linda Greenhouse, Supreme Court correspondent for the *New York Times* who has reviewed tens of thousands of documents in the Blackmun papers, suggests that McGeorge Bundy, who is now deceased, "may [have been] terrifically pleased to have endowed the affirmative action debate with such a pithy phrase." Linda Greenhouse, "At a Shrine of American Documents, Pathos, Poetry and Blackmun's 'Rosebud,'" *New York Times,* March 7, 2004, 7.

21. William G. Bowen and Derek Bok, *The Shape of the River: Long-Term Consequences of Considering Race in College and University Admissions* (Princeton, NJ: Princeton University Press, 1998).

22. Ibid., lv–lviii.

23. For a list of the figures and tables in *The Shape of the River,* see ibid., ix–xix.

24. Ibid., xxxvii–xxxviii, 15.

25. Ibid., liii–lv.

26. Ibid., xlix.

27. Ibid., 4–5.

28. Ibid., 7.

29. Ibid., 10.

30. Ibid., 31–39.

31. Ibid., 54–68.

32. Ibid., 66–68.

33. Ibid., 96–103.

34. Ibid., 175–77.

35. Ibid., 177–79.

36. Ibid., 180–92.

37. Quoted in ibid., 170.

38. Ibid., 268–69.

39. Ibid., 255. On policies to implement racial diversity at Ivy League institutions, see Jerome Karabel, *The Chosen: The Hidden History of Admission and Exclusion at Harvard, Yale, and Princeton* (Boston: Houghton Mifflin Company, 2005), 483–513.

40. Ibid., 15.

41. Ibid., 280–86.

42. Dinesh D'Souza, *Illiberal Education: The Politics of Race and Sex on Campus* (New York: The Free Press, 1991).

43. See also, Dinesh D'Souza Website, http://dineshdsouza.com/ (accessed March 20, 2008), and D'Souza, *Illiberal Education,* 22–23.

44. Quoted in D'Souza, *Illiberal Education,* 195.

45. Ibid., 24–58.

46. Ibid., 35–36. The passage of Proposition 209 (the California Civil Rights Initiative) in the mid-1990s effectively eliminated affirmative action at Berkeley and other California institutions of higher learning. An account of the passage and consequences of Proposition 209 is discussed later in this chapter.

47. Yat-pang Au's information is found in D'Souza, *Illiberal Education,* 24.

48. Ibid., 55.

49. The information on Melanie Lewis is found at ibid., 34.

50. Ibid., 36.

51. Ibid., 39.

52. Ibid., 38–51.

53. Ibid., 49.

54. Ibid., 52.

55. Ibid., 229–51.

56. Ibid., 230.

57. Ibid., 59–93.

58. Ibid., 94–123.

59. Ibid., 124–56.

60. Ibid., 157–93.

61. Ibid., 194–228.

62. Ibid., 251–53. His second modest proposal is for universities to refuse to recognize and or fund any group that practices racially separatist policies (ibid., 253–54). His third is for universities to maintain a significant place in their core curricula for the classics of Western civilization (ibid., 254–56).

63. William J. Clinton, Address delivered at the National Archives, July 19, 1965, *Public Papers of the President of the United States: William J. Clinton,* I (Washington, DC: Government Printing Office, 1995), 1106–14.

64. *Adarand Constructors, Inc. v. Pena,* 515 U.S. 200 (1995).

65. William J. Clinton, Address delivered at the National Archives, July 19, 1965, 1113.

66. Terry H. Anderson, *The Pursuit of Fairness: A History of Affirmative Action* (New York: Oxford University Press, 2004), 248.

67. "The California Black Regent Who Is Leading the Charge against Affirmative Action," *The Journal of Blacks in Higher Education* 9 (Autumn 1995): 30–31.

68. California Constitution, Article I, Section 31.

69. Guerrero, 98.

70. Anderson, 250.

71. These figures were culled from admissions data released by the Office of Student Research and the Office of Undergraduate Admissions at Berkeley and cited in Andrea Guerrero, *Silence at Boalt Hall: The Dismantling of Affirmative Action* (Berkeley: University of California Press, 2002), 147. Guerrero's book offers a powerful statistical and anecdotal portrait of the changing culture at the law school at UC Berkeley resulting from the end of affirmative action.

72. This description of the Texas affirmative action plan is drawn from the majority opinion of the circuit court that addressed the challenge to this plan, *Hopwood v. Texas,* 78 F.3d 932, 934–36 (1996).

73. Ibid., 938–39. See also Anderson, *The Pursuit of Fairness,* 253–54.

74. *Hopwood v. Texas,* 861 F. Supp. 551, 583 (1994).

75. *Hopwood v. Texas,* 78 F.3rd 932, 962 (1996).

76. *Hopwood v. Texas,* 78 F.3rd 932, 945 (1996).

77. Ibid., 946–47.

78. Ibid., 968.

79. Ibid., 968.

80. Jeffrey Rosen, "The Day the Quotas Died," *The New Republic,* April 22, 1996, 24.

81. *Texas v. Hopwood,* 518 U.S. 1033 (1996).

82. Martin Michaelson, "A Time to Increase Public Understanding of Affirmative Action," *The Chronicle of Higher Education,* July 19, 1996, A48.

7

Two Tales from One City: The Michigan Affirmative Action Cases

THREE ASPIRING STUDENTS

Jennifer Gratz and Patrick Hamacher, both Michigan residents, wanted to attend the highly selective undergraduate College of Literature, Science, and the Arts (LSA) at the University of Michigan's Ann Arbor campus. Gratz applied for admission for the fall semester of 1995. Although deemed "well qualified" by the undergraduate admissions committee, her application was ultimately rejected. She later enrolled at Michigan's less prestigious and less selective commuter campus at Dearborn, from which she received her baccalaureate degree in 1999. Hamacher applied to the LSA at Ann Arbor for admission for the fall semester of 1997. He was deemed "qualified" by the admissions committee. But, like Gratz, Hamacher was eventually rejected. He applied and was granted admission to Michigan State University, from which he graduated several years later. Both Gratz and Hamacher are white and were of "traditional college age"—that is, in their late teens at the time of their applications.[1]

Barbara Grutter, also a Michigan resident, was another individual hoping to attend the University of Michigan in the late 1990s. Grutter already held a baccalaureate degree. She now wanted admission to the Law School at Michigan's Ann Arbor campus, consistently ranked as one of the top law schools in the country. Grutter had achieved an impressive 3.8 undergraduate grade point average (on a scale of 4.0), and she had recorded a score of 161 (86th percentile) on the Law School Admissions Test (LSAT). At the age of 43, she was substantially older than most law school applicants. But, as was the case with Gratz and Hamacher, Grutter's application was rejected. Like Gratz and Hamacher, Grutter is white.[2]

All three Michigan residents suspected that the denials of their applications for admission to the University of Michigan had been dealt fatal blows by the university's affirmative action policies. Shortly after receiving the bad news about her application to the LSA, Jennifer Gratz and her parents happened to read a newspaper article describing a proposed class action challenge to affirmative action at the University of Michigan. Gratz quickly and enthusiastically enlisted in the cause, which was being mounted by the Center for Individual Rights (CIR), a conservative public interest law firm in Washington, DC. The CIR had successfully argued the case for Cheryl Hopwood a few years earlier that had resulted in the judicial termination of affirmative action in the Fifth Circuit (Texas, Mississippi, and Louisiana). The CIR had also successfully argued appeals court cases against affirmative action in Maryland and Georgia.[3]

Gratz appeared to be an ideal plaintiff to challenge the arbitrary and allegedly discriminatory affirmative action plan of the LSA at Ann Arbor. She was raised in a working-class suburb of Detroit by parents who were not college educated. She had excelled academically (3.8 GPA on a scale of 4.0) at a solid but not elite public high school. She participated in many extracurricular activities and had been selected in her senior year as homecoming queen. She was, thus, a poster child for the CIR's argument that an individual's hard work and achievement were frequently undercut by affirmative action. The CIR chose Gratz as its lead plaintiff to test the University of Michigan's undergraduate affirmative action plan. Hamacher's case was joined to the suit.[4]

Barbara Grutter was also an imminently sympathetic figure. As the single mother of two children, Grutter had been a health care consultant for most of her working career. Her undergraduate grades and her high LSAT score suggested that she possessed the ability to perform well in a competitive law school. Moreover, her age and life accomplishments promised that she would bring relatively unique experiences to a law school class of mostly twenty-somethings who could boast little work experience. In contrast to Gratz, however, Grutter had qualms about suing on the ground that her race (white) had placed her at a disadvantage in the admissions process to the Law School. In a 2001 interview, she commented that she had witnessed racial and sexual discrimination in her working lifetime, but she never dreamed that she herself would be a victim of "reverse discrimination." Ultimately, however, Grutter allowed the CIR to file a lawsuit on her behalf.[5]

GRIDS AND POINTS

In his *Bakke* opinion, Justice Lewis Powell had held that the separate admission pools for white and minority applicants employed by the University of California at Davis Medical School amounted to unconstitutional racial discrimination as forbidden by the Equal Protection Clause of the Fourteenth Amendment to the U.S. Constitution. By contrast, Powell had lauded the admissions policy of the Law School at Harvard University—essentially awarding it a constitutional seal of approval—for designating race as a "plus factor," along with other criteria that could be taken into account in making admissions decisions. The Law School at the University of Michigan adopted a plan for admission in 1992 that followed the spirit, if not the letter, of the Harvard plan. Powell had determined that designing an admissions policy to enhance the racial diversity of the law school classroom was a constitutionally permissible goal. The published rationale for the affirmative action policy at the University of Michigan Law School could almost have been lifted from Powell's opinion. According to the Law School's admissions bulletin, racial diversity in a law school classroom exposes all students to a variety of racial and ethnic perspectives of "special importance to our mission." Furthermore, the bulletin continued: "[W]e believe that the racial and ethnic diversity that has resulted [from affirmative action] has made the University of Michigan Law School a better law school than it could possibly have been otherwise. By enrolling a 'critical mass' of minority students, we have ensured their ability to make unique contributions to the character of the Law School."[6]

By what process did Michigan assemble a "critical mass" of minority students? It did it by fashioning a complex numerical "grid system" and then employing measures to mitigate the arbitrariness of the numerical scheme by taking race and other factors into account. The basic admissions grid displayed candidates' LSAT scores on a horizontal axis in three or four point increments and candidates' undergraduate grade point averages (UGPA) along a vertical axis. Virtually every combination of LSAT scores and UGPA appeared in a cell. The highest combinations of LSAT and UGPA were found in the cells in the upper right hand corner of the grid; applicants with scores represented in those cells had the highest probability of admission. The lowest achieving candidates had their scores represented in the lower left hand corner of the grid; they stood the least chance of admission. The Law School reported the number of students that made up each cell and the percentage in each cell offered places in the first-year class. That was the numerical side of the process. Then the admissions committee took into account nonquantifiable features of candidates' applications, such as the strength of reference letters, application essays, leadership experience, and, of course, race.[7] Dennis Shields, Director of Admissions in the Law School from 1991 to 1998, described the use of nonquantifiable factors in a memorandum that he whimsically titled "The Gospel According to Dennis": "Our mission is to pick winners. To make those selections requires more than a mere review of the numbers. . . . This is because many of the numbers will be so close to the same as to make the candidates indistinguishable from one another. . . . Rather we must begin with the numbers and go forward from there to scrutinize [nonquantifiable aspects of candidates' credentials]."[8] Shields, in his memorandum and in later court testimony in the *Grutter* litigation, did not single out race as a primary consideration in making admissions decisions.[9]

The affirmative action plan for the undergraduate college of the University of Michigan that Jennifer Gratz and Patrick Hamacher would challenge was modified during the course of their litigation. In 1995 and 1996, admissions decisions for the LSA were made pursuant to a grid system similar to that employed by the Law School. Standardized test scores (ACT or SAT) were mapped on the horizontal axis, and grade point averages were represented on the vertical axis. The various combinations of cells and the corresponding likelihood of admission to candidates in those cells were reported. Notably, however, separate grids were used for applicants based on residency (in-state versus out-of-state) and race (white versus under-represented minorities). Legacy status (having a relative who attended the LSA) was also factored in. So "regular applicants" and "minority applicants" were effectively evaluated in separate admissions pools. This factor would weigh heavily in the court proceedings.[10]

Beginning in 1998 and continuing through the course of the Gratz/Hamacher litigation, a point system was substituted for the grids to determine admission to the LSA. Applicants received points for different achievements or attributes. For example, high standardized test scores were accorded so many points, as were top grades, legacy status, strong application essays, and race. The highest number of possible points was 150, with a candidate's attainment of 100 points normally leading to admission. Most controversially, 20 points were automatically awarded to the file of a candidate from an underrepresented minority; this was the same number as received by an applicant who achieved a top score (1600) on the SAT. In addition, under the point system adopted in 1998, admissions officials were permitted to flag the files of underrepresented minority applicants to make sure those files were not discarded too easily from the pool of files designated for careful review.[11]

These were the admissions procedures challenged by the three would-be students and their public interest lawyers from the CIR. The cases would begin on parallel tracks in the federal district court in Michigan in the late

1990s, pass through the circuit court of appeals in 2001 and 2002, and finally reach culmination in a splintered set of opinions in the U.S. Supreme Court in 2003, somewhat reminiscent of the *Bakke* opinions a quarter century earlier.

GRUTTER AND GRATZ IN THE LOWER FEDERAL COURTS

On behalf of Barbara Grutter, the CIR filed a civil action against the University of Michigan in the U.S. District Court for the Eastern District of Michigan in December 1997. The principal named defendant in the suit, as in the parallel Gratz/Hamacher case, was Lee Bollinger, President of the University of Michigan. Grutter alleged that, by denying her admission to the Law School, she was discriminated against on the basis of race, thus violating her right to equal protection of the laws as guaranteed by the Fourteenth Amendment. She also asserted that the University of Michigan, a governmental institution that receives federal funds, violated her rights under Title VI of the Civil Rights Act of 1964. For almost three years, lawyers for Grutter and the Law School engaged in extensive discovery—that is, the gathering of evidence and the interviewing of witnesses. In addition, 41 individuals and three pro–affirmative action interest groups successfully sought permission to be heard as "interveners" on the side of the defendants. A bench trial took place over 15 days in early 2001 before Federal District Judge Bernard A. Friedman.[12]

In a written opinion issued on March 27, 2001, Judge Friedman held that the Law School's affirmative action plan violated the Equal Protection Clause of the Fourteenth Amendment and Title VI of the Civil Rights Act of 1964.[13] Given the controversy engendered by Grutter's suit, it was a forgone conclusion that the case would be appealed. So, at best, Barbara Grutter would have to wait several years longer to find out if the American court system would ultimately award her the opportunity to attend the law school of her choice.

The initial legal proceedings on behalf of Jennifer Gratz and Patrick Hamacher were conducted before Patrick J. Duggan, another federal judge in the Eastern District of Michigan. It commenced with the filing of a class action suit by Gratz and Hamacher on October 14, 1997. The plaintiffs in the undergraduate litigation raised similar legal concerns to that of Barbara Grutter. Similar groups of interveners successfully petitioned to be heard by the court. In contrast to the action before the district court in the *Grutter* case, the litigants in the *Gratz* case—Jennifer Gratz, Patrick Hamacher, and the University of Michigan's LSA—did not contest the facts in the case. Hence there was no bench trial; they only asked that the judge rule on matters of law via his summary judgment authority.[14]

The nub of Judge Duggan's opinion was his discussion of whether the University of Michigan's affirmative action plans—the 1992–1997 version and the 1998–2000 version—were narrowly enough tailored so as to be constitutional. He concluded that the plan that prevailed in the middle of the 1990s was constitutionally deficient. Duggan charged that this plan impermissibly "protected" some seats for under-representative minorities and operated with separate admissions pools. He characterized it as "the functional equivalent of a quota." On the other hand, the plan put into operation in 1998, the current admissions program for the purposes of the Gratz/Hamacher lawsuit, in which some applicants received a plus for being members of underrepresented minorities but were still kept in the same pool with all candidates for admission, met the constitutional requirements of an acceptable affirmative action admissions policy under Justice Powell's standard in *Bakke*.[15]

With the publication in late 2000 and early 2001 of the written opinions by the two district court judges in the Michigan cases, the viability of affirmative action in higher education remained as muddled as ever. One federal judge had found in favor of a female applicant to the Law School and ruled that the institution's affirmative action plan was unconstitutional. But a second federal judge had given two litigants desiring admissions to the LSA only a portion of what they had sought. The student plaintiffs, the University of Michigan, and the many other interested parties would now have to wait a little longer to see if an appellate court ruling would make their legal positions any clearer.

Parties losing at the federal district court level have an automatic right of appeal—should they wish to exercise it—to the Circuit Court of Appeals. Not surprisingly, given all that was at stake, the University of Michigan, together with Grutter, Gratz, and Hamacher, sought review of their legal rights by the Sixth Circuit Court of Appeals, headquartered in Cincinnati, Ohio, and charged with handling appeals from federal district courts in Kentucky, Michigan, Ohio, and Tennessee. Numerous interest groups clamored to be heard on one side or the other of the appeal. After substantial procedural wrangling, the cases found their way to an en banc panel of judges in the Sixth Circuit. An en banc panel—in which all the judges in the circuit sit—is only convened to adjudicate the most important appellate disputes.

The Grutter appeal was argued on December 6, 2001. The decision was not issued until May 14, 2002. The resulting majority opinion represented the views of five of the nine sitting judges. It reversed District Judge Friedman's decision in favor of Barbara Grutter and found the Law School's affirmative action program constitutionally acceptable. Boyce F. Martin, chief judge of the circuit and an appointee of President Jimmy Carter, wrote the majority opinion.[16] Two justices submitted concurring opinions, and all four dissenters filed separate opinions. Even for the reputedly contentious Sixth Circuit, the hostility that bubbled forth in the opinions in the *Grutter* case was extraordinary.

The most controversial opinion of the appeals court in *Grutter* was the dissent filed by Judge Danny Boggs, appointed to the Sixth Circuit by President Ronald Reagan. Its longest section contained both a principled critique of affirmative action and an analysis of the cases since *Bakke* that, in Boggs's view, undercut what little authority that he saw *Bakke* still possessing.[17] But it was not Boggs's legal analysis in the body of his dissent that would generate the most attention. In a "Procedural Appendix" following his opinion, Boggs took Boyce Martin, the author of the majority opinion in *Grutter* and the chief judge of the circuit, to task for allegedly holding up a full hearing of the case for five months so as to wait until two allegedly anti–affirmative action judges on the circuit assumed "senior status," thus effectively keeping them off the en banc panel.[18] One of the concurring justices, Karen Nelson Moore, strenuously objected to Boggs's Procedural Appendix because it made public what she and her colleagues in the majority perceived as internal Sixth Circuit matters.[19] Moore wrote: "[U]nhappiness over the outcome of the case cannot justify the dissenters' 'Procedural Appendix.' Judge Boggs's opinion marks a new low point in the history of the Sixth Circuit. It will irreparably damage the already strained working relationships among the judges of this court, and . . . serve to undermine public confidence in our ability to perform our important role in American democracy."[20]

Regardless of the merits of the charges in Judge Boggs's Procedural Appendix, it was clear that the *Grutter* case had rubbed raw the nerves of the judges in the Sixth Circuit.[21] What about the *Gratz* case? Although a Sixth Circuit panel conducted an oral argument on the appeal from Jennifer Gratz and Patrick Hamacher, it did not appear to be in any hurry to render a decision. Thus, shortly after the Sixth Circuit opinion in *Grutter,* Kirk O. Kolbo, the Minnesota lawyer coordinating the appeals for Gratz/Hamacher as well as Grutter in association with the CIR, decided to seek review of both cases by the U.S. Supreme Court. It was highly unusual for a lawyer to petition the Supreme Court to sit on a matter still pending in a lower-level court, but Kolbo felt that "the two cases considered together will present the court with a broader spectrum and more substantial record within which to consider the rule upon the common principles they involve."[22]

With few exceptions, most cases arrive at the nation's highest court via a largely discretionary process called certiorari. Thousands of petitions for a writ of certiorari to the Supreme Court are filed yearly. The Supreme Court consents to hear only what it considers the most important of these petitions, generally fewer than 100 a term.[23] Given the important public policy issues raised by *Grutter* and *Gratz,* and given the fact that the several judicial circuit courts of appeal had issued conflicting opinions on affirmative action in higher education, it seemed a good bet that the U.S. Supreme Court would agree to hear the appeals from Michigan. On December 2, 2002, the Court confirmed this speculation. Without explanation, it granted certiorari in *Grutter* and *Gratz.* Oral argument before the nine justices was scheduled for April 1, 2003.[24]

GRATZ AND *GRUTTER* IN THE SUPREME COURT

Of the nine justices who would hear and cast votes on the Michigan affirmative action cases, only two—Chief Justice William Rehnquist and Associate Justice John Paul Stevens—had been on the Supreme Court when *Bakke* had been decided a quarter century earlier. Rehnquist was a consistent opponent of affirmative action and a clear vote in favor of Gratz and Grutter. Stevens was harder to predict: he had written an opinion against affirmative action in *Bakke,* but in recent employment cases dealing with race-based preferences he had migrated toward an acceptance of affirmative action.

Appointees of Republican President Ronald Reagan, Antonin Scalia and Anthony Kennedy, had long been on record as opposed to affirmative action. Clarence Thomas, an appointee of George H. W. Bush and an African American, had benefited from affirmative action in his admission to Yale Law School. In addition, in the 1980s, Thomas had headed the Equal Employment Opportunity Commission, an agency charged with investigating employment discrimination and enforcing affirmative action orders. Thomas, who had long chafed at the claim that he got a jump start in the legal profession because of his law school's race-conscious admissions policies, spoke out against affirmative action on a number of occasions and took positions against race-based preferences in several employment and government contracting cases of the 1990s.[25]

The quiet and reclusive David Souter was thought to have been a conservative at the time of his nomination to the Court. But, soon after his appointment, this "stealth justice" began to write opinions applauded by political liberals; in the Michigan cases he was a likely vote in favor of affirmative action. Ruth Bader Ginsburg and Stephen Breyer, the two appointees of Democratic President Bill Clinton, joined the Court in the early 1990s and could be counted on as friends of affirmative action. The remaining justice, Sandra Day O'Connor, had been appointed by Ronald Reagan but was considered the swing vote on the Court.[26] The nose counting among Court watchers, thus, suggested that *Gratz* and *Grutter* had all the ingredients of closely-divided, split decisions with O'Connor being the deciding vote in each.

In anticipation of the Supreme Court's review of the Michigan affirmative action cases, almost 100 organizations prepared amicus curiae briefs. Three-quarters of the amici supported the University of Michigan's race-based admissions plans. One supportive document, dubbed the "military brief," highlighted the views of some of the country's most distinguished retired general officers, including Norman Schwarzkopf, John Shalikashvili, and Wesley Clark. It waxed eloquently on the need for a racially diverse officer corps to lead the even more diverse enlisted ranks of the modern American military. Another amicus brief was submitted on behalf of 65 of the nation's leading corporations. It advanced an argument similar to the military brief—that is, that large companies hire racially diverse pools of executives and other employees who benefit substantially from receiving college education in racially diverse classrooms. By contrast, the Department of Justice for the administration of President George W. Bush prepared an amicus brief opposing racial preferences in making admissions decisions in colleges and universities. Most leading educational associations submitted briefs supporting affirmative action in admissions in higher education. The major Jewish interest groups, however, were divided.[27]

The combined oral argument on *Gratz* and *Grutter* was conducted on April 1, 2003. From the questioning, several justices appeared to be impressed by the military brief. In fact, the members of the Court appeared to be more interested in asking the attorneys for the principals their views on the military brief than querying them on the points advanced in their own legal tomes. One journalist later suggested that the military brief might have been "the most influential *amicus* brief in the history of the Court."[28]

Maureen Mahoney, a former law clerk of Chief Justice Rehnquist, presented the oral argument for the University of Michigan in the *Grutter* case. Near the end of her time at the podium she was grilled by Justice O'Connor as to whether there was a problem with the Law School's affirmative action admissions plan because it did not specify a time at which the Law School would terminate race-based admissions. Mahoney dodged the question by answering that the Harvard plan, endorsed by a five-member bloc of the Court in *Bakke,* had been operating successfully since 1978—about 25 years. This response may have given O'Connor the inspiration for the conclusion to the decisive written opinion that she would soon be submitting for the Court to resolve the *Grutter* case.[29]

Many of the participating justices in *Gratz* and *Grutter* are still on the Supreme Court and, thus, have not yet placed their in-chambers materials in archives for scholars to examine. Hence we do not yet have access to the rich behind-the-scenes memoranda, notes, and draft opinions to illuminate these cases that were available for *DeFunis* and *Bakke*. We are left mainly with the public record and tidbits of Court gossip leaked to reporters.[30]

At the conference on *Gratz* and *Grutter* a few days after the oral argument, tentative votes were cast. They revealed a split of 5-4 in favor of the University of Michigan in *Grutter* but 6-3 in favor of the undergraduate plaintiffs in *Gratz*. Rehnquist, Scalia, Kennedy, and Thomas cast their lots with the plaintiffs in both cases; and Stevens, Souter, and Ginsburg supported the university in both cases. The swing votes were O'Connor and Breyer: they found in favor of the university in *Grutter* but went the other way in *Gratz*. The difference came down to the details of the two affirmative action plans. The inflexible point system for the LSA apparently troubled O'Connor and Breyer. It was not a quota in form, but it had the effect of a quota because it slammed the door on some white students who, were it not for the automatic points awarded for race, would have been admitted. Chief Justice Rehnquist, in the majority in *Gratz*, chose as was his right to prepare the Opinion of the Court in the undergraduate case. John Paul Stevens, the senior member of the Court in the majority in *Grutter*, could have elected to take the Opinion of the Court in that case for himself. But he wisely assigned it to Sandra Day O'Connor, a justice who was known for her conciliatory influence on the Court and who would likely be more successful than Stevens in keeping together the slender majority in the Law School case once the draft opinions began to circulate.[31]

AT LAST: THE DECISIONS IN THE MICHIGAN CASES

In what some legal experts saw as the two most important cases of the Supreme Court's 2002–3 term,[32] the long awaited opinions in *Gratz* and *Grutter* were presented by the justices in a public session on June 23, 2003. The word on *Gratz* came down first.

Chief Justice Rehnquist began his Opinion of the Court with the customary recitation of the facts. He then proceeded to a discussion of the procedural twists and turns in the case and rejected an argument raised in two of the dissenting opinions that the plaintiffs did not have standing to file a complaint.[33] Then, he quickly moved to the constitutional heart of the case. He cited the holding of *Adarand Constructors, Inc. v. Pena* that the Equal Protection Clause of the Fourteenth Amendment mandated that racial classifications could only be judged constitutional if they met the standard of strict scrutiny by satisfying "a compelling state interest" and were "narrowly tailored" to meet the objective being sought by the government policy.[34] He applied this principle to the facts in *Gratz* and found the LSA's affirmative action plan deficient. He pointed particularly to the feature of the LSA's plan that awarded 20 points to each applicant from an underrepresented minority solely on the basis of race, thereby granting such a candidate one-fifth of the total points needed to guarantee admission. He concluded that this flew in the face of the careful test for the constitutionality of affirmative action programs laid out by Justice Powell in *Bakke*. Thus, without a great deal of discussion, the Chief Justice and the other four justices joining his opinion struck down the LSA's admission policy as violating both the Equal Protection Clause of the Fourteenth Amendment and Title VI of the Civil Rights Act of 1964.[35]

The first concurring opinion was written by Sandra Day O'Connor and joined by Stephen Breyer. One purpose this opinion served was to distinguish *Gratz* from the case that O'Connor and most constitutional experts saw as more important, *Grutter v. Bollinger*. O'Connor emphasized that the admissions plan of the LSA, with its arbitrary point system and its flagging, was a much blunter instrument than the more individualized admissions plan of the Law School. As such, she was of the opinion that Michigan's undergraduate plan did not rise to the level of constitutional acceptability that had been set forth in Justice Powell's *Bakke* opinion 25 years earlier.[36] Justice Thomas filed a short concurring opinion, emphasizing his view that affirmative action, regardless of any laudable purposes, constitutes racial discrimination and should be "categorically prohibited by the Equal Protection Clause."[37]

Justice Stevens dissented in *Gratz* because he did not believe that either of the plaintiffs had standing to sue. Because Jennifer Gratz and Patrick Hamacher had successfully applied to, been admitted by, and then matriculated at other state institutions in Michigan, he believed that they had not suffered any appreciable loss. In turn, having completed their undergraduate degrees, Stevens maintained that Gratz and Hamacher would not now receive any tangible benefit if the admissions plan at the University of Michigan's LSA were struck down by the courts. Justice Souter joined in this dissent.[38] Souter and Justice Ginsburg also filed separate dissenting opinions on the constitutional merits of the LSA's admission plan. For Souter, the undergraduate admission plan permitted all applicants to compete for all places in the first-year class; thus it did not fall prey to the "quota problem" that caused the Court to void the admissions plan of the University of California at Davis Medical School at issue in *Bakke*.[39] Souter was also troubled by the fact that it was not clear in the lower court record just how the LSA's admissions committee administered its point system; but he did not see this as a constitutional infirmity.[40] In her separate dissent, Ginsburg emphasized that the LSA's plan was a straightforward attempt to implement race as a plus factor. This she saw as clearly permitted by *Bakke*. She concluded thusly: "If honesty is the best policy, surely Michigan's accurately described, fully disclosed . . . [undergraduate] affirmative action program is preferable to achieving similar numbers through winks, nods, and disguises."[41]

In speaking for the majority of the Supreme Court in the companion case of *Grutter v. Bollinger,* Justice O'Connor announced that the nation's highest court had agreed to hear this case in order to resolve a disagreement among the judicial circuits as to "[w]hether diversity is a compelling interest that can justify the narrowly tailored use of race in selecting applicants for admission to public universities."[42] Then she addressed the issue that had occupied much time and judicial brain power in the lower federal courts—that is, whether Justice Lewis Powell spoke just for himself or for the majority of the Court in *Bakke.* O'Connor dispatched this matter relatively quickly. She noted that Powell's opinion in *Bakke* "has served as the touchstone for constitutional analysis of race-conscious admissions policies" since 1978.[43] After explaining the Powell standard and reviewing its application over the previous quarter century, she concluded that the Court continues to "endorse Justice Powell's view that student body diversity is a compelling state interest that can justify the use of race in university admissions."[44] In short, the Supreme Court in 2003, just as in 1978, accepted Justice Powell's opinion in *Bakke* as controlling its affirmative action jurisprudence.

O'Connor noted that the language on strict scrutiny in *Adarand Constructors,* cited by Chief Justice Rehnquist in the Opinion of the Court in *Gratz,* also governed the racial component of the government policy in *Grutter.* However, she was quick to add that "[a]lthough all governmental uses of race are subject to strict scrutiny, not all are invalidated by it."[45] Then followed a long section of the opinion in which she cited cases decided since 1978 in which the Supreme Court had followed the *Bakke* principle that a narrowly tailored governmental program designed to enhance racial diversity offered a compelling governmental interest under the Equal Protection Clause of the Fourteenth Amendment.[46]

Near the midpoint of the opinion, O'Connor cited with favor the two key amicus briefs that had been the subject of pithy exchanges between the justices and lawyers for the parties in the oral argument. The military brief, which contained a myriad of pro–affirmative action statements of retired, high-ranking officers, impressed O'Connor and her like-minded cohort. If a selective institution like the military could benefit from affirmative action, she submitted, so could higher education. In addition, she found influential the brief from the leading American corporations, which lauded the importance of having a racially diverse student body so as to prepare young men and women for a global business world of many different races and nationalities.[47]

The longest section of O'Connor's opinion addressed the question of whether the Law School plan under review by the justices was narrowly enough tailored to be constitutional under the *Bakke* standard. She and the other justices making up the Court majority examined the Law School admissions plan closely and ruled that it, like the Harvard plan approved in *Bakke,* permitted a review of each student's individual student's credentials, employing race as a plus factor rather than indulging in the unconstitutional extreme of a racial quota.[48]

Although O'Connor came down solidly in favor of the constitutionality of the Law School's affirmative action plan, she concluded the Opinion of the Court with a plea to suspend racial preferences at some point in the future. The expression of this hope was, perhaps, triggered by her exchange in the oral argument with Maureen Mahoney, the attorney representing the University of Michigan. O'Connor wrote: "We take the Law School at its word that it would 'like nothing better than to find a race-neutral admissions formula' and will terminate its race-conscious admissions program as soon as practicable. . . . It has been 25 years since Justice Powell first approved the use of race to further an interest in student body diversity in the context of higher education. . . . We expect that 25 years from now, the use of racial preferences will no longer be necessary to further the interest approved today."[49] In their concurrence in *Grutter,* Justices Ginsburg and Breyer underlined O'Connor's call for a logical end to affirmative action.[50]

As an index of the strong feelings of the justices in the Michigan Law School case, all four dissenters filed separate opinions in *Grutter.* Chief Justice Rehnquist maintained that a careful review of how the Law School's admissions plan operated in fact suggested that there was a disguised racial quota at work. Making reference to the grids, he pointed out that "from 1995 to 2000 the percentage of admitted applicants who were members of . . . [underrepresented] minority groups closely tracked the percentage of individuals in the school's applicant pool who were from the same groups."[51] For example, the percentage of applicants to the Law School who were African American in 1996 was 9.3 percent; the percentage of African Americans who were admitted to the Law School that year was 9.2 percent.[52] Justice Kennedy, in his dissent, echoed the Chief Justice's arguments, chiding the majority for paying only lip service to strict scrutiny and awarding constitutional protection to race-conscious admissions programs that are "tantamount to quotas."[53] Justice Scalia, in typically quotable language, linked *Gratz* and *Grutter* and chided the Court majority for roiling constitutional waters for years to come: "Unlike a clear constitutional holding that racial preferences in state educational institutions are impermissible, or even a clear anti-constitutional holding that racial preferences in state educational institutions are OK, today's *Grutter-Gratz* split double header seems perversely designed to prolong the controversy and the litigation."[54]

The longest and angriest dissent in *Grutter* was filed by Justice Clarence Thomas. He commenced with a statement from the 19th-century black activist, Frederick Douglass: "The American people have always been anxious to know what they shall do with us. . . . I have had but one answer from the beginning. Do nothing with us! Your doing with us has already played the mischief with us. Do nothing with us!"[55] For Thomas, affirmative action sent the message that blacks and other "under-represented minorities" could not achieve in education "without the meddling of university administrators."[56] As he wrote in another Supreme Court opinion, race-conscious admissions programs "[engender] attitudes of superiority or . . . provoke resentment among those who believe that they have been wronged by the government's use of race."[57] For Thomas, the majority in *Grutter* did not interpret the U.S. Constitution; rather it "respond[ed] to a faddish slogan of the cognoscenti."[58] Affirmative action, he maintained, did not promote a true and valuable diversity; it only yielded "classroom aesthetics."[59]

The only part of the majority opinion with which Thomas agreed was Justice O'Connor's hope that affirmative action would not exist in 25 years. For Thomas, an America without affirmative action would be a better place for the education of minorities and a better place for the integrity of the U.S. Constitution. Why wait 25 years?[60]

REACTIONS TO *GRATZ* AND *GRUTTER*

Most of the immediate reactions to the two Michigan affirmative action decisions focused on Justice O'Connor's majority opinion in *Grutter*. The consensus of Court watchers was that race-conscious admissions policies had not only survived the acid test of Supreme Court review but had now received a clear blessing from a majority of the justices. The headline story in the *Washington Post* on the day after the announcement of the Court rulings heralded *Grutter v. Bollinger* as a "resounding endorsement of affirmative action in higher education."[61] Sheldon Steinbach, general counsel for the American Council on Education, saw *Grutter* as "an enormous victory for colleges and universities."[62] Perhaps a bit carried away by the power of the moment, Lee Bollinger, President of the University of Michigan in the early stages of the *Gratz* and *Grutter* litigation, characterizing the Supreme Court's decision in his former university's case as "the most important [decision] dealing with race in America . . . in a quarter century."[63]

Since *Regents v. Bakke* in 1978, some judges and constitutional experts had questioned whether Justice Powell's brokered opinion in that case actually commanded a majority of the Supreme Court. Any ambiguity on this point was dispelled with Justice O'Connor's 2003 opinion in *Grutter*. The *Washington Post* editorialized: *Grutter* placed affirmative action on a much more solid footing than did *Bakke* because in the Michigan decision five justices had "unambiguously rejected the claim that diversity is not a compelling interest."[64] Bollinger agreed: "Powell's famous opinion upholding the use of race under limited circumstances stood alone and required extensive analysis to make it into precedent. Now we have a clear majority and a clear precedent."[65] Cass Sunstein, University of Chicago law professor, however, noted that O'Connor's opinion remains within Powell's "universe" and continues to permit race to be a consideration in college admissions but does not permit race to be the key variable for a heavy-handed quota or point system.[66]

President George W. Bush, whose administration had presented an amicus brief in opposition to the University of Michigan's affirmative action plans in both the undergraduate and law school cases, put the best face on the *Grutter* decision. He lauded the justices for striking a "careful balance between the goal of campus diversity and the fundamental principle of equal treatment under the law. . . . Like the court," he added, "I look forward to the day when American will truly be a colorblind society."[67] Other opponents of affirmative action were not so cautious in expressing their feelings. For example, Edward Blum, a senior fellow at the Center for Equal Opportunity, an organization that had filed an amicus brief in favor of Grutter, termed O'Connor's decision on the Law School's affirmative action plan "a disaster."[68] And Ward Connerly, the man who led the charge against affirmative action in California, delivered this ominous statement shortly after learning of the *Grutter* decision: "They [the Supreme Court justices] dodged a bullet on explicit race preferences, but the gun is still loaded. If I didn't have a commitment tomorrow, I'd be in Michigan to see what it takes to get a referendum banning affirmative action on the ballot there."[69]

Although virtually all journalists and expert commentators agreed on the importance of Justice O'Connor's *Grutter* opinion, they divided markedly on the quality of her constitutional analysis. Nathan Glazer, a Harvard professor of sociology and a well-published scholar on race relations, gave O'Connor points for basing the case for affirmative action on the merits of racial diversity in the classroom as opposed to the more explosive and tougher to defend argument that race-conscious admissions were necessary to compensate for society's past discrimination against racial minorities.[70] Linda Greenhouse, the *New York Times*'s chief Supreme Court reporter, credited O'Connor with recognizing the broad "context" for race-conscious admissions programs by responding to the "societal consensus in favor of affirmative action" as expressed in the amicus briefs of the retired military leaders and the CEOs of America's largest corporations.[71]

A common theme among many writers in the immediate aftermath of *Grutter* was that O'Connor's opinion struck a compromise, reflecting the ambivalence of Americans regarding affirmative action. A 2003 opinion survey by the Pew Research Center revealed that Americans approved of college admissions programs "designed to increase the number of black and [other] minority students" by about a two to one majority, but were against programs "giving [minorities] preferential treatment" by a ratio of three to one.[72] According to TV journalist Jeffrey Toobin, the best defense of Justice O'Connor's *Grutter* opinion is that "she picked a result, and reached a compromise, that was broadly acceptable to most Americans."[73] A political cartoon in the *Michigan Daily,* which appeared a few days after the affirmative action decisions, aptly captured this constitutional balancing act. It portrays a robed and noticeably nervous Justice O'Connor, gingerly walking a tightrope over a football stadium (probably the "Big House" at Ann Arbor). The long steadying pole she is carrying has a weight on one end labeled "racial diversity" and a weight on the other marked "individual evaluation."[74]

O'Connor's critics saw little of value in her attempt to walk a fine line between accepting race as a plus factor while, at the same time, disowning discrete quotas or point systems. Longtime political commentator Michael Kinsley, in an opinion piece titled "Want Diversity? Think Fuzzy," charged O'Connor and the Court majority with believing "that a subjective judgment full of unquantifiable factors is obviously fairer than a straightforward formula. But confusion seems to be a purposeful strategy." In Kinsley's words, "The court's message to universities and other selective, government financed institutions is: We have fudged this dangerous issue. You should do the same."[75] Similarly, the *Washington Post*'s Richard Cohen concluded an op-ed column on *Grutter* with these sentences: "O'Connor's opinion is an intellectual mess. Given the nature and complexities of affirmative action, that's understandable. But the Supreme Court is supposed to clarify the very issues that befuddle the rest of us. O'Connor not only failed to do that, but she and her colleagues failed so spectacularly that maybe it is the high court that could use some affirmative action itself. Clear thinkers are underrepresented."[76]

The *Gratz* decision came in for press and expert comment primarily when it was linked to *Grutter.* Mary Sue Coleman, the President of the University of Michigan when the two cases were decided in June 2003, admitted that she was sorry the Supreme Court had struck down the affirmative action plan of the LSA in *Gratz,* but she expressed satisfaction that the Court had given Michigan "a road map" for redesigning a constitutionally acceptable undergraduate admissions program. She continued: "The central principle is that affirmative action may be used—and that's what we were fighting for."[77] College officials were quick to point out that most of America's institutions of higher learning did not employ quotas or points in race-conscious admissions plans. In commenting on the impact of *Gratz* and *Grutter,* Constantine W.

Curris, president of the American Association of State Colleges and Universities, noted that the tandem of decisions is "essentially an affirmation of policies that most institutions have followed. It underscores the importance of diversity and ensuring that graduate and professional schools are open to all students. It also offers a little clearer delineation of constitutionally permissible methods."[78]

RACE-BASED ADMISSIONS IN HIGHER EDUCATION AFTER THE MICHIGAN CASES

The immediate practical effect of *Gratz* and *Grutter* for most American colleges and universities was probably negligible: in 2003, just as today, only the top 10 to 15 percent of institutions of higher learning have competitive admissions policies. One writer on the case stated: "[F]or the vast majority of college admissions offices, last week's landmark rulings on affirmative action . . . are more likely to be the topic of applicant essays than a factor in admitting students."[79] For those few institutions that practiced competitive admissions, the impact of *Gratz* and *Grutter* was financial and bureaucratic. About two months after the *Gratz* ruling had struck down the LSA's affirmative action plan, the University of Michigan announced a new undergraduate admissions plan: it took race into account in much the way that the Supreme Court–certified Law School plan had been doing for several years. In the new LSA admissions plan, there was no rigid grid or point system as had been the case prior to the Supreme Court decision in *Gratz*. The new plan required hiring and training of additional admissions personnel so as to facilitate a more individualized review of applications for the undergraduate college than had been the case prior to June 2003. The university announced that the price tag for the new staff members would be between $1.5 and $2.0 million.[80] This was on top of the more than $10 million that Michigan had reportedly spent defending the suits filed by Gratz, Hamacher, and Grutter.[81] Racial diversity in Michigan clearly came at a very high price.

The pro-diversity euphoria that college and university officials expressed in the immediate aftermath of the Michigan affirmative action cases did not last very long. In Georgia, for example, where the anti–affirmative action appeals court ruling had been essentially reversed by *Grutter*, committees at the state's flagship university were still debating almost two years after the Michigan decisions whether to reinstitute an affirmative action plan.[82] In January 2005, Nancy E. Cantor, former Provost at Michigan who had since moved on to the position of Chancellor of Syracuse University, lamented: "Higher education has not taken up the victory that I believe we won in the Supreme Court. . . . I am worried about whether higher education will continue to be courageous."[83]

Part of the reason for the timidity on the part of the academy to capitalize on *Grutter* probably stemmed from the lawsuits and threats of lawsuits from anti–affirmative action advocacy groups. Prominent among these groups were four with annual budgets in excess of $1 million each: the CIR, the Washington-based legal organization that represented the plaintiffs in the Michigan case; the American Civil Rights Institute, Ward Connerly's California-based organization that favors state ballot initiatives to overturn affirmative action policies; the Virginia-based Center for Equal Opportunity, a group that has pressured state and federal officials to investigate race-based policies at colleges and universities that it finds questionable; and the National Association of Scholars, a conservative body of several thousand university faculty members that, among other causes, opposes race-conscious policies on campuses.[84]

A survey by the *Chronicle of Higher Education* of 29 American colleges and universities with highly competitive admissions compared their minority enrollments in the fall 2002 semester (the semester before the Supreme Court's ruling in *Grutter*) with fall 2004 semester minority enrollments. In 7 of these institutions, the number of black and Hispanic first-year students had declined in the two years surveyed; in 11 colleges and universities, both racial categories of beginning students had increased; and in the final 11 institutions, the enrollment of only one of the two groups of minority students had increased. Notable losses took place at the University of California, Berkeley, which sustained a two-year decline of 23.4 percent in black first-year students, and the University of Michigan, which witnessed a 21.0 percent decrease among black freshman in the same two-year period. By contrast, Harvard University saw more than a 20 percent two-year increase in freshman enrollment among both categories of minorities.[85] Clearly this scorecard showed mixed success for increasing the enrollment of minority students in the aftermath of *Grutter*.

The most telling setbacks to affirmative action, however, came from ballot initiatives. Ward Connerly's American Civil Rights Institute, the organization that had led the successful campaign to dispatch race-conscious programs in state institutions in California, brought his well-funded and battle-tested organization to Michigan. The Institute quickly succeeded in getting Proposition 2 on the ballot in Michigan for the November 2006 election. Proposition 2 was intended to "prohibit the University of Michigan and other state universities, the state, and all other state entities from discriminating against or granting preferential treatment based on race, sex, color, ethnicity or national origin." Despite vocal opposition from government, business, labor, education and religion, Proposition 2 received 1.8 million votes and passed by a clear majority, 58 percent to 42 percent.[86] Interestingly, both Jennifer Gratz and Barbara Grutter took active organizational and speaking roles in support of Proposition 2.[87]

As of mid-2008—whether as a result of ballot initiatives, legal decisions, or executive orders—fully 17 of the 50 states no longer permit race-based admissions in their public colleges and universities.[88] Emboldened by his success in Michigan and elsewhere, Connerly promised more ballot measures in the coming years.[89] The Supreme Court, by a thin majority in *Grutter*, may have found affirmative action to be constitutionally acceptable. But the public apparently does not want to see it practiced.

NOTES

1. Details on Gratz and Hamacher are drawn from the U.S. Supreme Court's opinion in *Gratz v. Bollinger*, 539 U.S. 244, 251 (2003). On the Michigan race-based admissions cases generally, see Barbara A. Perry, *The Michigan Affirmative Action Cases* (Lawrence: University Press of Kansas, 2007).

2. On Grutter's background, see the Supreme Court opinion in her case, *Grutter v. Bollinger*, 539 U.S. 306, 316 (2003) and Perry, *The Michigan Affirmative Action Cases*, 60–61, et passim.

3. Perry, 38–39.

4. Ibid., 58.

5. Ibid., 60.

6. Quoted in the District Court opinion, *Grutter v. Bollinger*, 137 F. Supp. 2d 821, 829 (2001).

7. Ibid., 825–26.

8. Ibid., 828.

9. Ibid., 831–32.

10. Ibid., 826–28.

11. Ibid., 827–30.

12. This procedural summary of the early stages of the *Grutter* case is drawn from Judge Friedman's opinion in ibid., 823–25.

13. Ibid., 872.

14. This procedural summary of the early stages in the *Gratz* case is drawn from Judge Duggan's opinion in *Gratz v. Bollinger*, 122 F. Supp. 2d 811, 813–16 (2000).

15. Ibid., 824–33.

16. *Grutter v. Bollinger*, 288 F.3d 732, 735–52 (2002).

17. Ibid., 773–810.

18. Ibid., 810–14.

19. Ibid., 753–58.

20. Ibid., 758.

21. On the acrimony in *Grutter* at the appellate level, see Perry, 76–87.

22. Quoted in Perry, 85.

23. On the certiorari process, see Kermit L. Hall, ed., *The Oxford Companion to the Supreme Court of the United States*, 2nd ed. (New York: Oxford University Press, 2005), 154–55.

24. *Gratz v. Bollinger,* 537 U.S. 1044 (2002) and *Grutter v. Bollinger,* 537 U.S. 1043 (2002).

25. See Kevin Merida and Michael A. Fletcher, *Supreme Discomfort: The Divided Soul of Clarence Thomas* (New York: Doubleday, 2007), 123, 149, 278, 375.

26. Short but substantive essay/entries on these nine justices are found in Melvin I. Urofsky, ed., *The Supreme Justices: A Biographical Dictionary* (New York: Garland Publishing, 1994).

27. On the amicus briefs in *Grutter and Gratz,* see Perry, 97–108; Ronald Dworkin, "The Court and the University," *The New York Review of Books,* May 15, 2003, 8–11; and Jeffrey Toobin, *The Nine: Inside the Secret World of the Supreme Court* (New York: Doubleday, 2007), 212–20.

28. Toobin, 224.

29. On the oral arguments in *Gratz* and *Grutter,* see Perry, 110–34 and Toobin, 218–21.

30. On reporters' accounts of recent Supreme Court activities and personalities, see especially Jeffrey Toobin, *The Nine;* and Jan Crawford Greenburg, *Supreme Conflict: The Inside Story of the Struggle for Control of the United States Supreme Court* (New York: The Penguin Press, 2007).

31. This brief account of what transpired in the conference on *Gratz* and *Grutter* is drawn from Toobin, 221–23.

32. See, for example, Dworkin, 8.

33. *Gratz v. Bollinger,* 539 U.S. 244, 249–68 (2003).

34. Ibid., 270.

35. Ibid., 268–75.

36. Ibid., 276–80.

37. Ibid., 281.

38. Ibid., 282–91.

39. Ibid., 293–94.

40. Ibid., 294–98.

41. Ibid., 304.

42. *Grutter v. Bollinger,* 539 U.S. 306, 322 (2003).

43. Ibid., 323.

44. Ibid., 325.

45. Ibid., 326–27.

46. Ibid., 326–30.

47. Ibid., 330–31.

48. Ibid., 333–43.

49. Ibid., 343.

50. Ibid., 344–46.

51. Ibid., 382–85.

52. Ibid., 384.

53. Ibid., 394.

54. Ibid., 348.

55. Quoted in ibid., 349–50.

56. Ibid., 350.

57. *Adarand Constructors Inc. v. Pena,* 515 U.S. 200, 241 (1995).

58. *Grutter v. Bollinger,* 350.

59. Ibid., 355.

60. Ibid., 375.

61. Charles Lane, "Affirmative Action for Diversity Is Upheld," *Washington Post,* June 24, 2003, A1.

62. Quoted in Perry Bacon, Jr., "And the Winner Is . . . Affirmative Action," *Time,* June 23, 2006, http://time.com/time/nation/printout/0,8816,460435,00.html (accessed October 18, 2006).

63. Lee C. Bollinger, "A Resounding Victory for Diversity on Campus," *Washington Post,* June 24, 2003, A21.

64. "Reaffirmative Action," *Washington Post,* June 24, 2003, A20.

65. Bollinger, "A Resounding Victory for Diversity on Campus," A21.

66. Bacon, "And the Winner Is . . . Affirmative Action."

67. Quoted in Lane, "Affirmative Action for Diversity Is Upheld," A8.

68. Quoted in Bacon, "And the Winner Is . . . Affirmative Action."

69. Quoted in Jeffrey Selingo, "Decisions May Prompt Return of Race-Conscious Admissions at Some Colleges," *Chronicle of Higher Education,* July 4, 2003, S5.

70. Charles Lane, "In Court's Ruling, a Nod to Notion of a Broader Elite," *Washington Post,* June 25, 2003, A1.

71. Linda Greenhouse, "The Supreme Court: The Justices; Context and the Court," *New York Times,* June 25, 2003, http://select.nytimes.com/search/restricted/article?res= (accessed October 12, 2006).

72. Quoted in David Von Drehle, "Court Mirrors Public Opinion," *Washington Post,* June 24, 2003, A1.

73. Jeffrey Toobin, *The Nine,* 225.

74. Pictured in "Editorial Pages and Columnists Weigh in on High Court's Rulings," *Chronicle of Higher Education,* July 4, 2003, S9.

75. Michael Kinsley, "Want Diversity? Think Fuzzy," *Washington Post,* June 25, 2003, A23.

76. Richard Cohen, "Confused O'Connor," *Washington Post,* June 26, 2003, A25.

77. "Court Rejects Quotas, But Says Race May Play a Factor in Admissions," June 23, 2003, http://cnn.law (accessed June 23, 2003).

78. Michael A. Fletcher, "Decision Means Most Colleges Will Stay Course," *Washington Post,* June 24, 2003, A9.

79. Jeffrey Selingo, "Decisions May Prompt Return of Race-Conscious Admissions at Some Colleges," S5.

80. Perry, *The Michigan Affirmative Action Cases,* 160–61.

81. Ibid., 163.

82. Jeffrey Selingo, "Michigan: Who Really Won?" *Chronicle of Higher Education,* January 14, 2005, A21.

83. Quoted in ibid., A21.

84. Peter Schmidt, "Behind the Fight over Race-Conscious Admissions," *Chronicle of Higher Education,* April 4, 2003, A22–A25. See also Peter Schmidt, "Affirmative Action Remains a Minefield, Mostly Unmapped," *Chronicle of Higher Education,* October 24, 2003, A22–A25; and Jeffrey Selingo, "Michigan: Who Really Won?" A21–A24.

85. Selingo, "Michigan: Who Really Won?" A21–A22.

86. Tamar Lewin, "Colleges Regroup after Voters Ban Race Preferences," *New York Times,* January 26, 2007, http://select.nytimes.com/search/restricted/article?res= (accessed January 28, 2007).

87. Perry, *The Michigan Affirmative Action Cases,* 167–70.

88. "Editor's Preface," Perry, *The Michigan Affirmative Action Cases,* ix.

89. Lewin, "Colleges Regroup after Voters Ban Race Preferences."

8

Desegregation, Resegregation, and Affirmative Action

HYBRID CASES

At the end of her majority opinion in *Grutter v. Bollinger,* Justice Sandra Day O'Connor sought to place affirmative action in a broad temporal context. She wrote: "It has been 25 years since Justice Powell first approved the use of race to further an interest in student body diversity in the context of public higher education. . . . We expect that 25 years from now, the use of racial preferences will no longer be necessary to further [that] interest."[1] Although other justices in their separate opinions in *Grutter* differed as to whether there would still be a need for affirmative action in 25 years,[2] there seemed to be general acquiescence on the Court in 2003 that affirmative action in education would not be revisited any time soon.

This consensus, however, would be soon abandoned. The dust had barely settled on the University of Michigan cases when the federal judiciary was forced to tackle affirmative action in the nation's elementary and secondary schools. Ever since the landmark desegregation decision of *Brown v. Board of Education* in 1954,[3] the courts and American society generally had struggled with how best to bring white and minority students together in the nation's public schools. Beginning in the 1960s, the Supreme Court began approving complicated desegregation plans—some mandated by lower federal courts and some worked out voluntarily by school districts.[4] But between 1970 and the late 1990s, with racial passions flaring in wildly idiosyncratic ways, the Supreme Court found reasons to strike down virtually as many plans as it approved.[5] By the late 1990s, scholars had begun to talk and write about a "re-segregation" of the country's public schools. They maintained that enrollment patterns across the nation disclosed that with every passing year increasing numbers of minority children were attending schools with over 50 percent minorities and, conversely, that in the same period of time increasing numbers of white children were attending schools with student bodies that were 90 percent or higher white.[6]

What did the alleged resegregation of the public schools have to do with affirmative action? None of the pupil placement plans adopted in the 1990s and the early years of the new century categorically barred minority students from enrolling in a public school district—as was the case in the Jim Crow era. However, some of the modern pupil placement schemes afforded priority in enrollment or transfer to students of color whose parents wished to have them attend a particular school (often a "magnet" or specialized school) within a district. What would be the constitutional fate of such "hybrid" desegregation/affirmative action plans?

Relying on the precedent of *Grutter v. Bollinger* that upheld race-based affirmative action if narrowly tailored in a college admission program, a circuit court of appeals in Massachusetts in 2005 ruled in favor of a pupil placement plan that afforded preference to minority students seeking transfer within a school district.[7] Later that year, without explanation, the U.S. Supreme Court denied certiorari in the case, thus upholding the race-based pupil placement plan.[8] This made it appear to Court watchers that Justice O'Connor's carefully crafted majority decision endorsing affirmative action in *Grutter* controlled pupil placement plans in elementary and secondary education as well as admissions to public institutions of higher learning.

Then random events sent a jolt through constitutional law. Justice O'Connor announced her intention to retire from the Supreme Court on July 1, 2005. O'Connor's replacement, after another nominee had withdrawn, was Samuel Alito, a circuit court of appeals court judge. Alito was confirmed and assumed his seat on the Court on January 31, 2006. Shortly after O'Connor announced her desire to leave the bench, Chief Justice Rehnquist, who had been ill for some time with thyroid cancer, died on September 3, 2005. His replacement, John W. Roberts, was nominated and confirmed swiftly. Roberts took over the Court's "center seat" on September 29, 2005. Thus, within a period of just seven months, two new justices began their tenures on a court that had had a stable membership for the 11 previous years. Roberts, a former law clerk for Chief Justice Rehnquist, appears to be following in the constitutional footsteps of his mentor. But Alito so far strikes Court watchers and scholars as much more of a conservative ideologue than the less doctrinaire, consensus-building Justice O'Connor.[9]

It would not take long for it to become apparent that the switch in the Court's membership might affect affirmative action jurisprudence. Whereas the Court had refused to disturb the appeals court decision upholding the Massachusetts pupil placement plan in late 2005, the new Supreme Court with Roberts and, especially, Alito on board tacked in a different direction. Two cases involving pupil placement plans had been working their way through the gauntlet of state and federal appellate courts during the months in which membership in the Supreme Court was in transition. One was from Seattle, Washington and the other was from Louisville, Kentucky. On June 5, 2006, near the end of the Supreme Court term that saw Roberts and Alito take their seats on the Court, the justices granted certiorari and agreed to hear in tandem the Seattle and Louisville cases.[10] These cases presented virtually the same issue as did the Massachusetts case that the Court refused to hear before Alito replaced O'Connor on the Court. This signaled to constitutional scholars and journalists that the newly configured Supreme Court might be prepared to reopen inquiry into the constitutionality of affirmative action.

THE SEATTLE AND LOUISVILLE CASES BEFORE THE SUPREME COURT

The plan at issue in the Seattle litigation involved 10 public high schools operated by the city's school board. Under the terms of the plan, entering ninth graders could choose from any of the schools in the district, but "tie-breakers" were employed to fill open seats in oversubscribed schools. The first tiebreaker gave preference to students with a sibling in the oversubscribed school. The second tiebreaker gave precedence to students who would bring a school closer to a preferred white/nonwhite racial balance. The Seattle district had never operated segregated schools or been under a court order to desegregate. The Seattle plaintiffs were a nonprofit corporation composed of parents of children who had been denied (or suspected they may have been denied) assignment in the high school of their choice. After a complicated tour through the state and federal courts, the Ninth Circuit Court of Appeals held that the Seattle plan served a compelling governmental interest and was narrowly enough tailored to be constitutional under the *Grutter* standard.[11]

Louisville, by contrast, had maintained a racially segregated school system until the 1970s. From 1975 to 1990 the city school system operated under a desegregation decree from the federal courts. In 2000 a federal court determined that Louisville had sufficiently eradicated segregation in its schools and, consequently, dissolved the former judicial decree. In 2001 Louisville adopted, without judicial pressure, a student assignment plan that prohibited a transfer within the system if such a transfer would contribute to racial imbalance in the school a student sought to attend. The plaintiff in the case was

Crystal Meredith, a single mother whose son did not receive a transfer to the kindergarten that his mother wished him to attend. The Sixth Circuit Court of Appeals upheld the plan.[12]

The cases were scheduled for a joint review by the U.S. Supreme Court. The constitutional question presented in each case was whether the pupil placement plans violated the Equal Protection Clause of the Fourteenth Amendment, Title VI of the Civil Rights Act of 1964, and parallel state laws prohibiting racial discrimination.[13] With a crowd estimated at several thousand outside the Supreme Court Building—most clamoring that the Seattle and Louisville plans be upheld—the justices presided at the oral argument on December 4, 2006.[14] The speculation of legal experts at that time was that Justice Anthony Kennedy held the key vote in the two cases. Kennedy appeared to be precariously perched at the ideological middle of the Court, a position formerly held by Justice O'Connor.[15] Given the justices' hostile questioning of the attorneys for the school districts, close followers of the oral argument saw little hope for the constitutional survival of either the Seattle or the Louisville pupil placement plans.[16] Even Justice Kennedy appeared skeptical of the validity of the two plans. In responding to a school district attorney, he mused: "The question is whether you can get into the school that you really prefer. And that in some cases depends solely on skin color. You know, it's like saying everybody can have a meal, but only people with separate skin can get the dessert."[17]

The decision in the combined cases of *Parents Involved v. Seattle* and *Meredith v. Jefferson County* was delivered on June 28, 2007, the final day of the 2006–2007 term of the Court. Although the decision was never in doubt, the Court wrote five separate, often angry, opinions. Speaking for himself and Justices Antonin Scalia, Clarence Thomas, and Samuel Alito, the new Chief Justice, John Roberts, wrote the Opinion of the Court and held both the Seattle and Louisville plans to be constitutionally flawed. Justice Thomas submitted a long concurring opinion. Justice Kennedy, confirming the speculation of those who saw him as staking out the middle of the new Roberts Court, concurred in part and dissented in part: he agreed with the Chief Justice that the plans were not narrowly enough tailored to be acceptable, but he was unwilling to abandon in principle the constitutional concept of affirmative action as announced in *Regents v. Bakke* and upheld in *Grutter v. Bollinger.* Justices John Paul Stevens, Ruth Ginsburg, David Souter, and Stephen Breyer filed dissents. Stevens wrote a short opinion, and Breyer wrote a long and powerful opinion, complete with an appendix.

Early in his decisive opinion, the Chief Justice gave a clear indication that the two city plans were not going to survive the review of a majority of the brethren. He pointed out that racial diversity constituted only one of the elements of true diversity sought in a student body. Cribbing language from Justice O'Connor's opinion in *Grutter* and Justice Lewis Powell's opinion in *Bakke,* he submitted that among the "broader array of qualifications and characteristics [of diversity] . . . racial or ethnic origin is but a single though important element."[18] The heart of his opinion emphasized that racial classifications, in order to be judged constitutional under the Equal Protection Clause of the Fourteenth Amendment and Title VI of the Civil Rights Act of 1964, must be "narrowly tailored to the goal of achieving the educational and social benefits asserted to flow from racial diversity." The problem with these two plans, he concluded, was that the broader perspective of diversity was lost in the crude quest for "racial balance, pure and simple," an end, he submitted, that "this Court has repeatedly condemned as illegitimate."[19] Roberts devoted several pages of his opinion to the point that there was no compelling evidence that "acceptable" percentages of whites versus racial minorities in Seattle or Louisville schools automatically resulted in the benefits of racial diversity.[20] In the final third of the opinion, the Chief Justice addressed many of the points advanced in the dissent of Stephen Breyer.[21]

Near the end of his opinion, Roberts made a curious allusion to the historic case of *Brown v. Board of Education.* He quoted with approval statements from the lawyers who argued on behalf of Linda Brown and the other plaintiffs in the case to the effect that classifications on the basis of race have no place in American constitutional law. For Seattle, which had never practiced segregation in its public schools, and for Louisville, which had effectively purged Jim Crow from its school system, Roberts submitted that racial balancing plans did not yield any appreciable benefits for the majority of students and, in fact, caused harms to students, like Crystal Meredith's son, who were not permitted to attend schools of their choice. Then, in a statement that the press would quote again and again over the next several days, Roberts concluded the Opinion of the Court with a powerful tautology: "The way to stop discrimination on the basis of race is to stop discriminating on the basis of race."[22]

RESEGREGATION?

Chief Justice Roberts's opinion and the separate opinions of Justices Clarence Thomas, Anthony Kennedy, and John Paul Stevens in *Parents Involved in Community Schools v. Seattle School District No. 1* and *Meredith v. Jefferson County Board of Education* all grappled with the points raised by Justice Stephen Breyer's long dissenting opinion. Breyer's opinion was essentially the statement around which all the other opinions in the case revolved. Breyer began by emphasizing that, despite countless well-meaning efforts of local school boards to implement desegregation in the wake of *Brown v. Board of Education*, that the progress toward this goal had been actually reversed in recent years. Citing the research of Gary Orfield and others, Breyer stated: "Between 1968 and 1980, the number of black children attending a school where minority children constituted more than half of the school fell from 77% to 63% in the Nation . . . but then reversed direction by the year 2000, rising from 63% to 72% in the Nation. Similarly, between 1968 and 1980, the number of black children attending schools that were more than 90% minority fell from 64% to 33% in the Nation, . . . but that too reversed direction, rising by the year 2000 from 33% to 37% in the Nation."[23]

Whether this resegregation was intentional or an unintended consequence of other social forces, Breyer accepted the argument of attorneys for the Seattle and Louisville school districts, as well as many of the amici, that it made sense to pursue voluntary integration efforts to meet the spirit of *Brown v. Board of Education* and other key decisions. Over several pages, he recounted the efforts of Seattle and Louisville to combat segregation and then resegregation with race-conscious pupil assignment programs.[24] Then, citing *Swann v. Charlotte-Mecklenburg Board of Education* (1971) and a variety of precedents, he maintained that an agency of the government, such as a school district, "may voluntarily adopt race-conscious measures to improve conditions of race even when it is not under a constitutional obligation to do so."[25] He next spent some time touring the Court's affirmative action opinions, arguing that a "contextual approach" to the review of race-based government programs is superior to the strict scrutiny standard employed by Roberts and the justices who signed on to the opinion of the Court.[26] Similarly, he applied the key affirmative action concepts—"compelling governmental interest" and "narrow tailoring"—to the Seattle and Louisville plans, ultimately concluding that both met the permitted standards for affirmative action set down by Justice O'Connor's holding for a majority of the Court in *Grutter*.[27]

The final substantive section of Breyer's dissent bemoaned the consequences of the Chief Justice's holding in the case. Hundreds, if not thousands, of local school districts with race-conscious pupil assignment plans, he maintained, will now have to scrap them in light of the Court's ruling in *Parents Involved* and *Meredith*. At a minimum, Breyer predicted, Roberts's decision will spawn "a surge of race-based litigation."[28] Breyer was saddened that the plurality decision that day had undercut local authority to address persistent, if not increasing, problems posed by segregation in the nation's public schools. In his final paragraphs, Breyer took his leader, Chief Justice Roberts, to task for a distortion of history. According to Breyer, Roberts and the justices signing his opinion were essentially saying that the racial segregation of the 1950s that kept Linda Brown and countless African Americans from attending integrated schools was constitutionally identical to the pupil placement plans in Seattle and Louisville in the early 21st century that voluntarily sought to break down resegregation in the public schools.[29] To the contrary, Breyer concluded that "[t]o invalidate the plans under review is to threaten the promise of *Brown*. The plurality's position, I fear, would break that promise. This is a decision that the Court and the Nation will come to regret."[30]

In his concurring opinion, Justice Clarence Thomas sought to rebut many of the points raised in Breyer's dissent. Without directly contesting Breyer's analysis of national racial patterns, Thomas correctly noted that his dissenting colleague had not demonstrated that the Seattle and Louisville districts themselves were undergoing resegregation. "Contrary to the dissent's rhetoric," Thomas intoned, "neither of these school districts is threatened with resegregation, and neither is constitutionally compelled or permitted to undertake race-based remediation. Racial imbalance is not segregation, and the mere incantation of terms like resegregation and remediation cannot make up the difference."[31] At another point in his opinion, Thomas clearly stated this position: "racial imbalance without intentional state action to separate the races does not amount to segregation."[32] In Thomas's view, both the Seattle and Louisville pupil placement plans voluntarily sought to remedy racial imbalance not legally enforced conditions of racial segregation.[33] Thus, neither plan could survive the Court's strict scrutiny standard for evaluating racial classifications under the Fourteenth Amendment. Thomas was insistent that the strict scrutiny standard, not Breyer's contextual approach, was the proper constitutional tool to employ.[34]

Thomas also objected to Breyer's citation of social science research to support the proposition that black children excel in racially balanced schools. At best, Thomas observed, this view is "hotly disputed among social scientists."[35] Near the end of his concurrence, in a sentence that would be quoted extensively in the days following the pupil placement decisions, Thomas admonished Breyer and his dissenting colleagues: "Indeed, if our history has taught us anything, it has taught us to beware of elites bearing racial theories."[36]

Perhaps the most interesting and, ultimately, disputed portion of Thomas's dissent was the section in which he asserted that Breyer's confidence in local school boards to do the right thing in adopting pupil assignment plans with a racial component was tantamount to the racial bigotry of segregationists in the 1950s and 1960s who sought to circumvent the thrust of *Brown v. Board of Education*. Thomas wrote: "The segregationists in *Brown* embraced the arguments the Court endorsed [in 1896 in *Plessy v. Ferguson*]. . . . Though *Brown* decisively rejected those arguments, today's dissent replicates them to a distressing extent."[37]

Although it might appear to be impossible to locate middle ground between the views of Breyer and Thomas in *Parents Involved* and *Meredith,* Justice Anthony Kennedy did his best to try to find it, concurring in part and
dissenting in part. He agreed with the Chief Justice and Justice Thomas that
the two pupil placement plans at issue were constitutionally defective, but he
clung to the belief that affirmative action, particularly as articulated by Justice
O'Connor in *Grutter,* possessed constitutional validity.

Kennedy found neither the Seattle nor the Louisville pupil assignment
plans to be narrowly tailored: they contained ambiguities and depended on
arbitrary criteria.[38] Each plan, he correctly noted, resulted in only a few dozen
students being shunted for purposes of racial balance to schools other than
those they would normally have attended given their places of residence. This
suggested to him that two the school districts, with a little more creativity,
could have achieved the end of racial diversity through different and, arguably, constitutional means.[39] One of the problems of Breyer's dissent, according to Kennedy, was that the contextual approach to state action under the
Fourteenth Amendment that Breyer championed was not consonant with the
Court's affirmative action precedents, particularly that of *Grutter.*[40]

In spite of his differences with Breyer over the standard of constitutional
analysis under the Equal Protection Clause of the Fourteenth Amendment,
Kennedy was still inclined to agree with the dissenters on the fundamental
point that an affirmative action plan, if narrowly tailored and in support of
a compelling state interest, was constitutional. As a result, he concluded that
Chief Justice Roberts's plurality opinion of the Court was "too dismissive of
the legitimate interest government has in ensuring all people have equal opportunity regardless of their race. The . . . postulate that '[t]he way to stop
discrimination on the basis of race is to stop discriminating on the basis of
race,' . . . is not sufficient to decide these cases. . . . To the extent the plurality opinion suggests the Constitution mandates that state and local school
authorities must accept the status quo of racial isolation in schools, it is, in
my view, profoundly mistaken."[41] Later in his opinion, Kennedy made even
clearer his support of affirmative action: "The decision today should not prevent school districts from continuing the important work of bringing together
students of different racial, ethnic, and economic backgrounds."[42] With these
words, Kennedy staked out the middle ground on affirmative action, preserv-
ing the legacy of Justice O'Connor's majority opinion in *Grutter.*

The final opinion in *Parents Involved* and *Meredith* was submitted by Justice John Paul Stevens, the most senior member of the Court and the only
sitting justice who had had a hand in the key affirmative action decision
of *Bakke v. Board of Regents.* Stevens began by expressing his complete support for Breyer's "eloquent and unanswerable dissent."[43] The main reason, he

indicated, for taking the time and effort to submit a separate opinion was because he strongly objected to what he saw as Chief Justice Roberts's unacceptable historical revisionism. In referring to the Jim Crow era before the *Brown* decision, Roberts had stated that school children were compelled to attend schools based on their race. Although Roberts was technically correct, Stevens emphasized that in the years before *Brown* only black children were subject to discriminatory and offensive pupil placement policies. "[T]he history books," Stevens noted, "do not tell stories of white children struggling to attend black schools. In this and other ways, the Chief Justice rewrites the history of one of this Court's most important decisions."[44] Stevens concluded his brief opinion with this powerful exit line: "It is my firm conviction that no Member of the Court that I joined in 1975 would have agreed with today's decision."[45] These words may well have been a personal slap at Chief Justice Roberts because the Supreme Court in 1975 included among its members William Rehnquist, the justice for whom Roberts had worked as a law clerk in the late 1970s and for whom he had served as a pallbearer in 2005.

THE PROPER LEGACY OF *BROWN V. BOARD OF EDUCATION?*

Shortly after the announcement of the combined decision in *Parents Involved* and *Meredith,* the online version of the *Washington Post* dubbed it "the most important opinion of . . . [Chief Justice John Roberts's] two terms leading the Court."[46] Similarly, *USA Today* asserted that "no case revealed the chasm between the conservatives and the liberals [on the Supreme Court] as much as . . . [the] decision preventing the use of race in school assignments."[47] Several news reports repeated the statement delivered extemporaneously from the bench by Justice Stephen Breyer: "It is not often in the law that so few have so quickly changed so much."[48] The "few" Breyer had in mind were John Roberts and Samuel Alito. The pupil placement decisions made clear to many observers that, with these two appointments, President George W. Bush had tilted the Court farther to the ideological right. One reporter called this shift "a significant achievement and likely enduring legacy for President Bush."[49]

Sharon L. Browne, the lead attorney for the Pacific Legal Foundation, a conservative public interest law firm that assisted in the appeal of the parents challenging the race-based pupil placement plans in Seattle and Louisville, hailed the decision as a positive step for education and parental choice: "Schools across the country must get the message loud and clear," she stated: "Our young people should not be assigned to a school based on the color of their skin."[50] The consensus of the media reaction, however, was critical of the Court's ruling. Typical was the lead editorial, titled "Resegregation Now," in the June 29, 2007 issue of the *New York Times:* "The Supreme Court ruled

53 years ago in *Brown v. Board of Education* that segregated education is inherently unequal, and it ordered the nation's schools to integrate. Yesterday the Court switched sides and told two cities that they cannot take modest steps to bring public school students of different races together. It was a sad day for the Court and for the ideal of racial equality."[51]

A number of television and newspaper reporters focused on the clash in open court between the Chief Justice and Justice Stephen Breyer. For example, Jeffrey Toobin, the legal affairs analyst for CNN and the author of *The Nine: Inside the Secret World of the Supreme Court*,[52] reported just moments after the decision was rendered that "the Supreme Court was at war with itself in a drama that is rarely seen inside that room." Toobin noted that Roberts had characterized the white students who did not get the school assignments they desired under the Seattle and Louisville plans as "equivalent to the black students in *Brown v. Board of Education*." Toobin then paraphrased Breyer's response to Roberts in a colloquial fashion: "You have got to be kidding me. . . . [H]ow dare you compare [the racial balancing plans in Seattle and Louisville] to the discrimination of Jim Crow?"[53]

Roberts's comparison of the legal argument made by the aggrieved white parents in Seattle and Louisville to the arguments of the lawyers for the National Association for the Advancement of Colored People (NAACP) on behalf of the black parents in *Brown v. Board of Education* drew the ire of a number of Court watchers. Nancy MacLean, a history professor at Northwestern University and the author of an important book on affirmative action, *Freedom Is Not Enough: The Opening of the American Workplace*,[54] had this to say about the Chief Justice's reasoning in *Parents Involved* and *Meredith*: "Chief Justice John G. Roberts reversed a half-century of precedent and progress on civil rights with his decision. . . . Roberts claimed to be upholding the spirit of *Brown v. Board of Education*. Yet the conservative movement that put him on the bench bitterly opposed the *Brown* decision and has fought every serious civil rights initiative since."[55] Even more telling, a few of the lawyers who had participated on behalf of the plaintiffs in *Brown* a half century earlier were asked by reporters to respond to the Chief Justice's contention that the white parents and their children in the Seattle and Louisville cases were acting in the same cause of racial justice as the black parents and students in the *Brown* case. Robert L. Carter, one of the plaintiff's attorneys in *Brown* was quoted by name in the Chief Justice's opinion in *Parents Involved*. Carter, then 90 years old, was incensed: "All that race was used for at that . . . time was to deny equal opportunity to black people. It's to stand that argument on its head to use race the way they use it now." Jack Greenberg, another lawyer who helped prepare the case for the plaintiffs in *Brown,* simply characterized Roberts's historical linkage as "preposterous." But Roberts had his supporters. Roger

Clegg, general counsel of the Center for Equal Opportunity, an organization that had consistently fought against affirmative action, commented: "There's no question but that the principle of *Brown* is that a child's skin color should not determine what school he or she should be assigned to."[56]

Some who did not agree with the Chief Justice's decision in *Parents Involved* were still able to take solace in the long and passionately argued apologia for affirmative action in the dissent of Justice Breyer. The *New York Times,* for example, termed Breyer's opinion "eloquent."[57] For those who believed in the constitutional validity of race-conscious government programs, Breyer's opinion in *Parents Involved* was every bit as powerfully argued and as studded with factual evidence as any of the pro–affirmative action opinions in *Bakke* or *Grutter.*

It was Justice Kennedy's separate opinion, however, that sparked the most commentary by journalists and legal scholars. The pupil assignment plans in the two cases may have been voided by the Court's decision in *Parents Involved* and *Meredith,* but it was Kennedy's separate opinion that actually preserved the principle that race could still be taken into account in government-sponsored programs. The *Chronicle of Higher Education,* for example, noted that, despite the decision in *Parents Involved,* the *Grutter* precedent permitting affirmative action at the college level was "left solidly intact."[58] Even Terence J. Pell, president of the Center for Individual Rights—a group that had supported the plaintiffs in *Grutter* and *Gratz*—acknowledged that the holding in *Parents Involved* would likely have little adverse impact at the college level because most institutions of higher learning were "more or less in compliance" with *Grutter.*[59] A discordant view, however, was expressed by Gary Orfield, the scholar most responsible for identifying resegregation in the public schools. Orfield lamented that "the dike protecting affirmative action has held but the river that brings diverse groups of students to colleges may be drying up as a result of the latest [Supreme Court] decision."[60]

A CASE STUDY FROM THE HEARTLAND

One of the first questions asked in the aftermath of *Parents Involved* and *Meredith* was: "What would happen to the numerous school districts across the country that had pupil assignment plans based, at least in part, on race?" Education officials reported on the day after the decision that there were no reliable numbers as to how many school districts were following plans that took race into account in matching students with schools: According to school administrators quoted in the *Chronicle of Higher Education,* "estimates range[d] from a few hundred to nearly 1000."[61] Stephen Imhoff, a member of the Jefferson Country school board, which had been the subject of the

Louisville litigation in *Meredith,* confessed that his district did not have a "Plan B." However, Imhoff did anticipate that his board would have to look into economic diversity, as opposed to race, as the main basis for pupil assignment.[62] Justice Kennedy's opinion in *Parents Involved* had left the door open for public schools to devise narrowly tailored and, hence, constitutional methods of taking race into account in pupil assignment cases. Some legal experts predicted that there would be more litigation to test existing modes of pupil assignment; others speculated that school boards around the country would scramble quickly to come up with new enrollment plans.[63]

The case of the medium-sized city of Des Moines, Iowa (population of about 200,000) offers an example of how the 2007 pupil assignment decisions caused one municipality to voluntarily take steps to devise an acceptable open enrollment/parental choice plan for its public schools. Because the state of Iowa provides a school district with financial support for the students it serves (currently about $6,000 per student), it is in the financial interest of a school district to have a net inflow of students under open enrollment policies.

Des Moines has never intentionally discriminated on the basis of race to keep minorities from attending integrated schools. However, as was the case with most northern cities, the residences of black and other racial minority families have been clustered in a few parts of the city, thus leading several schools to be de facto segregated. For a time in the late 1960s and early 1970s, some black students within Des Moines were bused within the district to attempt to achieve a preferred level of racial balance. But busing did not generate a sufficient degree of integration to suit school administrators. Consequently, in 1976 Des Moines adopted a voluntary desegregation plan, in accord with a "Memorandum of Understanding" with the U.S. Office of Civil Rights, in which the city pledged to reduce the number of minority students at certain city schools and to stop assigning black and other minority teachers and administrators to schools with the largest minority enrollments.

The 1976 agreement led to the closing of some schools, mainly in the center of the city, and the redrawing of attendance lines. Most importantly, a parent who wished to open enroll a child outside of the Des Moines district to a nearby suburb was often kept from doing so if her child's enrollment would exacerbate racial imbalance in the preferred school. The Iowa desegregation plan was upheld by a state court in the mid-1990s and was still in force at the time of the Supreme Court decisions in *Parents Involved* and *Meredith.* In the five years before these decisions were issued, about one-third of the total number of requests to enroll outside of the Des Moines district had been denied on racial grounds.[64]

In the immediate aftermath of the 2007 ruling in the pupil placement cases, Carol Gretta, an attorney for the Iowa Department of Education, was charged with writing new guidelines to assist Iowa schools in conforming with the terms of the Supreme Court ruling in *Parents Involved* and *Meredith*. Paraphrasing Justice Kennedy, Gretta emphasized that whatever pupil assignment plan Des Moines devised could not "classify by race" but still could be "race-conscious." To walk this fine line, she suggested that an acceptable plan to promote the diversity favored by the Supreme Court would have to take into account—in addition to race—such factors as income level, language skills, special needs, and test scores.[65] The *Des Moines Register* editorialized in favor of a nuanced approach to diversity that took into account the factors identified by Gretta: "The Supreme Court has made the job harder, but not impossible."[66] In sympathy with Justice Kennedy's opinion, the *Register* maintained that "children benefit from learning alongside classmates with a variety of backgrounds. It helps them succeed in a global economy."[67]

In November 2007, the Iowa Board of Education unanimously approved new guidelines for pupil placement in the school districts within the state. As Carol Gretta had predicted, the new guidelines were weighted more heavily on income, language, and disability than on race. Des Moines and the five other districts in the state that had in force pupil assignment plans with racial components at the time of the *Parents Involved* decision were charged with coming up with new plans by March 1, 2008. The alternative was to adopt no diversity plan and, therefore, not be able to take race into account in any way in guiding open enrollment. In addition, school districts that chose voluntarily for the first time to adopt open enrollment plans with diversity components were required to meet the same deadline.[68]

The *Des Moines Register* continued to focus attention on the issue as the March 1 deadline approached. On January 24, the newspaper once again editorialized in favor of a new diversity plan for the capital city.[69] On Sunday, February 17, 2008, the *Register* published a long editorial on diversity on the front page of its opinion section. In it, the newspaper endorsed the approval of a diversity plan as "a test of conscience" for Des Moines.[70] Two pages later, the paper aired an exchange among four Des Moines residents arguing various sides of the diversity issue. One of the discussants, a young African American woman named Mary Ann Spicer, saw a diversity plan as a boon to quality education: it would allow students, she argued, to be taught in clear, well-equipped classrooms with well-trained teachers. The alternative, as she saw it, was that the poorest city schools would face "teacher turnover, resegregation and academic stagnation as well as student flight out of the district." In opposition, Les Cason, Jr.—also an African American—urged the Des Moines school district to refuse to adopt any diversity plan because he saw such plans as excuses to bus minority students to schools emphasizing special education. Cason's solution was to allow children to attend schools in their neighborhoods and to direct more resources to schools in the poorest parts of the city.[71]

On February 19, a front page story in the *Register* reported that fully two-thirds of 1,030 respondents to a Des Moines school district survey favored creating a diversity plan to be filed with the state Department of Education. The same story announced that a majority of the city's school board supported a diversity plan.[72] The following day one of the *Register*'s regular columnists wrote a strong defense of adopting a diversity plan that incorporated income and race as key variables in regulating transfers into and out of the Des Moines schools.[73] A few days later, the much debated Des Moines diversity plan—which emphasized income inequality more than race in directing student movement in and out of the district—was adopted by the city school board.[74]

At the same time Des Moines and other Iowa cities were contemplating the wisdom of adopting diversity pupil assignment plans comporting with the Supreme Court's decision in *Parents Involved,* the Iowa legislature was debating a bill that, if adopted, would essentially ratify the diversity guidelines promulgated in late 2007 by the state Department of Education. The bill, House File 2164, was introduced on February 6, 2008. It passed the Iowa House 97-0 and the Iowa Senate by a vote of 40-9. It was signed into law by Governor Chet Culver on April 11, 2008. The new Iowa law eliminates any reference to racial minority or nonracial minority pupil ratios under a school district's open enrollment plan. The law permits taking race into account as but one factor in a diversity plan. Besides requiring the state board of education to adopt diversity guidelines (which by April had already taken place), the law gives school districts adopting Department of Education–approved diversity plans until July 1, 2009 to fully implement those plans.[75]

How successful the new Iowa law will be in promoting diversity, finessing the race issue, and still being consonant with the Supreme Court's rulings in *Parents Involved* and *Meredith* remains to be seen.

NOTES

1. *Grutter v. Bollinger,* 539 U.S. 306, 343 (2003).
2. See ibid., 346 (Justice Ruth Ginsburg, concurring); ibid., 386–87 (Chief Justice William Rehnquist, dissenting); 377–78 (Justice Clarence Thomas, dissenting).
3. *Brown v. Board of Education,* 347 U.S. 483 (1954).
4. The key case here was *Swann v. Charlotte-Mecklenburg Board of Education,* 402 U.S. 1 (1971).

5. See the discussion of the ebb and flow of desegregation in these years in Donald G. Nieman, *Promises to Keep: African-Americans and the Constitutional Order, 1776 to the Present* (New York: Oxford University Press, 1991), 189–200.

6. See, especially, Gary Orfield and C. Lee, *Racial Transformation and the Changing Nature of Segregation* (Cambridge, MA: The Civil Rights Project at Harvard University, 2006).

7. *Comfort v. Lynn School Comm.*, 418 F.3d 1 (2005).

8. *Comfort v. Lynn School Comm*, 546 U.S. 1061 (2005).

9. On the 2005–6 shift in Supreme Court membership and its consequences for the law, see Jan Crawford Greenburg, *Supreme Conflict: The Inside Story of the Struggle for Control of the United States Supreme Court* (New York: The Penguin Press, 2007).

10. *Parents Involved in Community Schools v. Seattle School District No. 1* and *Meredith v. Jefferson County Board of Education*, 547 U.S. 1178 (2006).

11. This description of the Seattle plan is drawn from *Parents Involved in Community Schools v. Seattle School District No. 1* and *Meredith v. Jefferson County Board of Education*, 127 S. Ct. 2738 (2007), 2–7 of slip opinion of Chief Justice John Roberts. Here and elsewhere in this chapter where specific passages of the opinions in *Parents Involved* are cited, the references are to the "slip opinions" issued by the Supreme Court shortly after the decision was announced.

12. The description of the Louisville plan is drawn from ibid., 7–9 of slip opinion of Roberts.

13. Ibid., 5 of slip opinion of Roberts.

14. "High Court Weighs Race in Assigning Schools," MSNBC.Com, December 4, 2006, http://www.msnbc.msn.com/id/16036037 (accessed December 14, 2006).

15. Peter Schmidt, "Supreme Court Shows Increased Skepticism toward Affirmative Action," *Chronicle of Higher Education,* December 15, 2006, 20.

16. Linda Greenhouse, "Court Reviews Race as Factor in School Plans," *New York Times,* December 5, 2006, http://www.nytimes.com/2006/12/05 (accessed December 7, 2006).

17. "Excerpts from Arguments in School Race Cases," *The Seattle Times,* December 5, 2006, http://.seattletimes.nwsource.com/gci-bin (accessed December 14, 2006).

18. *Parents Involved in Community Schools v. Seattle School District No. 1* and *Meredith v. Jefferson County Board of Education*, 127 S. Ct. 2738 (2007), 14 of slip opinion of Chief Justice John Roberts.

19. Ibid., 17–18 of slip opinion of Roberts.

20. Ibid., 17–25 of slip opinion of Roberts.

21. Ibid., 28–39 of slip opinion of Roberts.

22. Ibid., 40–41 of slip opinion of Roberts.

23. Ibid., 1–4, 69–72 of slip opinion of Justice Stephen Breyer.

24. Ibid., 4–18, 73–77 of slip opinion of Breyer.

25. Ibid., 27 of slip opinion of Breyer.

26. Ibid., 27–37 of slip opinion of Breyer.

27. Ibid., 37–55 of slip opinion of Breyer.

28. Ibid., 61 of slip opinion of Breyer.

29. Ibid., 66–68 of slip opinion of Breyer.

30. Ibid., 68 of slip opinion of Breyer.

31. Ibid., 2 of slip opinion of Justice Clarence Thomas.

32. Ibid, 4 of slip opinion of Thomas.

33. Ibid., 5–6 of slip opinion of Thomas.

34. Ibid., 11–13 of slip opinion of Thomas.

35. Ibid., 15 of slip opinion of Thomas.

36. Ibid., 35–36 of slip opinion of Thomas.

37. Ibid., 28 of slip opinion of Thomas.

38. Ibid., 3–7 of slip opinion of Justice Anthony Kennedy.

39. Ibid., 9–10 of slip opinion of Kennedy.

40. Ibid., 8–13 of slip opinion of Kennedy.

41. Ibid., 7–8 of slip opinion of Kennedy.

42. Ibid., 18 of slip opinion of Kennedy.

43. Ibid, 1 of slip opinion of Justice John Paul Stevens.

44. Ibid., 1–2 of slip opinion of Stevens.

45. Ibid., 6 of slip opinion of Stevens.

46. Robert Barnes, "Court Limits Use of Race to Achieve Diversity in Schools," *Washington Post,* June 28, 2007, http://www.washingtonpost.com/wp-dyn (accessed June 28, 2007).

47. Joan Biskupic, "Roberts Steers Court Right Back to Reagan," *USA Today,* June 29, 2007, 8A.

48. Ibid., 8A.

49. Ibid., 8A. See also Robert Barnes, "Newest Justice tips High Court to Right," *Washington Post,* June 28, 2007, http://www.washingtonpost.com/wp-dyn (accessed June 28, 2007).

50. Quoted in Joan Biskupic, "School Vote Marked by Intense Discord," *USA Today,* June 29, 2007, 9A; and Sharon L. Browne, "Ruling Sends Clear Message," *USA Today,* June 29, 2007, 14A.

51. "Resegregation Now" [editorial], *New York Times,* June 29, 2007, A26.

52. Jeffrey Toobin, *The Nine: Inside the Secret World of the Supreme Court* (New York: Doubleday, 2007).

53. Jeffrey Toobin, "School Ruling 'a Victory for Conservatives,'" CNN.Com, June 28, 2007, http://www.cnn.com/2007/LAW/06/28/toobin.ots/index (accessed June 28, 2007).

54. Nancy MacLean, *Freedom Is Not Enough: The Opening of the American Workplace* (Cambridge, MA: Harvard University Press, 2006).

55. Nancy MacLean, "The Scary Origins of Chief Justice Roberts's Decision Opposing the Use of Race to Promote Integration," *History News Network,* August 6, 2007, http://hnn.us/articles/41501.html (accessed August 8, 2007).

56. The statements of Robert Carter, Jack Greenberg, and Roger Clegg are quoted in Adam Liptak, "The Same Words, but Differing Views," *New York Times,* June 29, 2007, A20.

57. "Resegregation Now" [editorial], *New York Times,* June 29, 2007, A26.

58. Peter Schmidt, "High Court Leaves Michigan Cases Intact," *Chronicle of Higher Education,* July 6, 2007, A1.

59. Quoted in ibid., A19.

60. Quoted in Robert O'Neill, "The Supreme Court, Affirmative Action, and Higher Education," *AAUP Academic Online,* January/February 2008, http://aaup.org (accessed February 15, 2008).

61. Tamar Lewin, "Across U.S., a New Look at School Integration Efforts," *New York Times,* June 29, 2007, A21.

62. Quoted in ibid., A21.

63. Linda Greenhouse, "Justices, 5–4, Limit Use of Race for School Integration Plans," *New York Times,* June 29, 2007, A1, A20.

64. This plan is described in Megan Hawkins, "Court Ruling Raises Questions for School," *Des Moines Register,* June 29, 2007, 1A, 3A.

65. Quoted in ibid., 3A.

66. "Racial Balance in Schools Still Possible, and Iowa School Districts Should Still Pursue It" [editorial], *Des Moines Register,* June 29, 2007, 8A.

67. Ibid., 8A.

68. Megan Hawkins, "State Advances School Diversity Rules," *Des Moines Register,* November 15, 2007, 4B.

69. "Little Time, Big Decision: OK School Diversity Plan?" [editorial], *Des Moines Register,* January 24, 2008, 8A.

70. "A Broader View of Diversity" [editorial], *Des Moines Register,* February 17, 2008, 1OP.

71. "Should Des Moines Adopt Diversity Plan?" *Des Moines Register,* February 17, 2008, 3OP.

72. Megan Hawkins, "Most on D.M. School Board Back Diversity Effort," *Des Moines Register,* February 19, 2008, 1A.

73. Rekha Basu, "Greater Good Should Be Goal of Desegregation Plan," *Des Moines Register,* February 20, 2008, 9A.

74. Jason Clayworth, "Bill Advances to Eliminate Race in Diversity Efforts," *Des Moines Register,* March 12, 2008, 2B.

75. Iowa House File 2164, "An Act Relating to Voluntary Diversity of Court-Ordered School Desegregation Plans under the State's Open Enrollment Law," http://.coolice.legis.state.ia.us/Cool-ICE (accessed June 29, 2008).

Conclusion

Where the Affirmative Action Debate Stands Today

THE TWISTING COURSE OF AFFIRMATIVE ACTION

Born in the black anger and white guilt of the 1960s, affirmative action is now more than 40 years old. Intended initially as a set of government programs to redress inequities resulting from racial discrimination (and, to a lesser degree, discrimination on the basis of gender), when affirmative action is defended today its advocates principally stress the benefits of racial and gender diversity to all Americans, in the classroom as well as in the workforce. Or, to put it another way: after more than 40 years of judicial rulings, executive orders, employment patterns, agency decisions, changing college and public school admissions policies, and social practices, affirmative action is now more grounded in social and educational theory than in the history of racial or gender discrimination.

A recent front page article in *The Chronicle of Higher Education,* published on the 30th anniversary of the Supreme Court decision in *Bakke v. Regents,* noted that Justice Lewis Powell's opinion in the now famous California case constituted a key moment in the debate over race-conscious government programs. Powell grounded his apologia for using race as a plus factor on the benefits of racial diversity to *all* students in an integrated professional school. Twenty-five years later, in *Grutter v. Bollinger,* Justice Sandra Day O'Connor said much the same thing. In her key opinion in the Michigan case, she relied heavily on the arguments mounted for racial diversity in amicus briefs submitted by high-ranking military officers and business leaders.[1]

The most profound and most empirically grounded defense of affirmative action—William Bowen and Derek Bok's *The Shape of the River*—provides solid evidence that the gap between the scholastic achievement of whites and most racial minorities can effectively be addressed by race-conscious admissions programs. In the years before race-based admissions policies were instituted, the nation's leading colleges and universities admitted only a token number of minority students. But, after three decades of affirmative action, the number of minorities admitted to colleges, universities, and professional schools is approaching the percentage of minorities in the population as a whole. The authors of *The Shape of the River* also stress that the number of white students who have been denied places in particular institutions of higher learning by affirmative action has been minimal: if affirmative action had not been practiced from the 1970s through the1990s, only about two percent more white students would have been admitted to this country's most competitive colleges and universities. And the benefit to all students from being educated in diverse classrooms outweighs the fact that a small percentage of white men and women might not have been able to attend top-tier schools.

In the eyes of its critics, however, the case against affirmative action rests as much on principle as it does on evidence. The Fourteenth Amendment's Equal Protection Clause, the critics maintain, demands color blindness in the treatment of the races. This view is as strongly embraced today as it was when affirmative action was in the talking stage in the 1960s. There is a clear thread running through the conservative hostility to the EEOC, the campaign to pass California's Proposition 209, and the 2007 opinion of Chief Justice John Roberts in the Seattle and Louisville pupil placement cases. The Chief Justice's injunction in *Parents Involved v. Seattle*—"The way to stop discrimination on the basis of race is to stop discriminating on the basis of race"[2]—could just as easily have been uttered by James J. Kilpatrick or Allan Bakke in the 1970s, by Ward Connerly in the 1980s, or by Dinesh D'Souza in the 1990s.

In addition, the critics of affirmative action are quick to add that race-based policies stigmatize minorities who are afforded special consideration. They argue: How can one be sure that a person of color who was hired for the job or given a seat in a classroom is truly qualified? Or was he or she merely an "affirmative action hire" or an "affirmative action student"? Finally, the critics question the rationale of diversity. Should diversity by race trump all other forms of diversity? Perhaps a diversity of ideas, as D'Souza and Connerly have argued, is more important in a college classroom than diversity of skin color.

Affirmative action still hangs on in America—but barely so. Complex permutations of U.S. Supreme Court opinions from the 1970s to 2007 have resulted in a slender majority of the nation's highest court holding that race may be taken into account in hiring, government contracting, admissions to colleges, and the placement of students in public elementary and secondary schools. But severe limitations have been placed on when race may be considered: it may only be done so in narrowly tailored programs or plans to satisfy a compelling governmental interest. Racial quotas are prohibited in educational settings. Flying under the banner of diversity, race-consciousness is still widely practiced in admissions to institutions of higher education and permitted in the placement and transfers of public school students. In the spheres of employment and government contracting, race- and gender-based preferences are still legally tolerable. But such preferences, particularly after the 1995 Supreme Court decision in *Adarand Constructors v. Pena,* are narrowly and tightly circumscribed.

RACE-BASED PUBLIC POLICY: SUCCESS, FAILURE, OR A DISTRACTION?

Justice Sandra Day O'Connor, at the end of her 2003 opinion in *Grutter v. Bollinger,* expressed the hope that affirmative action would no longer be necessary to further the interest of diversity a quarter century down the road. However one feels about affirmative action, if present trends continue it may in fact vanish from the American scene long before Justice O'Connor's predicted sunset date of 2028. As of this writing, 18 of the country's 50 states have on their books legislative enactments or constitutional amendments prohibiting race-based admissions policies in public education and other government programs. In fact, four of the five times that the public has been given the opportunity to go to the polls to vote to maintain a state's race-conscious policies in education or employment, a majority of the electorate has responded with a resounding "No."[3] Ironically, among the states that now prohibit race-conscious public policy are California and Michigan, the two states that spawned the leading Supreme Court opinions endorsing affirmative action in higher education. If California, the nation's most racially diverse state, no longer practices affirmative action, what does the future hold for other states still under the constitutional sway of *Grutter*?

What accounts for the retreat from affirmative action as expressed in state referenda voiding race-based policies in education and employment? A reasonable hypothesis is that well-organized and well-funded anti–affirmative action interest groups, such as Ward Connerly's Center for Individual Rights, have seized on the passions expressed over socially divisive "wedge issues," such as affirmative action, and have been successful in rallying a majority of the voting electorate around their cause.[4] Conversely, defenders of race-conscious programs, such as educators and various liberal interest groups, have been conspicuously unsuccessful in marshalling their partisans to support referenda votes favoring affirmative action.

There is a further irony in the public policy debate over affirmative action. In the same period that the organized resistance to race-based public policy has caused a third of the states in America to turn their backs on affirmative action, support for preferential treatment of minorities among the public at large has never been higher. Since 1987, the Pew Research Center for People and the Press has been conducting public opinion polls on a variety of issues facing Americans. Most of these polls have included a query on affirmative action. In 2007 as in 1995, those sampled were asked "Do you favor or oppose affirmative action programs designed to help blacks, women and other minorities get better jobs and education?" In 1995, 58 percent responded that they favored such programs. In 2007 the number favoring affirmative action had jumped to 70 percent. If the question is framed a little differently, however, the support for affirmative action is much weaker. To the statement, "We should make every effort to improve the position of blacks and minorities, even if it means giving preferential treatment," only 34 percent of the respondents in 2007 indicated their agreement. Still, as low as this number is, it is higher than the mere 24 percent who agreed with the identically worded statement in 1995. By either phrasing, then, general support for race-based consideration in employment and education has increased since the mid-1990s.[5]

Stephen Carter, a professor of law at Yale University, writing an opinion piece for the *New York Times* on July 6, 2008, pointed to several examples of minority success in the 30 years since Justice Powell's opinion in *Bakke:* (1) the number of African Americans with advanced degrees has nearly doubled; (2) the number of minority students in baccalaureate programs has grown substantially; (3) the median income of black families has increased by almost 20 percent; (4) the gap between black and white scores on standardized tests has narrowed considerably; and, most notably, (5) the nation was presented with an opportunity to elect Barack Obama, an African American, as the 44th president of the United States (Obama was in fact elected on November 4, 2008, with almost 53% of the popular vote and the vast majority of the electoral vote).[6]

Without necessarily crediting race-based public policy for these gains, Carter argued that these positive changes should offer only a small cause for celebration for those who favor affirmative action. Carter, an African American himself, termed affirmative action a "distraction." It may have helped the black middle class improve its relative standing in America since the *Bakke* decision, and it may have made the white majority more conscious of the benefits of diversity in American life, but it did not fundamentally improve the plight of the poorest Americans of color. Citing figures well-known to sociologists, Carter observed that one in three black students still fails to graduate from high school, and the murder rate among black men in the United States continues to escalate.[7]

Back in 1965, Daniel Patrick Moynihan had attempted to convince America's elected leaders of the need to institute race-based policies in education and employment. He saw these measures as necessary in order to keep the country from descending further into racial violence. The Great Society of Lyndon Johnson accepted this argument as, to an extent, did the administration of Richard Nixon that followed. Beginning with the *Bakke* decision and continuing through the key Supreme Court rulings of the last 30 years, however, Moynihan's arguments for affirmative action were placed on distant back burners. Front and center emerged the assertion that affirmative action made good public policy sense because racial and gender diversity in the workplace and in the classroom were good for all Americans.

Professor Carter may be right that affirmative action predicated on diversity has not done much to ameliorate the plight of the poorest people of color in the United States. But the gains for middle-class people of color and white women, as we have seen in these pages, have been significant. Moreover, the case for diversity has been made powerfully—perhaps most notably in the amicus briefs of military and corporate leaders in *Grutter*— and then accepted, however tenuously, by the Supreme Court in *Bakke, Grutter,* and *Parents Involved.* What the future holds for affirmative action is far from clear. A shift in membership on the precariously balanced Supreme Court could bolster race and gender-conscious public policy or lead to its demise. Or the justices could avoid the issue altogether. Whatever transpires in the courts, the public debate over affirmative action is destined to continue.

NOTES

1. Peter Schmidt, "'*Bakke*' Set a New Path to Diversity for Colleges," *Chronicle of Higher Education,* June 20, 2008, A1, A18–A19.

2. *Parents Involved in Community Schools v. Seattle School District No. 1* and *Meredith v. Jefferson County Board of Education,* 127 S. Ct. 2738 (2007), at 39–40 of slip opinion of Chief Justice Roberts.

3. The exception occurred in the November 2008 election when Colorado voters defeated, by a 51 percent to 49 percent margin, a ballot measure crafted to prohibit affirmative action programs in the state. On that same day, however, Nebraska voters joined California, Michigan, and Washington as the fourth state to pass a ballot proposition banning race-conscious education and employment programs. The 2008 Colorado affirmative action vote might have been muddied because of the large number of proposals on the state's ballot, thus leading confused and impatient voters to "just vote no." Colleen Slevin, "Colorado Voters Reject Affirmative Action Ban,"

Associated Press, November 7, 2008, http://cbs4denver.com/politics/affirmative.action.ban.2.858976.html (accessed February 21, 2009).

4. An intriguing analysis of affirmative action as a wedge issue is provided by the linguistic philosopher George Lakoff. See Lakoff's *Moral Politics: How Liberals and Conservatives Think,* 2nd ed. (Chicago: The University of Chicago Press, 2002), 222–25; and his *Don't Think of an Elephant: Know Your Values and Frame the Debate* (White River Junction, VT: Chelsea Green Publishing, 2004), 81–88.

5. Pew Research Center for People and the Press, "Trends in Political Values and Core Attitudes: 1987–2007," http://people-press.org/report, March 22, 2007 (accessed July 2, 2008).

6. Stephen L. Carter, "Affirmative Distraction," *New York Times,* July 6, 2008, http://www.nytimes.com/2008/07/06/opinion (accessed July 6, 2008).

7. Ibid.

Affirmative Action Time Line

1866	Civil Rights Act of 1866
	Congress passes first federal civil rights legislation over President Andrew Johnson's veto
1868	Fourteenth Amendment
	States ratify historic constitutional amendment
	Equal Protection Clause will become the constitutional standard for testing laws dealing with race
	Includes brief definitions of federal and state citizenship
1873	*Slaughterhouse Cases*
	First judicial interpretation of the Fourteenth Amendment
	Supreme Court identifies dual citizenship rights, national and state
	Court leaves the protection of fundamental rights (e.g., life and property) to the states
1875	Civil Rights Act of 1875
	Congress passes federal legislation prohibiting racial discrimination in public accommodations
1876	*United States v. Cruikshank*
	Supreme Court rules that racial discrimination by individuals cannot be prohibited by Fourteenth Amendment

Only state action may be proscribed under Fourteenth Amendment

1883   *Civil Rights Cases*

Rules public accommodations sections of Civil Rights Act of 1875 unconstitutional

Another statement of the state action doctrine

1896   *Plessy v. Ferguson*

Famous Supreme Court enunciation of separate but equal

Separate state facilities for blacks and whites found constitutionally acceptable, provided that they are substantially equal

1905   *Lochner v. New York*

Supreme Court strikes down law limiting the number of hours per week that bakers may work

Gives the Fourteenth Amendment a substantive economic interpretation probably not intended by its framers or by the majority in the *Slaughterhouse Cases*

1908   *Muller v. Oregon:*

State maximum hours law for women upheld

First "Brandeis Brief," heavily statistical legal argument

Supreme Court finds it constitutional to treat women differently from men in employment cases, due to the "delicate nature" of women

1923   Equal Rights Amendment

Introduced in Congress for first time

Would be regularly introduced in Congress until the 1970s

1935   National Labor Relations Act

First use of term "affirmative action" in American public policy

1941   President Franklin Roosevelt's Executive Order 8802

Mandates nondiscrimination in defense and government employment

Establishes Fair Employment Practices Committee (FEPC)

1944   Gunnar Myrdal's *An American Dilemma*

Major study published, emphasizing that African Americans in the United States suffer from widespread discrimination and injustice

1948	President Harry Truman's Executive Order 9981
	Orders an end to racial discrimination in the military
1950	*Sweatt v. Painter*
	Supreme Court rules separate but equal practice in a state law school unconstitutional
1954	*Brown v. Board of Education*
	Supreme Court rules separate but equal in public elementary and secondary schools unconstitutional
1955	Montgomery bus boycott
	Major act of civil disobedience against segregated buses in the city of Montgomery, Alabama, begins and continues for over a year
1957	Civil Rights Act of 1957
	Congress passes first federal civil rights legislation since Reconstruction
1961	President John F. Kennedy's Executive Order 10925
	Mandates nondiscrimination by federal contractors
	First use of the term "affirmative action" by a president in regard to race
1963	Betty Friedan's *The Feminine Mystique*
	Publication of the most important book in the modern women's movement
	Equal Pay Act
	Congress passes law prohibiting unequal pay for men and women for performing equal jobs
1964	Civil Rights Act of 1964
	Congress passes the most important civil rights bill in the nation's history
	Title II: forbids discrimination by race in public accommodations
	Title VI: forbids discrimination by race in programs receiving federal funds
	Title VII: forbids discrimination by race and sex in employment
	Equal Employment Opportunity Commission (EEOC) established

President Lyndon Johnson's University of Michigan Commencement Address

> Outlines the principles of his "Great Society"

1965   President Johnson's Howard University Commencement Address

> Declares freedom is not enough.

> Considered the main presidential impetus for affirmative action

Watts Riots

> Bloodiest racial riot in American history takes place in Los Angeles, California

> Commences several summers of racial rioting

Moynihan Report

> Publication of semisecret government report

> Attributes the lack of progress by African Americans principally to weaknesses in the black family

President Johnson's Executive Order 11246

> Reinstates President Kennedy's Executive Order 10925

Department of Labor creates the Office of Federal Contract Compliance (OFCC)

1968   Report of the National Advisory Commission on Civil Disorders (Kerner Commission Report)

> Concludes that white racism was the principal cause of the racial violence of the 1960s

Quarles v. Philip Morris, Inc.

> Federal District Court upholds the challenge of African American workers to a departmental seniority system within a large company

1969   Revised Philadelphia Plan

> Administration of President Richard Nixon issues order requiring bidders for government contracts to incorporate in their bids targets and timetables for employment of racial minorities

1971   *Contractors Association of Eastern Pennsylvania v. Secretary of Labor*

> Circuit Court of Appeals upholds revised Philadelphia Plan

Griggs, et al. v. Duke Power

Supreme Court rules that disparate impact racial discrimination violates EEOC mandates

Phillips v. Martin Marietta Corp.

Supreme Court rules that persons of like qualifications be afforded equal employment opportunities regardless of sex

Swann v. Charlotte-Mecklenburg Board of Education

Supreme Court upholds county-wide busing plan to achieve racial balance

1972   Equal Employment Opportunity Act of 1972

Title IX, Education Amendments

Prohibits exclusion on the basis of sex from participation in any education program receiving federal financial assistance

Equal Rights Amendment passes Congress

Sent to the states for ratification

1974   *DeFunis v. Odegaard*

Supreme Court rules moot first challenge to an affirmative action admissions plan at a state university

1976   *General Electric Co. v. Gilbert*

Supreme Court rules that the denial of disability insurance benefits to women who miss work while pregnant does not deny women equal protection of the laws

1977   Federal Public Works Employment Act of 1977

Requires at least 10 percent of federal funds for public works projects be set aside for services and materials of minority business enterprises (MBEs)

McGeorge Bundy's "Who Gets Ahead in America?"

Published by *The Atlantic Monthly*

Influences Justice Harry Blackmun's opinion in *Regents v. Bakke*

Dothard v. Rawlinson

Supreme Court extends the disparate impact principle of *Griggs v. Duke Power* to women

1978   *Regents of the University of California v. Bakke*

Justice Powell's Solomonic compromise

Alan Bakke: yes; quotas: no; race-based admissions: it depends

Diversity becomes key justification for affirmative action

Pregnancy Disability Act of 1978

Congress passes legislation essentially overturning *General Electric Co. v. Gilbert*

Women missing work due to pregnancy may not be denied disability insurance benefits

1979   *United Steelworkers of America v. Weber*

The blue collar *Bakke* decision

Supreme Court rules that a voluntary affirmative action plan negotiated by a company and a labor union does not violate Title VII of the Civil Rights Act of 1964

1980   *Fullilove v. Klutznick*

Supreme Court upholds 10 percent set-asides for MBEs under Public Works Employment Act of 1977

1981   *County of Washington v. Gunther*

Supreme Court rules that women may sue over sex-based wage discrimination even if jobs at issue between men and women are not equal

1982   Equal Rights Amendment dies

A sufficient number of states fail to ratify the ERA

1983   *Newport News Shipbuilding and Drydock Co. v. EEOC*

Supreme Court rules that the Pregnancy Disability Act applies to pregnant spouses of male employees

1984   *Firefighters v. Stotts*

Supreme Court protects the seniority of white firefighters in the face of layoffs

Court finds that bona fide seniority systems trump affirmative action plans designed to aid African American firefighters

1986   *Wygant v. Jackson Board of Education*

Supreme Court protects the seniority of white teachers in the face of layoffs

Court finds that affirmative action incorporating dismissal of whites places too great a burden on innocent third parties

Sheet Metal Workers v. EEOC

Supreme Court upholds an EEOC fine and a mandated affirmative action hiring goal in the steel industry

Racial benchmarks acceptable, but racial quotas still considered unconstitutional

Meritor Savings Bank, FSB v. Vinson

Supreme Court adopts the EEOC's position that sexual discrimination under Title VII of the Civil Rights Act of 1964 is not limited to economic discrimination (such as a loss of employment status) but may also include the creation of a hostile or abusive working environment

1987   *United States v. Paradise*

Supreme Court upholds a district court order requiring promotion of one black for every white patrolman promoted in a public safety department with a history of racial discrimination

Johnson v. Transportation Agency of Santa Clara County

Supreme Court upholds a voluntary affirmative action plan to address the historic underrepresentation of women and minorities in a state agency

California Federal Savings and Loan Assn. v. Guerra

Supreme Court rejects argument that a state law requiring employers to grant pregnancy leaves without pay violated the equal treatment language of Title VII.

1989   *City of Richmond v. J.A. Croson Company*

Supreme Court strikes down a municipal ordinance requiring nonminority contractors to require a certain percentage of minority set-asides in the selection of subcontractors

Court applies strict scrutiny standard and finds no compelling state interest or narrowly tailored policies for such hiring

Wards Cove v. Atonio

Supreme Court rules against unskilled cannery workers alleging racial discrimination in selection of employees for skilled positions

Essentially reverses the disparate impact test of *Griggs v. Duke Power*

1990   *Metro Broadcasting, Inc. v. Federal Communications Commission*

Supreme Court majority holds that the Congressional goal of achieving racial diversity in broadcasting should be judged by an intermediate (as opposed to a strict) standard of review

1991   Dinesh D'Souza's *Illiberal Education* published

Civil Rights Act of 1991

Congress repudiates Supreme Court decision of *Wards Cove v. Antonio*

Disparate impact test of *Griggs v. Duke Power* reinstated

UAW v. Johnson Controls, Inc.

Supreme Court rules that an employer's policy excluding women of childbearing age from a job with potential health hazards to their unborn children violated Title VII of the Civil Rights Act of 1964

1995   *Adarand Constructors, Inc. v. Pena*

Supreme Court adopts strict scrutiny as the appropriate standard of review for determining whether a federal set-aside program is constitutional

Essentially overrules *Metro Broadcasting v. Federal Communications Commission*

Serves as key precedent limiting affirmative action in subsequent cases

President Bill Clinton's National Archives Address

"Mend it, don't end it" language on affirmative action sends mixed message

Accepts the principles of *Adarand Constructors, Inc. v. Pena*

1996   Proposition 209, California Civil Rights Initiative (CCRI)

California anti–affirmative action ballot referendum passes

Essentially eliminates affirmative action from California public law

Texas v. Hopwood

Supreme Court refuses to hear case in which an affirmative action admissions plan at the University of Texas law school was ruled unconstitutional by a federal appeals court

Follows precedent applying strict scrutiny standard to affirmative action measures as set forth in *Adarand Constructors, Inc. v. Pena*

1998   William Bowen and Derek Bok's *The Shape of the River* published

2003   *Grutter v. Bollinger*

Supreme Court upholds principle of race-based admissions in opinion by Justice Sandra Day O'Connor

Michigan law school's affirmative action plan found constitutionally acceptable

Gratz v. Bollinger

Supreme Court rules undergraduate affirmative action admissions plan at University of Michigan unconstitutional

2006   Proposition 2, Michigan Ballot Initiative

Michigan electorate votes down affirmative action in Michigan public law

Grutter v. Bollinger essentially reversed for Michigan

2007   *Parents Involved v. Seattle School District* and *Meredith v. Jefferson County Board*

Supreme Court upholds principle of using race in pupil placement in public elementary and secondary schools

But city-wide race-based pupil placement plans in Seattle and Louisville ruled unconstitutional

2008   Thirtieth anniversary of *Bakke v. Board of Regents*

Selected Materials and Readings on Affirmative Action

PRIMARY SOURCES

The most important primary materials on affirmative action are judicial decisions, especially those of the U.S. Supreme Court. Not only have these decisions affected the legal course of affirmative action, but they also provide useful windows into virtually all the issues in the debate over race and gender-based public policy. See especially the following decisions. With the exception of one recent decision, the citations for all of the Supreme Court cases discussed in these pages are to the *U.S. Reports,* the official compendium of Supreme Court opinions.

Adarand Constructors, Inc. v. Pena, 515 U.S. 200 (1995).
California Federal Savings and Loan Assn. v. Guerra, 479 U.S. 272 (1987).
City of Richmond v. J. A. Croson Company, 488 U.S. 469 (1989).
County of Washington v. Gunther, 452 U.S. 161 (1981).
DeFunis v. Odegaard, 416 U.S. 312 (1974).
Dothard v. Rawlinson, 433 U.S. 321 (1977).
Firefighters Local Union #1784 v. Stotts, 467 U.S. 561 (1984).
Fullilove v. Klutznick, 448 U.S. 448 (1980).
General Electric Co. v. Gilbert, 429 U.S. 125 (1976).
Gratz v. Bollinger, 539 U.S. 244 (2003).
Griggs, et al. v. Duke Power, 401 U.S. 424 (1971).
Grutter v. Bollinger, 539 U.S. 306 (2003).
Johnson v. Transportation Agency of Santa Clara County, 480 U.S. 616 (1987).
Meredith v. Jefferson County Board, 127 S. Ct. 2738 (2007) [Same citation as connected case *Parents Involved v. Seattle*].

Meritor Savings Bank, FSB v. Vinson, 477 U.S. 57 (1986).
Metro Broadcasting, Inc. v. FCC, 497 U.S. 547 (1990).
Newport News Shipbuilding and Drydock Co. v. EEC, 462 U.S. 669 (1983).
Parents Involved v. Seattle School District, 127 S. Ct. 2738 (2007) [Same citation as connected case *Meredith v. Jefferson County Board*].
Phillips v. Martin Marietta Corp., 400 U.S. 542 (1971).
Regents of the University of California v. Bakke, 438 U.S. 265 (1978).
Sheet Metal Workers v. EEOC, 478 U.S. 421 (1986).
Texas v. Hopwood, 518 U.S. 1033 (1996).
UAW v. Johnson Controls, Inc., 499 U.S. 187 (1991).
United States v. Paradise, 480 U.S. 149 (1987).
United Steelworkers of America v. Weber, 443 U.S. 193 (1979).
Wards Cove v. Atonio, 490 U.S. 642 (1989).
Wygant v. Jackson Board of Education, 476 U.S. 267 (1986).

In addition to the published Supreme Court decisions, the following behind-the-scenes collections of primary documents proved useful in this study:

Blackmun, Harry A. *The Public Papers of Harry A. Blackmun* (Folders 260–62). Washington, DC: Library of Congress.
Dickson, Del, ed. *The Supreme Court in Conference (1940–1985): The Private Discussions Behind Nearly 300 Supreme Court Decisions.* Oxford: Oxford University Press, 2001.
Douglas, William O. *The Public Papers of William O. Douglas* (Folder 1655). Washington, DC: Library of Congress.
Marshall, Thurgood. *The Public Papers of Thurgood Marshall* (Folders 203–4). Washington, DC: Library of Congress.

Collections of primary materials on affirmative action and race, especially accessible to general readers, include the following.

Green, Robert P., Jr. *Equal Protection and the African American Constitutional Experience: A Documentary History.* Westport, CT: Greenwood Press, 2000.
Robinson, Jo Ann Ooiman. *Affirmative Action: A Documentary History.* Westport, CT: Greenwood Press, 2001.

SECONDARY SOURCES

Scores of secondary studies of affirmative action are available in libraries, in bookstores, and on the World Wide Web. We found the following six books to be the most insightful of the many we perused.

Anderson, Terry H. *The Pursuit of Fairness: A History of Affirmative Action.* New York: Oxford University Press, 2004.

Blumrosen, Alfred W. *Modern Law: The Law Transmissions System and Equal Employment Opportunity.* Madison: University of Wisconsin Press, 1993.

Bowen, William G., and Derek Bok. *The Shape of the River: Long-Term Consequences of Considering Race in College and University Admissions.* Princeton, NJ: Princeton University Press, 1998.

D'Souza, Dinesh. *Illiberal Education: The Politics of Race and Sex on Campus.* New York: The Free Press, 1991.

MacLean, Nancy. *Freedom Is Not Enough: The Opening of the American Workplace.* Cambridge, MA: Harvard University Press, 2006.

Skrentny, John David. *The Ironies of Affirmative Action: Politics, Culture, and Justice in America.* Chicago: University of Chicago Press, 1996.

Readers interested in technical analyses of specific court cases should access law review articles through search portals such as LexisNexis or Westlaw. Law review articles tend to be detailed and often quite tedious. Those interested in substantive but lucid studies of U.S. Supreme Court decisions on affirmative action and race and gender would be better served by examining the following books.

Ball, Howard. *The Bakke Case: Race, Education, and Affirmative Action.* Lawrence: University Press of Kansas, 2000.

Cottrol, Robert J., Raymond T. Diamond, and Leland B. Ware. *Brown v. Board of Education: Caste Culture, and the Constitution.* Lawrence: University Press of Kansas, 2003.

Perry, Barbara A. *The Michigan Affirmative Action Cases.* Lawrence: University Press of Kansas, 2007.

Schwartz, Bernard. *Behind Bakke: Affirmative Action and the Supreme Court.* New York: New York University Press, 1988.

Schwartz, Bernard. *Swann's Way: The School Busing Case and the Supreme Court.* New York: Oxford University Press, 1986.

Sindler, Allan P. *Bakke, DeFunis, and Minority Admissions: The Quest for Equal Opportunity.* New York: Longman, 1978.

Urofsky, Melvin I. *Affirmative Action on Trial: Sex Discrimination in Johnson v. Santa Clara.* Lawrence: University Press of Kansas, 1997.

Wilkinson, J. Harvie, III. *From Brown to Bakke: The Supreme Court and School Integration: 1954–1978.* New York: Oxford University Press, 1979.

Useful reference tools on the Supreme Court and its most important decisions, available in many public and university libraries, include the following.

Hall, Kermit L., ed. *The Oxford Companion to the Supreme Court of the United States,* 2nd ed. New York: Oxford University Press, 2005.

Hall, Kermit L., ed. *The Oxford Guide to United States Supreme Court Decisions.* New York: Oxford University Press, 1999.

Johnson, John W., ed. *Historic U.S. Court Cases: An Encyclopedia,* 2nd ed. 2 vols. New York: Routledge, 2001.

Urofsky, Melvin I., ed. *The Public Debate over Controversial Supreme Court Decisions.* Washington, DC: CQ Press, 2006.

Urofsky, Melvin I., ed. *The Supreme Court Justices: A Biographical Dictionary.* New York: Garland Publishing, 1994.

The historical context out of which affirmative action was launched and then developed is treated in a number of books. The best of them include the following.

Graham, Hugh Davis. *The Civil Rights Era: Origins and Development of National Policy, 1960–1972.* New York: Oxford University Press, 1990.

Karabel, Jerome. *The Chosen: The Hidden History of Admission and Exclusion at Harvard, Yale, and Princeton.* Boston: Houghton Mifflin Company, 2005.

Katznelson, Ira. *When Affirmative Action Was White: An Untold History of Racial Inequality in Twentieth-Century America.* New York: W. W. Norton & Company, 2005.

Myrdal, Gunnar. *An American Dilemma: The Negro Problem and Modern Democracy.* New York: Harper & Bros., 1944.

Nieman, Donald G. *Promises to Keep: African-Americans and the Constitutional Order, 1776 to the Present.* New York: Oxford University Press, 1991.

Rainwater, Lee, and William L. Yancey. *The Moynihan Report and the Politics of Controversy.* Cambridge, MA: The M.I.T. Press, 1967.

Schulman, Bruce J. *Lyndon B. Johnson and American Liberalism: A Brief Biography with Documents,* 2nd ed. Boston: Bedford/St. Martin's, 2007.

Other worthwhile books on aspects of the affirmative action history and controversy are the following.

Belz, Herman. *Equality Transformed: A Quarter-Century of Affirmative Action.* New Brunswick, CT: Transaction Publishers, 1991.

Burstein, Paul. *Discrimination, Jobs, and Politics: The Struggle for Equal Employment Opportunity in the United States since the New Deal.* Chicago: The University of Chicago Press, 1998.

Chavez, Lydia. *The Color Bind: California's Battle to End Affirmative Action.* Berkeley: University of California Press, 1998.

Curry, George E., ed. *The Affirmative Action Debate.* Cambridge, MA: Perseus Publishing, 1996.

Eastland, Terry. *Ending Affirmative Action: The Case for Colorblind Justice.* New York: Basic Books, 1997.

Guerrero, Andrea. *Silence at Boalt Hall: The Dismantling of Affirmative Action.* Berkeley: University of California Press, 2002.

Leiter, Samuel, and William M. Leiter. *Affirmative Action in Antidiscrimination Law and Policy.* Albany: State University of New York Press, 2002.

Moreno, Paul D. *From Direct Action to Affirmative Action: Fair Employment Law and Policy in America, 1933–1972.* Baton Rouge: Louisiana State University Press, 1997.

Orfield, Gary, ed. *Diversity Challenged: Evidence on the Impact of Affirmative Action.* Cambridge, MA: Harvard Education Publishing Group, 2001.

The best journalism treating the affirmative action controversy can be found in the pages of the *New York Times,* the *Washington Post,* and the *New Republic.* See specific references in the endnotes to our chapters.

Index

About the Authors

JOHN W. JOHNSON is Interim Dean of the College of Social and Behavioral Sciences and Professor of History at the University of Northern Iowa. He has written widely on U.S. Constitutional and legal history. He is the author of *American Legal Culture, 1908–1940* (Greenwood Press, 1981); *Insuring Against Disaster: The Nuclear Industry on Trial* (1986); *The Struggle for Student Rights: Tinker v. Des Moines and the 1960s* (1997); and *Griswold v. Connecticut: Birth Control and the Constitutional Right of Privacy* (2005). He is also the editor of *Historic U.S. Court Cases: An Encyclopedia* (1993; second edition, two volumes, 2001), both editions of which won the Thomas Jefferson Prize of the Society for History in the Federal Government.

ROBERT P. GREEN, JR., is Alumni Distinguished Professor of Education, Educational Foundations, at Clemson University's School of Education. He is the author/editor of *Equal Protection and the African American Constitutional Experience: A Documentary History* (Greenwood Press, 2000) and coauthor/editor of the forthcoming *The American Civil Rights Movement: A Documentary History* (2009). He has contributed to several U.S. history textbooks.